C++ Nuts & Bolts:
For Experienced Programmers

Herbert Schildt

Osborne **McGraw-Hill**

Berkeley New York St. Louis San Francisco Auckland Bogotá
Hamburg London Madrid Mexico City Milan Montreal New Delhi
Panama City Paris São Paulo Singapore Sydney Tokyo Toronto

Osborne **McGraw-Hill**
2600 Tenth Street
Berkeley, California 94710
U.S.A.

For information on translations or book distributors outside the U.S.A., or to arrange bulk purchase discounts for sales promotions, premiums, or fundraisers, please contact Osborne **McGraw-Hill** at the above address.

C++ Nuts & Bolts: For Experienced Programmers

1234567890 DOC 998765

ISBN 0-07-882140-1

Publisher   *Larry Levitsky*
Acquisitions Editor   *Wendy Rinaldi*
Project Editor   *Cindy Brown*
Copy Editor   *Madhu Prasher*
Proofreader   *Pat Mannion*
Computer Designer   *Roberta Steele*
Illustrator   *Lance Ravella*
Quality Control Specialist   *Joe Scuderi*
Cover Design   *Ted Mader Associates*

Contents

About the Author...

Herbert Schildt is the world's leading C/C++ author. His programming books have sold more than one and a half million copies worldwide and have been translated into all major foreign languages. He is author of several best sellers, including **C++: The Complete Reference, C++ From The Ground Up**, **C: The Complete Reference**, and **The Annotated ANSI C Standard**. He has also written **Schildt's Windows 95 Programming in C and C++** and **Windows 95 Programming Nuts & Bolts: For Experienced Programmers**, as well as numerous other books. Schildt is president of Universal Computing Laboratories, a software consulting firm in Mahomet, Illinois. He holds a master's degree in computer science from the University of Illinois.

Introduction

This book teaches you how to program in the most exciting and powerful computer language invented to date: C++.

C++ is fast becoming the universal language of professional programmers. In fact, to be a professional programmer today virtually implies that you are fluent in C++. C++ represents the current state of the art as applied to computer programming languages and contains a wealth of features that make it applicable to any type of programming task. Unlike many other computer languages, C++ exists for only one reason: to enable the production of commercial quality applications. If your goal is to produce the tightest, fastest, leanest, and most efficient code possible, then you have chosen the right language.

To fully appreciate C++, it is necessary to understand how and why it came into existence.

C++ Is Built on C

As you may already know, C++ is built upon the foundation of C. In fact, C++ is a superset of C. (Indeed, all C++ compilers can also be used to compile C programs!) Specifically, C++ is an expanded and enhanced version of C that embodies the philosophy of object-oriented programming. C++ also includes several other improvements to the C language. However, much of the spirit and flavor of C++ is inherited directly from C.

C was invented and first implemented by Dennis Ritchie in the 1970s on a DEC PDP-11 using the UNIX operating system. C was the first mainstream computer language to be created by and for programmers. That is, it was a "programmer's language." Its features were honed, tested, thought about and rethought by the people who actually used the language. The result of this process was a language highly optimized for the people it serves: programmers. It is this reason more than anything else that lead to the rapid rise in the popularity of C.

For many years, the de facto standard for C was the version described in **The C Programming Language** by Brian Kernighan and Dennis Ritchie (Prentice-Hall, 1978). In December of 1989, C finally became standardized with the adoption of the ANSI (American National Standards Institute) standard for C. This is important because ANSI standard C is the foundation upon which C++ is built.

Why C++?

Since C is a successful and popular computer programming language, why was there a need for C++? The answer is complexity. Throughout the history of programming, the increasing complexity of programs has driven the need for better ways to manage that complexity. C++ is a response to that need. To better understand why managing program complexity is fundamental to the creation of C++, consider the following.

Approaches to programming have changed dramatically since the invention of the computer. The primary reason for change is to accommodate the increasing complexity of programs. For example, when computers were first invented, programming was done by toggling in the binary machine instructions using the front panel. As long as programs were just a few hundred instructions long, this approach worked. As programs grew, assembly language was invented so that a programmer could deal with larger, increasingly complex programs using symbolic representations of the machine instructions. As programs continued to grow, high-level languages were introduced which gave the programmer more tools with which to handle complexity.

In the final analysis, although C is one of the most liked and widely used professional programming languages in the world, there comes a time when its ability to handle complexity is exceeded. In response to the need to manage greater complexity, C++ was born. It was invented by Bjarne Stroustrup in 1980, while working at Bell Laboratories at Murray Hill, New Jersey. He initially called the new langauge "C with Classes." However, in 1983 the name was changed to C++.

C++ contains the entire C language. It also adheres to C's philosophy that the programmer, not the language, is in charge. At this point, it is critical to understand that the invention of C++ was not an attempt to create a new programming language. Instead, it was an enhancement to an already highly successful language.

Since C++ was first invented, it has gone through three major revisions, one in 1985, one in 1989, and the third when work began on the ANSI standard for C++. The first draft of the proposed standard was created on January 25, 1994. The ANSI C++ committee (of which I am a member) has kept virtually all of the features defined by Stroustrup and has added several new ones, as well.

The standardization process is typically a slow one and it will probably be years before the C++ standard is finally adopted. Therefore, keep in mind that C++ is still a "work in progress" and some features are still being developed and added. However, the material presented in this book is stable. It is applicable to all contemporary C++ compilers and is in compliance with the currently proposed ANSI standard for C++. Therefore, you can learn with confidence.

Who Is This Book For?

This book is designed specifically for experienced programmers who are moving to C++. This book assumes that you have had substantial experience writing programs using another computer language, such as FORTRAN, Pascal, or BASIC. Although this book covers all necessary C++ fundamentals, it moves quickly. Put directly, there is a lot of material packed into this book and its pace is quite rapid.

Watch for the Boxes

Throughout this book you will find two special types of boxed text. The first is called a ***Fast Track Tip***. Fast Track Tips tell you about things that you will want to explore on your own. That is, they contain brief descriptions of special C++ features not described in the text, proper. In essence, Fast Track Tips are pointers to interesting aspects of C++ that you will want to examine in detail, when you have time.

The second type of box is called ***Nuts & Bolts.*** Typically, a Nuts & Bolts box contains options, enhancements, or alternative methods. For example, one Nuts & Bolts box describes how to overload the dynamic allocation operators. Another shows how to rotate an integer. In general, the Nuts & Bolts boxes contain programming tips that you can apply immediately.

What Programming Tools You Will Need

The code in this book complies with the current draft of the ANSI C++ standard. It was written, compiled, and tested using both Borland C++ and Microsoft C++ . Because it is standard code, it can be compiled using any standard, mainstream C++ compiler.

Diskette Offer

There are many useful and interesting functions, algorithms, and programs contained in this book. If you're like me, you probably would like to try them, but hate typing them into the computer. When I key in routines from a book it always seems that I type something wrong and spend hours trying to get the program to work. For this reason, I am offering the source code on diskette for all the programs contained in this book for $24.95. Just fill in the order blank on the next page and mail it, along with your payment, to the address shown. Or, if you're in a hurry, just call (217) 586-4021 (the number of my consulting office) and place your order by telephone. You can FAX your order to (217) 586-4997. (Visa and Mastercard accepted.)

Please send me _____ copies, at $24.95 each, of the programs in *C++ Nuts & Bolts: For Experienced Programmers* on an IBM compatible diskette.

Foreign orders only: Checks must be drawn on a U.S bank and please add $5 shipping and handling.

_____

Name

_____

Address

_____   _____   _____

City   State   ZIP

_____

Telephone

Diskette size (check one): 5.25"_____   3.5"_____

Method of payment: Check_____   VISA_____   MC_____
Credit card number: _____
Expiration date: _____

Signature: _____

Send to:

Herbert Schildt
398 County Rd 2500 N
Mahomet, IL 61853

or phone: (217) 586-4021
FAX: (217) 586-4997

This offer subject to change or cancellation at any time.

For Further Study

C++ Nuts & Bolts: For Experienced Programmers is just one of the many programming books written by Herbert Schildt. Here are some others that you will find of interest.

To learn more about C++, we recommend:

> *C++: The Complete Reference, Second Edition*
> *Teach Yourself C++, Second Edition*
> *C++ From the Ground Up*

If you want to learn more about C (which forms the foundation for C++), then the following titles will be of interest.

> *The Annotated ANSI C Standard*
> *C: The Complete Reference, Third Edition*
> *Teach Yourself C, Second Edition*

If you are interested in programming for Windows 95, Schildt has written the definitive guides to this latest version of Windows:

> *Schildt's Windows 95 Programming in C and C++*
> *Windows 95 Programming Nuts & Bolts: For Experienced*
> *Programmers*

To learn more about Windows programming, we recommend the ***Osborne Windows Programming Series***, co-authored by Herbert Schildt. You will find it to be invaluable when trying to understand the complexities of Windows. The series titles are:

> *Volume 1: Programming Fundamentals*
> *Volume 2: General Purpose API Functions*
> *Volume 3: Special Purpose API Functions*

Finally, here are some other interesting and useful books about C and C++ written by Herbert Schildt.

> *The Art of C*
> *The Craft of C*
> *Turbo C/C++: The Complete Reference*

When you need solid answers, fast, turn to Herbert Schildt, the recognized authority on programming.

CHAPTER 1

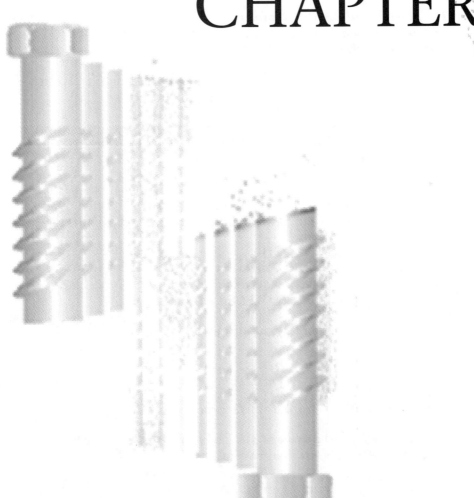

C++ Fundamentals

This chapter describes the basic elements of a C++ program. As you know, the elements of a computer language do not exist in a void, separate from one another. Instead, they work together, complementing and reinforcing each other. However, this interrelatedness is even more pronounced in C++. In fact, it is difficult to discuss one aspect of C++ in isolation because the features of C++ are highly integrated. To help overcome this problem, this chapter provides a brief overview of several C++ features. This overview gives you a general idea about how C++ works and how a C++ program is constructed.

It also supplies the necessary background to allow you to examine each aspect of C++ in detail. Keep in mind that most topics discussed here will be more thoroughly explored in later chapters.

As you probably know, C++ is an enhanced and expanded version of the C language. Many of its features are designed to support object-oriented programming (OOP for short). However, C++ also contains many improvements and features that simply make it a "better C," independent of object-oriented programming. To a large extent, C++ is a superset of C. If you already know how to program in C, then everything that you know about the C language is fully applicable to C++. If you don't know how to program in C, don't worry. This book covers the entire C++ language, including its C-like features. That is, prior knowledge of C is not a requirement.

Although C++ is more powerful and flexible, it still works in more or less the same way as other computer languages with which you are already familiar. In fact, C++ uses the same basic types of loops and control structures found in most computer languages. However, as you will soon see, C++ does not provide the "hand-holding" common to many other computer languages. It also does not prevent you from doing things that may be questionable or dangerous, from a programming perspective. For example, in C++ it is permissible (although, wrong) to index an array past its boundary! As you progress through this book keep one fact in mind: C++ is a professional programming language. It *does not* provide training wheels and guide rails. It *will do* what you tell it to do—even if what you want is inherently unsound.

This chapter begins with two example C++ programs. While both are quite short, they illustrate the basic elements common to all C++ programs. This chapter also describes C++'s most important building block: the function. As you will see, functions are at the core of a C++ program. Other items described include identifiers, the basic data types, and the arithmetic operators. Since C++ was invented to support object-oriented programming, this chapter ends with a description of OOP. As you will see, many features of C++ are related to OOP in one way or another. In fact, the theory of OOP permeates much of C++. Thus, a general understanding of the major tenets of OOP will make it easier for you to understand why certain features of C++ work the way they do. However, it is important to remember that C++ can be used to write programs that are and are *not* object oriented. How you use C++ is completely up to you.

A Simple C++ Program

The best way to gain a basic understanding of how C++ programs are written is to start with an example. Therefore, let's begin with the simple C++ program shown here.

```
/*
  A Simple C++ Program.

  Although it is quite simple, this program contains all
  of the basic elements found in any C++ program.
*/

#include <iostream.h>

// main() is where program execution begins.
main()
{
  cout << "This is a very simple C++ program.";

  return 0;
}
```

When run, this program displays **This is a very simple C++ program.** on the screen.

Let's examine each line in this program. First, the program begins with the lines

```
/*
  A Simple C++ Program.

  Although it is quite simple, this program contains all
  of the basic elements found in any C++ program.
*/
```

This is a *comment*. Like most other programming languages, C++ lets you enter a remark into a program's source code. The contents of a comment are ignored by the compiler. The purpose of a comment is to describe or explain the operation of a program to anyone reading its source code. In the case of this comment, it identifies the program. In more complex programs, you will use comments to help explain what each feature of the program is for and how it goes about doing its work. In other words, you can use comments to provide a "play-by-play" description of what your program does.

In C++, there are two types of comments. The one just shown is called a *multiline comment*. This type of comment begins with a **/*** (a slash followed by an asterisk). It ends only when a ***/** is encountered. Anything that is within the comment symbols is completely ignored by the compiler. Multiline comments may be one or more lines long. The second type of comment is found a little further on in the program.

The next line of code looks like this:

```
#include <iostream.h>
```

The C++ language defines several files, called *header files*, which contain information that is either necessary or useful to your program. For this program the file IOSTREAM.H is needed. (It is used to support the C++ I/O system.) This file is provided along with your compiler. Later in this book you will learn more about header files and why they are important.

The next line in the program is

```
// main() is where program execution begins.
```

This is also a comment. It uses the second type of comment available in C++: the *single-line comment*. Single-line comments are begun using **//** and stop at the end of the line. Typically, C++ programmers use multiline comments when writing larger, multiple line commentaries and single-line comments when short remarks are needed. However, this is a matter of personal style.

The next line, as the preceding comment suggests, is where program execution begins.

```
main()
```

As you will learn more about shortly, all C++ programs are composed of one or more functions. (Loosely speaking, a function is a subroutine.) All C++ functions must have a name and the only function that any C++ program *must* have is the one called **main( ).** The **main( )** function is where program execution begins and (most commonly) ends. (Technically speaking, a C++ program begins with a call to **main( )** and ends (in most cases) when **main( )** returns.) The opening curly brace which follows **main( )** marks the start of the **main( )** function's code.

The next line in the program is

```
cout << "This is a very simple C++ program.";
```

This is a console output statement. It causes the message **This is a very simple C++ program.** to be displayed on the screen. It accomplishes this by using the output operator **<<**. The **<<** causes whatever expression is on its right side to be output to the device specified on its left side. **cout** is a predefined identifier that stands for console output and (in general) refers to the computer's screen. Thus, this statement causes the message to be output to the screen. Notice that this statement ends with a semicolon. In fact, all C++ statements end with a semicolon.

In C++, a *string* is created when you enclose a sequence of characters between quotation marks. Thus "This is a very simple C++ program." is a string. As you might expect, strings are used frequently in C++.

The next line in the program is

```
return 0;
```

This line terminates **main( )** and causes it to return the value 0 to the calling process (which is typically the operating system). For most operating systems, a return value of 0 signifies that the program terminated normally. Other values indicate that the program terminated because of some error. **return** is one of C++'s keywords and it is used to return a value from a function. (**return** will be discussed in great detail later in this book.) Technically, a return value from **main( )** is optional, but desirable. Generally, all of your programs should return 0 when they terminate normally (that is, without error).

The closing curly brace at the end of the program formally concludes the program. Although the brace is not actually part of the object code of the program, conceptually you can think of a C++ program ending when the closing curly brace of **main( )** is executed. In fact, if the **return** statement had not been part of the program, the program would have automatically ended when the closing curly brace was encountered.

A Second Simple Program

Let's take a look at another sample program. It introduces two new features of C++. Specifically, it shows you how to declare a variable, and it demonstrates how to assign that variable a value. As you probably know, a variable is a named memory location that may be assigned a value. Further, the value of a variable may be changed one or more times during the execution of the program. That is, the content of a variable is changeable, not fixed.

The following program creates a variable called **num**, gives it the value 99, and then displays this value on the screen.

```
// Using a variable

#include <iostream.h>

main()
{
   int num; // this declares a variable

   num = 99; // this assigns 99 to num

   cout << "The value of num is: ";
   cout << num; // This displays 99

   return 0;
}
```

This program displays **The value of num is : 99**. Let's take a closer look at the new parts of this program. The first new item is shown here.

```
int num; // this declares a variable
```

This statement declares a variable called **num** to be of type integer. In C++ all variables must be declared before they are used. Further, the type of values the variable may hold must also be specified. This is called the *type* of the variable. In this case, **num** may hold integer values. For most compilers, this means the whole number values between –32,768 and 32,767. In C++, to declare a variable to be of type integer, precede its name with the keyword **int**. Later, you will see that C++ supports a wide range of built-in variable types. (You can create your own data types, too.)

The second new feature is found in the next line of code:

```
num = 99; // this assigns 99 to num
```

As the comment suggests, this assigns the value 99 to **num**. In C++, the assignment operator is the single equal sign. It copies the value on its right side into the variable on its left. After the assignment, the variable **num** will contain the number 99.

The two **cout** statements display the output generated by the program. Notice how the value of **num** is output using the statement:

```
cout << num; // This displays 99
```

As this example shows, if you want to display the value of a variable, simply put it on the right side of **<<** in a **cout** statement. In this specific case, because **num** contains the value 99, it is this number that is displayed on the screen.

More About Output

Since almost all useful C++ programs output information to the user, a closer look at the **<<** operator is warranted. In general, the **<<** operator can be used to display any type of data. It can also be used to output the value of arithmetic expressions. For example, this is a perfectly valid **cout** statement:

```
cout << num + 2;
```

Try substituting this statement into the previous program. As you will see, it displays the value of **num**, plus 2.

C++ arithmetic expressions use the same operators as do most other computer languages. Specifically, the basic arithmetic operators are

Operator	Operation
+	addition
–	subtraction
*	multiplication
/	division
%	modulus (yields the remainder of an integer division)

As you will see in subsequent chapters, C++ provides a rich set of operators, including some additional arithmetic ones.

Up to this point, output created by the sample programs has all been on one line. (A **cout** statement does not automatically advance to the next line.) If you want to advance to the next line, you must do so explicitly by outputting a carriage return, linefeed sequence. In C++, the carriage return, linefeed sequence is generated using the *newline* character. One way to output a newline character is to embed a newline character into a string. This is done by using the following code: **\n**. For example, try the following program.

```
#include <iostream.h>

main()
```

```
{
  cout << "This is on the first line.\n";
  cout << "This is on the second line.\n";
  cout << "\n\n\n"; // output three newlines
  cout << "This is several lines down.";

  return 0;
}
```

This program displays the following output.

```
This is on the first line.
This is on the second line.



This is several lines down.
```

The newline character can go anywhere in the string—not just at the end. For example, this is a perfectly valid **cout** statement.

```
cout << "one\ntwo\nthree\n";
```

This statement displays this output:

```
one
two
three
```

You might want to try experimenting with the **\n** now, just to make sure you understand exactly what it does. We will be using it frequently in programs throughout this book.

It is possible to string together two or more output operations in one **cout** statement. For example, the following statements

```
cout << "one";
cout << "two";
cout << "three";
```

could be rewritten like this:

```
cout << "one" << "two" << "three";
```

In general, you can string together as many **<<** output operations within one **cout** statement as you can conveniently fit on a line. Using this feature, the following lines from the second sample program

```
cout << "The value of num is: ";
cout << num; // This displays 99
```

could be rewritten like this:

```
cout << "The value of num is: " << num;
```

The Basic Data Types

The preceding example introduced the **int** data type. As you will see, C++ supports a wide variety of data types that range from the most basic to quite complex. However, all C++ data types are derived from the seven basic types, shown here.

Keyword	Typical Range	Purpose
bool	**true** or **false**	Holds only true and false values
char	-128 to 127	Holds a character value
int	-32,768 to 32,767	Holds integer values
float	3.4E-38 to 3.4E+38	Holds floating-point values
double	1.7E-308 to 1.7E+308	Holds double floating-point values
void	Not applicable	Represents a valueless expression
wchar_t	0 to 65,535	Holds wide characters

All variables in C++ must be declared prior to their use. This is necessary because the compiler must know the type of a variable before it can properly compile any statement that uses it. The keywords used to declare variables of the basic types are **bool**, **char**, **int**, **float**, **double**, **void**, and **wchar_t**.

Variables of type **char** are used to hold 8-bit ASCII characters such as 'A', 'B', or 'C' or any other 8-bit quantity. To specify a character you must enclose it between single quotes. Variables of type **int** can hold integer quantities that do not require a fractional component. Variables of this type are often used for controlling loops and conditional statements. Variables of the types

float and **double** are employed either when a fractional component is required or when your application requires large numbers. The difference between a **float** and a **double** variable is the magnitude of the largest (and smallest) number that they can hold. As the table shows, a **double** in C++ can store a number substantially larger than a **float**. **void** is used to explicitly tell the compiler that something has no value. You will see a use of **void** soon, when functions are discussed. Other purposes of **void** are discussed later in this book.

The types **bool** and **wchar_t** have been recently added to C++ and may not be supported by your compiler. Values of type **bool** may hold only the values **true** and **false**. (**true** and **false** are keywords defined by C++.) **wchar_t** is used to declare wide (16-bit) character types. Wide characters are used to hold the character sets of certain human languages which have a large number of characters, such as Chinese. Both **bool** and **wchar_t** are special-use types and are discussed later in this book.

Declaring Variables

To declare a variable, use this general form:

type variable_list;

Here, *type* must be a valid C++ data type and *variable_list* may consist of one or more variable names separated by commas. Some declarations are shown here, for example.

```
int counter, size, i, j, k;

char ch, chr, i27;

float f, balance, overdraft;

double result, dividend;
```

In C++, the name of a variable has nothing to do with its type.

At least the first 1024 characters of any variable name will be significant. This means that if two variable names differ in at least one character within the first 1024 characters, then they will be seen as being different names by the compiler.

Inputting Information from the User

So far, the sample programs have displayed information, but have not allowed user input. As you will see, C++ provides an easy means by which the program can input information. Again, let's begin with an example.

```cpp
// Reading user input.
#include <iostream.h>

main()
{
  int num;

  cout << "Enter a value: ";

  cin >> num; // input a number from the user

  cout << "The value of num is: " << num;

  return 0;
}
```

In this program, the value of the variable **num** is set by user input. The program first prompts the user to enter a value. Then, the following statement is executed.

```cpp
cin >> num; // input a number from the user
```

This statement inputs a number entered by the user. **cin** is another of C++'s predefined identifiers. It stands for *console input*, which generally refers to the keyboard. The **>>** is the input operator. It reads the input device specified on its left and assigns that input to the variable on its right. For example, if you run this program and enter the number 1088, then the program will respond with **The value of num is: 1088**.

The input operator **>>** can be used to input most types of data. For example, the following fragment inputs a floating-point value.

```cpp
float result;

cin >> result; // read a floating-point value
```

It is permissible to specify more than one input operation within a **cin** statement. For example, this program intputs two integers.

```
// Input two integers.
#include <iostream.h>

main()
{
  int a, b;

  cout << "Enter two values: ";

  cin >> a >> b; // input two numbers from the user

  cout << "The value of a is: " << a << "\n";
  cout << "The value of b is: " << b;

  return 0;
}
```

When inputting two or more items, you will generally need to separate each item with a space or by pressing ENTER.

Semicolons, Syntax, and Indentation

As mentioned, all C++ statements end with a semicolon. In C++, the semicolon is a statement *terminator*. It indicates the end of one logical entity. However, a function does not end with a semicolon. The reason for this is that a function definition is not a statement. Unlike some other computer languages, C++ does not recognize the end of the line as a terminator. Also, it does not matter where on a line you put a statement. For example,

```
x = y;
y = y+1;
cout << x * y;
```

is the same as

```
x = y;   y = y+1; cout << x * y;
```

to a C++ compiler.

You may have noticed from the previous examples that certain statements were indented. In C++, it does not matter where you place statements relative to each other on a line. However, over the years, a common and accepted indentation style has developed that allows for very readable programs. This book will follow that style and it is recommended that you do as well. Using this style you indent one level after each opening brace and back up one level at each closing brace. There are certain statements that encourage some additional indenting and these will be covered later.

Functions

Now that you know some of the basic elements of C++, it is time to move on to its single most important feature: the function. Functions are the building blocks of C++. A function is a subroutine that contains one or more C++ statements and performs a specific task. Each function has a name and it is this name that is used to call the function. (To *call* a function means to execute it.) In general, you can give a function whatever name you please. However, remember that **main( )** is reserved for the function that begins execution of your program.

In C++, one function cannot be created within another function. Unlike Pascal, Modula-2, and some other programming languages which allow the nesting of functions, all C++ functions are separate entities. (Of course, one function may call another.)

When denoting functions in the text, this book has used and will continue to use a convention which has become common when writing about C++. A function will have parentheses after the function name. For example, if a function's name is **initdevice** then it will be written **initdevice( )** when its name is used in a sentence. This notation will help you distinguish variable names from function names in this book.

In the preceding examples, **main( )** was the only function contained in the program. As stated earlier, **main( )** is the first function executed when your program begins to run and it must be in all C++ programs. There are two types of functions that will be used by your programs. The first type is written by you. **main( )** is an example of this type of function. The other type of function is implemented by the compiler and is found in the compiler's *standard library*. (The standard library is discussed shortly, but in general terms, it is a collection of predefined functions.) Programs you write will consist of a mix between functions you create and those supplied by the compiler.

Since functions form the foundation of C++, let's take a closer look at them at this time, beginning with an example.

A Program with Three Functions

The following program contains three functions: **main( )**, **myfunc1( )**,
and **myfunc2( )**. Before running this program (or reading the description
that follows), try to figure out exactly what it prints on the screen.

```
/* This program contains three functions: main(),
     myfunc1(), and myfunc2().
*/
#include <iostream.h>

void myfunc1(); // myfunc1's prototype
void myfunc2(); // myfunc2's prototype

main()
{
  cout << "In main() ";
  myfunc1(); // call myfunc1()
  cout << "Back in main()";

  return 0;
}

void myfunc1()
{
  cout << "Inside myfunc1() ";
  myfunc2(); // call myfunc2()
  cout << "Back in myfunc1() ";
}

void myfunc2()
{
  cout << "Inside myfunc2() ";
}
```

As you can see, the functions **myfunc1( )** and **myfunc2( )** have the same
general form as **main( )**. The program works like this. First, **main( )** begins
and it executes the first **cout** statement. Next, **main( )** calls **myfunc1( )**.
Notice how this is achieved. In the program, the function's name,
myfunc1, followed by parentheses generates a call to **myfunc1( )**. A
function call is a C++ statement and, therefore, must be ended with a
semicolon. Next, **myfunc1( )** executes its first **cout** statement and then
calls **myfunc2( )**. Inside **myfunc2( )**, the message **Inside myfunc2( )** is
displayed and then **myfunc2( )** returns to **myfunc1( )** at the line of code
immediately following the call. At this point, **myfunc1( )** outputs the
message **Back in myfunc1( )**. Then, **myfunc1( )** returns to **main( )**.

Finally, **main( )** executes its second **cout** statement and then the program terminates. Hence, the output on the screen is

```
In main() Inside myfunc1() Inside myfunc2() Back in myfunc1()
Back in main()
```

1

There is one other important feature introduced by the preceding program. It is found in the following lines:

```
void myfunc1(); // myfunc1's prototype
void myfunc2(); // myfunc2's prototype
```

As the comment states, these are the *prototypes* for **myfunc1( )** and **myfunc2( )**. Although we will discuss prototypes in detail later in this book, a few words are necessary now. A function prototype declares the function prior to its definition. The prototype allows the compiler to know the return type and the number and type of any parameters which the function may have. The compiler needs to know this information prior to the first time the function is called. This is why the prototype occurs before **main( )**.

As you can see, neither **myfunc1( )** nor **myfunc2( )** contains a **return** statement. The keyword **void**, which precedes both the prototypes and their definitions, formally states that these functions do not return a value. In C++, functions that don't return values are declared as **void**.

Function Arguments

It is possible to pass one or more values to a function. A value passed to a function is called an *argument*. In the programs that you have used so far, no function has taken any arguments. Specifically, neither **main( )**, nor **myfunc1( ),** nor **myfunc2( )** in the preceding examples have an argument. However, functions in C++ can have from zero to several arguments. The upper limit is determined by the compiler you are using, but at least 256 arguments will be allowed by any standard compiler.

Here is a short program that uses one of C++'s standard library (i.e., built-in) functions, called **abs( )**, to display the absolute value of number. The **abs( )** function takes one argument, converts it into its absolute value, and returns the result.

```
// Use the abs() function.
#include <iostream.h>
#include <stdlib.h> // required by abs()
```

```
main()
{
  cout << abs(-10);

  return 0;
}
```

Here, the value –10 is passed as an argument to **abs( )**. The **abs( )** function receives the argument that it is called with and returns its absolute value, which is 10 in this case. Although **abs( )** only takes one argument, functions can have several. The key point here is that when a function requires an argument, it is passed by specifying it between the parentheses that follow the function's name.

The return value of **abs( )** is used by the **cout** statement to display the absolute value of –10 on the screen. The reason this works is that whenever a function is part of a larger expression, it is automatically called so that its return value can be obtained. In this case, **abs( )**'s return value becomes the value of the right side of the **<<** operator and is, therefore, displayed on the screen.

Notice one other thing about the preceding program. It also includes the header file STDLIB.H. This is the header file required by **abs( )**. In general, whenever you use a library function, you must include its header file. Among other things, header files provide the prototypes for the library functions.

When you create a function that takes one or more arguments, the variables that will receive those arguments must also be declared. These are called the *parameters* of the function. The parameters to a function are declared within the parentheses that follow its name. For example, the function shown here displays the area of a triangle, given the length of its base and its height. It declares two parameters: **base** and **height**.

```
void AreaOfTriangle(int base, int height)
{
  cout << "Area of triangle is ";
  cout << base * height / 2;
  cout << "\n"; // output a linefeed
}
```

Each time **AreaOfTriangle( )** is called, it will display the area of a triangle whose base is passed as the first argument and whose height is passed in the second argument. Remember, however, that **base** and **height** are simply the function's operational variables that receive the values you use when calling the function. Consider this short program, which illustrates how to call **AreaOfTriangle( )**.

```
// A simple program that demonstrates AreaOfTriangle().
#include <iostream.h>

// This is the prototype for AreaOfTriangle().
void AreaOfTriangle(int base, int height);

main()
{
  AreaOfTriangle(10, 20);
  AreaOfTriangle(5, 6);
  AreaOfTriangle(8, 9);

  return 0;
}

void AreaOfTriangle(int base, int height)
{
  cout << "Area of triangle is ";
  cout << base * height / 2;
  cout << "\n"; // output a linefeed
}
```

This program displays the areas 100, 15, and 36 on the screen. When **AreaOfTriangle( )** is called, the C++ compiler copies the value of each argument into the matching parameter. That is, in the first call to **AreaOfTriangle( )**, 10 is copied into **base** and 20 is copied into **height**. In the second call, 5 is copied into **base** and 6 into **height**. In the third call, 8 is copied into **base** and 9 into **height**.

Notice that the parameters to **AreaOfTriangle( )** are also declared within its prototype. This can be generalized. When you create the prototype for a function, it must also include the declaration of any parameters used by the function.

If you have never worked with a language that allows parameterized functions, then the preceding process may seem a bit strange. Don't worry. As you see more examples of C++ programs, the concept of arguments, parameters, and functions will become clear.

Remember: The term *argument* refers to the value that is used to call a function. The variable that receives the value of an argument is called a *parameter*. In fact, functions that take arguments are called *parameterized functions*.

In C++ functions, when there are two or more arguments, they are separated by commas. In this book, the term *argument list* will refer to comma-separated arguments.

Functions Returning Values

Many of the C++ library functions that you will use return a value. For example, the **abs( )** function used earlier returns the absolute value of its argument. Also, functions you write may return values to the calling routine. In C++, a function returns a value using a **return** statement. The general form of **return** is

　　return *value*;

where *value* is the value being returned.

To illustrate functions returning values, the foregoing program can be rewritten as follows. In this version, **AreaOfTriangle( )** returns the area instead of displaying it. Notice that the return value is assigned to a variable by placing the function on the right side of an assignment statement.

```
// Returning a value.
#include <iostream.h>

int AreaOfTriangle(int base, int height);

main()
{
  int area;

  area = AreaOfTriangle(9, 12); // assign return value
  cout << "The area is " <<  area;

  return 0;
}

int AreaOfTriangle(int base, int height)
{
  return base * height / 2;
}
```

In this example, **AreaOfTriangle( )** returns the value of **base*height/2** using the **return** statement. This value is then assigned to **area**. That is, the value returned by the **return** statement becomes **AreaOfTriangle( )**'s value in the calling routine.

Since **AreaOfTriangle( )** now returns a value, it is not preceded by the keyword **void**. (Remember, **void** is only used when a function does *not* return a value.) Instead, it is preceded by the type **int.** Just as there are different types of variables, there are different types of return values. In this case, **AreaOfTriangle( )** returns data of type integer. The return type of a function precedes its name in both its prototype and definition.

When declaring a function, if no return type is specified, then the function is assumed to return an integer value. For example, the **AreaOfTriangle( )** function just shown could have been written like this:

```
AreaOfTriangle(int base, int height)
{
  return base * height / 2;
}
```

In this case, the return type of integer is assumed, by default. In professionally written C++ programs, functions that return integer values seldom explicitly specify **int**. Most simply default to integer.

Look back at the **main( )** function in any of the preceding programs. Since it contains no explicit return type specifier, its return type also defaults to **int**. This implies (and rightfully so) that **main( )** returns an integer to the operating system when it terminates. If you want, you could write the **main( )** function like this:

```
int main()
{
  // ...
```

with the integer return type explicitly specified. However, most C++ programmers simply allow **main( )** to default to a return type of **int**. (This is, of course, a matter of taste.)

It is possible to cause a function to return by using the **return** statement without any value attached to it. However, this form of **return** can only be used with functions that have no return values and that are declared as **void**. Also, there can be more than one **return** in a function.

Improving AreaOfTriangle( )

Although the **AreaOfTriangle( )** function is syntactically correct, it does not always produce an accurate answer. As you know, integer data types cannot represent a fractional value. This means that when you try to use

AreaOfTriangle( ) to compute the area of a triangle that has a base of 5 and a height of 7, you will receive the answer 17, instead of the proper answer of 17.5. However, it is an easy matter to improve **AreaOfTriangle( )** so that it produces an accurate answer for all triangles. Simply convert its return type and the type of its parameters to **float.** Operations on floating-point numbers preserve any fractional part of the outcome and, hence, provide a precise computation.

The following program shows how **AreaOfTriangle( )** can be converted to handle floating-point values.

```cpp
// An improved version of AreaOfTriangle().
#include <iostream.h>

float AreaOfTriangle(float base, float height);

main()
{
  float area;

  area = AreaOfTriangle(9.5, 12.01); // assign return value
  cout << "The area is " <<  area;

  return 0;
}

float AreaOfTriangle(float base, float height)
{
  return base * height / 2;
}
```

In the program, the variable **area,** the parameters to **AreaOfTriangle( )** and its return type have been converted to type **float**. The program will now correctly compute the area of any size triangle.

Passing Variables to Functions

An argument to a function can be any object that produces a value that is compatible with the type specified by the parameter. In the examples in this chapter, function arguments have been constants. However, you may use variables and/or expressions, too. For example, here is another version of the **AreaOfTriangle( )** program that uses variables as arguments.

```
#include <iostream.h>

float AreaOfTriangle(float base, float height);

main()
{
  float base, height;
  float area;

  cout << "Enter base: ";
  cin >> base;

  cout << "Enter height: ";
  cin >> height;

  area = AreaOfTriangle(base, height);
  cout << "The area is " <<  area;

  return 0;
}

float AreaOfTriangle(float base, float height)
{
  return base * height / 2;
}
```

In this version, the variables **base** and **height** are set by the user and then used to call **AreaOfTriangle( ).**

Remember, arguments may be expressions, too. For example, to find the area of a triangle that is twice as big as the dimensions entered by the user, substitute this statement:

```
area = AreaOfTriangle(base * 2, height * 2);
```

In this statement, the arguments to **AreaOfTriangle( )** are expressions rather than constants or single variables.

The main( ) Function

As you know, the **main( )** function is special because it is the first function called when your program executes. It signifies the beginning of your program. Unlike some programming languages that always begin at the "top" of the program, a C++ program begins with a call to the **main( )** function, no matter where that function is located in your program. (However, it is good form for **main( )** to be the first function in your program so that it can be easily found.)

There can only be one **main( )** in a program. If there were more than one, your program would not know where to begin execution. Actually, most compilers will catch an error like that and report it.

The General Form of C++ Functions

The preceding examples have shown some specific types of functions. However, all C++ functions share a common form, which is shown here.

```
return-type function_name(parameter list)
{
.
. // body of the function
.
}
```

Let's look closely at the different parts that make up a function.

The return type of a function is integer by default, but you can specify any return type you like. Keep in mind, however, that no function has to return a value. If it does not return a value, its return type is **void**. But if it does return a value, then the value returned must be of a type that is compatible with the function's return type.

All functions must have a name. After the name is a parenthesized parameter list. The parameter list specifies the names and types of variables that will be passed information. If a function has no parameters, the parentheses are empty.

Next, braces surround the body of the function. The body of the function is composed of the C++ statements that define what the function does. The function terminates and returns to the calling procedure when the closing curly brace is reached or when a **return** statement is encountered.

The C++ Keywords

There are 61 keywords currently defined for C++. These are shown in Table 1-1. However, the keywords **bool, const_cast, dynamic_cast, explicit, false, mutable, namespace, reinterpret_cast, static_cast, true, typeid, using,** and **wchar_t** have been recently added to C++ and may not be fully implemented by your compiler. Also, old versions of C++ include the **overload** keyword, which is now obsolete. You will want to

1

asm	auto	bool	break
case	catch	char	class
const	const_cast	continue	default
delete	do	double	dynamic_cast
else	enum	extern	explicit
false	float	for	friend
goto	if	inline	int
long	mutable	namespace	new
operator	private	protected	public
register	reinterpret_cast	return	short
signed	sizeof	static	static_cast
struct	switch	template	this
throw	true	try	typedef
typeid	union	unsigned	using
virtual	void	volatile	wchar_t
while			

The C++
Keywords
Table 1-1.

check your compiler user's manual to determine precisely what C++ keywords it supports.

The case of the keywords is significant. C++ requires that all keywords be in lowercase. For example, **RETURN** will *not* be recognized as the keyword **return**.

Identifiers in C++

In C++ an identifier is a name for a function, a variable, or any other user-defined item. Identifiers can be from one to several characters long. The first 1024 characters will be significant. Identifiers may start with any letter of the alphabet or an underscore. Next may be either a letter, a digit, or the underscore. (The underscore can be used to enhance the readability of a name, as in **first_name**.) Uppercase and lowercase are different; that is, to C++, **count** and **COUNT** are separate names. Here are some examples of acceptable identifiers:

```
first   last  Addr1  top_of_file
name23  _temp  s23e3   MyVar
```

You cannot use any of the C++ keywords as identifier names. Also, you should not use the name of a standard function, such as **abs**, for an identifier. Beyond these two restrictions, good programming practice dictates that you should use identifier names that reflect the item's meaning or usage.

The Standard C++ Library

In the discussion of the sample programs, it was mentioned that **abs( )** was provided with your C++ compiler. **abs( )** is not part of the C++ language, per se, yet you will find it included with every C++ compiler. This function, and many others, are found in the *standard library*. We will be making extensive use of library functions in the example programs throughout this book.

C++ defines a rather large set of functions that will be contained in the standard library. These functions are designed to perform many commonly needed tasks, including I/O operations, mathematical computations, and string handling. When you use a library function, the C++ compiler automatically links the object code for that function to the object code of your program.

Because the C++ standard library is so large, it already contains many of the functions that you will use in your programs. They act as building blocks that you simply assemble. You should explore your compiler's library manual. You may be surprised at how varied the library functions are. If you write a function that you will use again and again, it too can be placed into a library. Some compilers will allow you to place this in the standard library; others will make you create an additional one. Either way, the code will be there for you to use whenever you need it.

One last point: All C++ compilers also contain a *class library*, which contains object-oriented functions. However, you will need to wait until you learn about classes and objects before you can make use of the class library.

FAST TRACK TIP

Exploring the Standard Library

As mentioned, the C++ standard library contains hundreds of general purpose functions which your programs may use. In the course of this book, we will be examining several of the most commonly used library functions. However, you will also want to explore the standard library on your own. The first thing to understand about the standard library is that it is grouped into subsystems. For example, there is a subsystem for mathematical functions, one for I/O functions, and another for string handling. Each subsystem requires its own header file. One of the best ways to become familiar with the standard library is to examine its header files. The following table lists the header files for the standard library subsystems.

Header File	Purpose
ASSERT.H	Supports debugging (defines the **assert( )** macro)
CTYPE.H	Supports character handling
ERRNO.H	Supports error reporting
FLOAT.H	Defines implementation-dependent floating-point values
LIMITS.H	Defines various implementation-dependent limits
LOCALE.H	Supports localization functions
MATH.H	Supports the mathematical functions
SETJMP.H	Supports nonlocal jumps
SIGNAL.H	Supports signal handling
STDARG.H	Supports variable-length argument lists
STDDEF.H	Defines some commonly used constants
STDIO.H	Supports the C-based file and console I/O functions
STDLIB.H	Supports various miscellaneous functions
STRING.H	Supports string handling
TIME.H	Supports the time and date functions

When you examine these header files remember two important points. First, above all else, do not modify these files. They contain precise declarations which must not be changed. Second, don't worry if much of what you see makes no sense. As you progress through this book, the contents of these header files will become clear.

An Overview of Object-Oriented Programming

To conclude this chapter, a short overview of object-oriented programming is presented. As stated at the start of this chapter, C++ was invented to support object-oriented programming. Although actual object-oriented techniques and features will not be discussed until later in this book, it is valuable for you to understand, in a general way, what object-oriented programming is and why it has emerged as an important approach to software engineering. As you will see as you advance through this book, several features of C++ are designed expressly for the purpose of supporting OOP.

Object-oriented programming is a new way to approach the task of programming. Since its early beginnings, programming has been governed by various methodologies. At each critical point in the evolution of programming, a new approach was created to help the programmer handle increasingly complex programs. The first programs were created by toggling switches on the front panel of the computer. Obviously, this approach is suitable for only the smallest programs. Next, assembly language was invented, which allowed longer programs to be written. The next advance happened in the 1950s when the first high-level language (FORTRAN) was invented.

By using a high-level language, a programmer was able to write programs that were several thousands of lines long. However, the method of programming used early on was an ad hoc, anything-goes approach. While this is fine for relatively short programs, it yields unreadable (and unmanageable) "spaghetti code" when applied to larger programs. The elimination of spaghetti code waited until the invention of *structured programming languages* in the 1960s. These languages include Algol and Pascal. C, C++'s predecessor, is also a structured language. Most likely the type of programming you have been doing would be called structured programming. Structured programming relies on well-defined control structures, code blocks, the absence (or at least minimal use) of the GOTO, and stand-alone subroutines that support recursion and local variables. The essence of structured programming is the reduction of a program into its constituent elements. Using structured programming, the average programmer can create and maintain programs that are up to approximately 50,000 lines long.

Although structured programming has yielded excellent results when applied to moderately complex programs, even it fails at some point, after a program reaches a certain size. To allow more complex programs to be written, a new approach to the job of programming was needed. Towards this end, object-oriented programming was invented. OOP takes the best of the ideas embodied in structured programming and combines them with powerful new concepts that allow you to organize your programs in a different way. Object-oriented programming encourages you to decompose a problem into related subgroups. Each subgroup becomes a self-contained object that includes its own code and data that relate to that object. In this way, complexity is reduced and the programmer can manage larger programs.

All OOP languages, including C++, share three common defining traits: encapsulation, polymorphism, and inheritance. Let's look at these concepts now.

Encapsulation

Encapsulation is the mechanism that binds together code and the data it manipulates and keeps both safe from outside interference and misuse. In an object-oriented language, code and data may be bound together in such a way that a self-contained "black box" is created. Within the box are all necessary data and code. When code and data are linked together in this fashion, an *object* is created. In other words, an object is the device that supports encapsulation.

Within an object, code, data, or both may be *private* to that object or *public*. Private code or data is known to and accessible only by another part of the object. That is, private code or data may not be accessed by a piece of the program that exists outside the object. In contrast, when code or data is public, other parts of your program may access it even though it is defined within an object. Typically, the public parts of an object are used to provide a controlled interface to the private elements of the object.

For all intents and purposes, an object is a variable of a user-defined type. It may seem strange that an object that links both code and data can be thought of as a variable. However, in object-oriented programming, this is precisely the case. Each time you define a new object, you are creating a new data type. Each specific instance of this data type is a compound variable.

Polymorphism

Object-oriented programming languages support *polymorphism*, which is characterized by the phrase "one interface, multiple methods." In simple terms, polymorphism is the attribute that allows one interface to be used with a general class of actions. The specific action selected is determined by the exact nature of the situation. A real-world example of polymorphism is a thermostat. No matter what type of furnace your house has (gas, oil, electric, and so on) the thermostat works the same way. In this case, the thermostat (which is the interface) is the same no matter what type of furnace (method) you have. For example, if you want a 70 degree temperature, you set the thermostat to 70 degrees. It doesn't matter what type of furnace actually provides the heat. This same principle can also apply to programming. For example, you might have a program that defines three different types of stacks. One stack is used for integer values, one for character values, and one for floating-point values. Because of polymorphism, you can create three sets of functions called **push( )** and **pop( )**—one set for each type of data. The general concept (interface) is that of pushing and popping data onto and from a stack. The functions define the specific ways (methods) this is done for each type of data. When you push data on the stack, it is the type of the data that will determine which specific version of the **push( )** function will be called.

The advantage of polymorphism is that it helps to reduce complexity by allowing the same interface to be used to specify a *general class of action*. It is the compiler's job to select the *specific action* as it applies to each situation. You, the programmer, don't need to do this selection manually. You need only remember and utilize the general interface.

Polymorphism can be applied to both functions and operators. Virtually all programming languages contain a limited application of polymorphism as it relates to the arithmetic operators. For example, in virtually all computer languages, the + sign is used to add integers, long integers, characters, and floating-point values. In these cases, the compiler automatically knows which type of arithmetic to apply. In C++, you can extend this concept to other types of data that you define. This type of polymorphism is called *operator overloading*.

The first object-oriented programming languages were interpreters, so polymorphism was, of course, supported at run time. However, C++ is a compiled language. Therefore, in C++, both run-time and compile-time polymorphism are supported.

The key point to remember about polymorphism is that it allows you to handle greater complexity by allowing the creation of standard interfaces to related activities.

Inheritance

Inheritance is the process by which one object can acquire the properties of another. More precisely, an object can inherit a general set of properties to which it can add those features that are specific only to itself. Inheritance is important because it allows an object to support the concept of *hierarchical classification*. Most information is made manageable by hierarchical classification. For example, think about the description of a house. A house is part of the general class called **building**. In turn, **building** is part of the more general class **structure**, which is part of the even more general class of objects that we call **man-made**. In each case, the child class inherits all those qualities associated with the parent and adds to them its own defining characteristics. Without the use of ordered classifications, each object would have to define all characteristics that relate to it explicitly. However, by using inheritance, it is possible to describe an object by stating what general class (or classes) it belongs to along with those specific traits that make it unique. As you will see, inheritance plays a very important role in OOP.

CHAPTER 2

Control Statements

Perhaps the single most defining characteristic of a language is its control statements. These are the mechanisms by which the flow of execution is directed. C++ defines three specific categories of program control statements: *selection* statements, which include the **if** and the **switch**; *iteration* statements, which include the **for**, **while**, and **do-while** loops; and *jump* statements, which include **break**, **continue**, **return**, and **goto**. Except for the **return** statement (which is examined in a later chapter) the control statements are described here. In addition to control statements, this chapter also discusses the relational and logical operators.

These operators are typically used in the expressions that govern the control statements.

This chapter begins with the most fundamental control statement: the **if**.

The if Statement

The **if** statement is one of C++'s selection statements. Its operation is governed by the outcome of a conditional expression. (For this reason, the **if** is also referred to as a *conditional statement*.) The simplest form of the **if** is shown here.

if (*expression*) *statement*;

The *expression* may be any valid C++ expression. If the expression evaluates as true, the statement will be executed. If it does not, the statement is bypassed, and the line of code following the **if** is executed. In C++, an expression is true if it evaluates to any nonzero value. If it evaluates to zero, it is false. The statement that follows an **if** is commonly referred to as its *target*.

Often, the expression inside the **if** compares one value to another using a *relational operator*. Although you will learn about all the relational operators later in this chapter, three are introduced here so that we can create some example programs. A relational operator determines how one value relates to another. For example, to see if one value is greater than another, C++ uses the **>** relational operator. The outcome of this comparison is either true or false. For example, **10 > 9** is true, but **9 > 10** is false. Therefore, this **if** will cause the message **true** to be displayed.

```
if(10 > 9) cout << "true";
```

However, because the expression in the following statement is false, the **if** does not execute its target statement.

```
if(3 > 11) cout << "this will not print";
```

The less-than operator is **<**. For example, **10 < 11** is true. To test for equality, C++ provides the **==** operator. (There can be no space between the two equal signs.) For example, **10 == 10** is true, but **10 == 11** is not. Of course, the expression inside the **if** may involve variables. For example, in the following fragment, the **cout** statement is executed only if **max** is greater than **size**.

```
if(max > size) cout << "Still running process.";
```

Here is an example that uses the **if**. This program converts feet to meters or meters to feet, depending upon which option the user requests.

```cpp
#include <iostream.h>

main()
{
  float num;
  int choice;

  cout << "Enter value: ";
  cin >> num;

  cout << "1: Feet to meters, 2: Meters to feet\n";
  cout << "Enter choice: ";
  cin >> choice;

  if(choice == 1) cout << num / 3.28;
  if(choice == 2) cout << num * 3.28;

  return 0;
}
```

It is important to understand that in C++, true is any nonzero value and false is zero. This means that the expression controlling the **if** may be of any type. That is, it need not involve a relational operator. For example, the following **if** statement is perfectly valid.

```cpp
if(size+1) cout << "Size is non-negative.";
```

As long as **size+1** is nonzero, the **cout** statement will execute. However, if **size** is –1, then the condition is false and the **cout** statement will not execute.

The else Option

You can add an **else** statement to the **if**. When this is done, the **if** statement looks like this:

if (*expression*) *statement1*;
else *statement2*;

If the expression is true, then the target of the **if** will execute, and the **else** portion will be skipped. However, if the expression is false, then the target of the **if** is bypassed, and the target of the **else** will execute. Under no

2

circumstances will both statements execute. Thus, the addition of the **else** provides a two-way decision path.

You can use the **else** to create more efficient code in some cases. For example, here the **else** is used in place of a second **if** in the feet/meters conversion program from the preceding section.

```
#include <iostream.h>

main()
{
  float num;
  int choice;

  cout << "Enter value: ";
  cin >> num;

  cout << "1: Feet to meters, 2: Meters to feet\n";
  cout << "Enter choice: ";
  cin >> choice;

  if(choice == 1) cout << num / 3.28;
  else cout << num * 3.28;

  return 0;
}
```

Since there are only two possibilities, there is no reason to see if **choice** is 2. Because of the way a C++ compiler generates code, the **else** requires far fewer machine instructions than an additional **if**. (Of course, this program assumes that the user always enters either 1 or 2.)

Blocks of Code

Before continuing our exploration of the **if** a small but important digression is required. Because C++ is a structured (as well as an object-oriented) language it supports the creation of blocks of code. A *block* is a logically connected group of program statements that is treated as a unit. In C++, a code block is created by placing a sequence of statements between opening and closing curly braces. In this example,

```
if(counter > 100) {
  cout << "Too Large! Enter another number.";
  cin >> counter;
}
```

the two statements after the **if** and between the curly braces are both executed only if **counter** is greater than 100. These two statements together with the braces represent a block of code. They are a logical unit: one of the statements cannot execute without the other also executing. In C++, the target of most commands may be either a single statement or a code block. Code blocks allow many algorithms to be implemented with greater clarity and efficiency. They can also help you better conceptualize the true nature of the algorithm.

The program that follows uses a block of code. It is an improved version of the feet-to-meters, meters-to-feet conversion program. Notice how the use of code blocks allows the program to prompt specifically for each unit.

```
#include <iostream.h>

main()
{
  float num;
  int choice;

  cout << "1: feet to meters, 2: meters to feet ";
  cout << "Enter choice: ";
  cin >> choice;

  if(choice == 1) {
    cout << "Enter number of feet: ";
    cin >> num;
    cout << "meters: " << num / 3.28;
  }
  else {
    cout << "Enter number of meters: ";
    cin >> num;
    cout << "feet: " << num * 3.28;
  }

  return 0;
}
```

Remember: A block of code is begun with a **{** and ends when its matching **}** is encountered. Also, one block of code may be nested within another block. Blocks may be nested to at least 256 levels.

Nested if Statements

When an **if** statement is the target of another **if** or **else**, it is said to be *nested* within the outer **if**. Here is a simple example of a nested **if**.

```
if(count>max) // outer if
  if(error == 26) cout << "Error, try again."; // nested if
```

Here, the **cout** statement will only execute if **count** is greater than **max** and if **error** is equal to 26. Notice how the nested **if** is indented. This is common practice. It enables anyone reading your program to know quickly that the **if** is nested and what actions are nested.

A nested **if** is also created when one **if** appears inside a block of statements that are the target of the outer **if**. For example,

```
if(count>max) { // outer if
  max = count;
  if(error == 26) cout << "Error, try again."; // nested if
  count = count + 3;
}
```

In C++ you may nest **if**s at least 256 levels deep. (However, it would be rare to find such deep nesting.)

One confusing aspect of nested **if**s is illustrated by the following fragment.

```
if(p<10)
  if(q>100) cout << "Both if statements are true.";
  else cout << "To which statement does this else apply?";
```

The question, as suggested by the second **cout** statement, is: which **if** is associated with the **else**? Fortunately, the answer is quite easy: an **else** always associates with the nearest **if** within the same block that does not already have an **else** associated with it. In this example, the **else** is associated with the second **if**.

It is possible to string together several **if**s and **else**s into what is sometimes called an *if-else-if ladder* or *if-else-if staircase* because of its visual appearance. In this situation a nested **if** has as its target another **if**. The general form of the if-else-if ladder is shown here.

2

```
  if (expression)
    statement;
  else if (expression)
    statement;
  else if (expression)
    statement;

    .
    .
    .

  else
    statement;
```

The conditions are evaluated from the top downward. As soon as a true condition is found, the statement associated with it is executed, and the rest of the ladder is bypassed. If none of the conditions is true, the final **else** will be executed. That is, if all other conditional tests fail, the last **else** statement is performed. If the final **else** is not present, no action will take place if all other conditions are false.

Here is an example that uses an if-else-if ladder. It asks the user for two numbers and then for the arithmetic operation to apply. It uses the if-else-if ladder to select the proper operation.

```
#include <iostream.h>

main()
{
  float a, b;
  char operation;

  cout << "Enter first number: ";
  cin >>  a;
  cout << "Enter second number: ";
  cin >> b;

  cout << "Do you want to:\n";
  cout << "Add, Subtract, Multiply, or Divide?\n";
  cout << "Enter letter (A, S, M or D): ";
  cin >> operation;

  if(operation == 'A') cout << a+b;
  else if(operation == 'S') cout << a-b;
  else if(operation == 'M') cout << a*b;
  else if(operation == 'D') cout << a/b;
  else cout << "Invalid operation!";
```

```
    return 0;
}
```

There is one other thing to be aware of in the preceding program. It uses a **cin** statement to read a single character entered at the keyword. When using **cin** to read a character, you may need to press ENTER after pressing the character key before that character is sent to your program. (For example, to select Add, you may need to press **A** followed by ENTER.) By default, most C++ compilers *line-buffer* console input operations. This means that no input will be sent to your program until you press ENTER—even when reading a single character. Later in this book you will learn how to perform interactive I/O using C++. Also notice that the **if** statements compare the value in **operation** to the character constants 'A', 'S', 'M', and 'D'. As mentioned in Chapter 1, character constants are specified in C++ by enclosing them between single quotes. Also, character constants are case-sensitive (as are all elements of C++). Therefore, the constant 'A' is separate from 'a'.

Relational and Logical Operators

A few of C++'s relational operators were introduced in the discussion of the **if**. Because they are tightly intertwined with the control statements, a complete discussion of them is warranted now. Closely related to the relational operators are the logical operators, which are also described here.

In the terms *relational operator* and *logical operator*, relational refers to the relationships which values can have with one another and logical refers to the ways these relationships can be connected together. Because the relational and logical operators often work together, they will be discussed together.

The key to using the relational and logical operators is the idea of *true* and *false*. As mentioned, in C++, true is any value other than 0. False is 0. Thus, only expressions that evaluate to 0 are false. Any other value is true. As you learn more about C++, you will see that this concept of true and false makes certain algorithms much easier to write.

The relational and logical operators are shown in Table 2-1. Notice that in C++, *not equal* is **!=** and *equality* is the double equal sign, **==**.

The Relational Operators	
Operator	**Action**
>	greater than
>=	greater than or equal
<	less than
<=	less than or equal
==	equal
!=	not equal
Logical Operators	
Operator	**Action**
&&	AND
||	OR
!	NOT

The Relational
and Logical
Operators
Table 2-1.

2

The logical operators are used to support the basic logical operations of AND, OR, and NOT according to this truth table. The table uses 1 for true and 0 for false.

p	q	p AND q	p OR q	NOT p
0	0	0	0	1
0	1	0	1	1
1	1	1	1	0
1	0	0	1	0

Although C++ does not contain a built-in exclusive OR (XOR) operator, it is easy to construct one. (And doing so provides an interesting way to demonstrate the logical operators.) The XOR operation uses this truth table.

p	q	p XOR q
0	0	0
0	1	1
1	0	1
1	1	0

In words, the XOR operation produces a true result when one and only one operand is true. The following function uses the **&&**, **||**, and **!** operators to construct an XOR operation. The result is returned by the function.

```
xor(int a, int b)
{
  return (a || b) && !(a && b);
}
```

The following program uses this function. It displays the results of AND, OR, and XOR on the values you enter.

```
// This program demonstrates the xor() function.
#include <iostream.h>

xor(int a, int b);

main()
{
  int p, q;

  cout << "Enter P (0 or 1): ";
  cin >> p;
  cout << "Enter Q (0 or 1): ";
  cin >> q;

  cout << "P AND Q: " << (p && q) << '\n';
  cout << "P OR Q: " << (p || q) << '\n';
  cout << "P XOR Q: " << xor(p, q) << '\n';

  return 0;
}

xor(int a, int b)
{
  return (a || b) && !(a && b);
}
```

Both the relational and logical operators are lower in precedence than the arithmetic operators. This means that an expression like 10 > 1+12 is evaluated as if it were written 10 > (1+12). The result is, of course, false. Also, the parentheses surrounding **p && q** and **p || q** in the preceding program are necessary because the **&&** and the **||** are lower in precedence than the output operator.

You may link any number of relational operations together using logical operators. For example, this expression joins three relational operations.

var>15 || !(10<count) && 3<=item

The table below shows the relative precedence of the relational and logical operators.

highest	!
	> >= < <=
	== !=
	&&
lowest	||

2

All relational and logical expressions produce a result of either true or false. Generally, the value 1 is used for true and (of course) 0 is false. Therefore, the following program is not only correct, but will also print the number 1 on the screen.

```
#include <iostream.h>

main()
{
  int x;

  x = 100;
  cout << (x>10);

  return 0;
}
```

Note: The proposed ANSI C++ standard states that the outcome of a relational or logical expression is a value of type **bool**, which may be either **true** or **false**. However, these values automatically convert into integers that are nonzero and zero, respectively.

Testing for Zero

When testing for zero in a conditional expression, most beginning C++ programmers will write a statement such as this:

```
If(size == 0) cout << "size is zero.";
```

However, this is actually an overly complicated way of doing things. Since false in C++ is any expression that evaluates to zero, the preceding statement is more efficiently written like this:

```
if(!size) cout << "size is zero.";
```

This is the way you will normally see a test for zero done in professionally written C++ code. If **size** is zero, then **!size** is true. If **size** is nonzero, then **!size** is false.

Here is another example. This program prompts the user for two numbers, divides the first by the second, and displays the result. However, division by zero is undefined, so the program prevents division by zero from occurring by testing **num2** for zero.

```
#include <iostream.h>

main()
{
  int num1, num2;

  cout << "Enter first number: ";
  cin >> num1;
  cout << "Enter second number: ";
  cin >> num2;

  if(!num2) cout << "Cannot divide by zero.";
  else cout << num1 / num2;

  return 0;
}
```

As you will see, in C++ tests for zero are quite common and you should adopt the method shown here because it is the way such tests are normally written.

Testing for nonzero (i.e. true) is also performed the same way. For example, the following fragment.

```
if(error != 0) cout >> "Error occurred";
```

can be better written like this:

```
if(error) cout >> "Error occurred";
```

The **cout** statement will execute if and only if the variable **error** is nonzero.

The switch Statement

While **if** is good for choosing between two alternatives, it quickly becomes cumbersome when several alternatives are needed. C++'s solution to this problem is the **switch** statement. The **switch** statement is C++'s multiway selection statement. It is used to select one of several alternative paths in program execution. It works like this: A variable is successively tested against a list of integer or character constants. When a match is found, the statement sequence associated with that match is executed. The general form of the **switch** statement is

2

```
switch(variable) {
  case constant1:
    statement sequence
    break;
  case constant2:
    statement sequence
    break;
  case constant3:
    statement sequence
    break;
     .
     .
     .
  default:
    statement sequence
}
```

where the **default** statement sequence is performed if no matches are found. The **default** is optional. If all matches fail and **default** is absent, no action takes place. When a match is found, the statements associated with that **case** are executed until **break** is encountered or, in the case of **default** or the last **case**, the end of the **switch** is reached.

Here is a simple example. This program recognizes the numbers 1,2,3, and 4 and prints the name of the one you enter. That is, if you enter **2**, the program displays **Two**.

```
#include <iostream.h>

main()
{
  int i;

  cout << "Enter a number between 1 and 4: ";
  cin >> i;
```

```
switch(i) {
  case 1:
    cout << "One";
    break;
  case 2:
    cout << "Two";
    break;
  case 3:
    cout << "Three";
    break;
  case 4:
    cout << "Four";
    break;
  default:
    cout << "Unrecognized number";
}

return 0;
}
```

The **switch** statement differs from **if** in that **switch** can only test for
equality, whereas the **if** conditional expression can be of any type. Also,
switch will work with only **int** or **char** types. You cannot, for example, use
floating-point numbers.

The statement sequences associated with each **case** *do not* form a code block;
they are not enclosed by curly braces.

C++ allows at least 16,384 **case** statements within any single **switch**. In
practice, you should limit the amount of **case** statements to a much smaller
number for efficiency reasons. Also, no two **case** constants in the same
switch can have identical values.

It is possible to have a **switch** as part of the statement sequence of an outer
switch. This is called a *nested switch*. If the **case** constants of the inner and
outer **switch** contain common values, no conflicts will arise. For example,
the following code fragment is perfectly acceptable.

```
switch(a) {
  case 1:
    switch(b) {
      case 0: cout << "b is false";
              break;
      case 1: cout << "b is true";
    }
```

```
    break;
  case 2:
    .

    .

    .
```

C++ will allow at least 256 levels of nesting for **switch** statements.

The **switch** statement is often used to process menu commands. For example, the arithmetic program shown earlier can be recoded as shown here, using the **switch**. Notice that it also prevents a divide-by-zero error.

2

```cpp
#include <iostream.h>

main()
{
  float a, b;
  char ch;

  cout << "Do you want to:\n";
  cout << "Add, Subtract, Multiply, or Divide?\n";

  cout << "Enter letter (A, S, M, or D): ";
  cin >> ch;

  cout << "Enter first number: ";
  cin >> a;
  cout << "Enter second number: ";
  cin >> b;

  switch(ch) {
    case 'A':
      cout << a+b;
      break;
    case 'S':
      cout << a-b;
      break;
    case 'M':
      cout << a*b;
      break;
    case 'D':
      if(b!=0) cout << a/b;
  }

  return 0;
}
```

The break Is Optional

Technically, the **break** statement in a **switch** is optional. The **break** statement, when encountered within a **switch**, causes the program flow to exit from the entire **switch** statement and continue on to the next statement outside the **switch**. However, if a **break** statement is omitted, the execution continues into the following **case** or **default** statement (if either exists). That is, when a **break** statement is missing, execution "falls through" into the next **case** and stops only when a subsequent **break** statement or the end of the **switch** is encountered. For example, study this program carefully.

```cpp
#include <iostream.h>

main()
{
  int num;

  cout << "Enter an integer between 1 and 4: ";
  cin >> num;

  switch(num) {
    case 1:
      cout << "The switch statement provides ";
    case 2:
      cout << "a convenient means of ";
    case 3:
      cout << "selecting between several options.";
      break;
    case 4:
      cout << "The if statement ";
    default:
      cout << "selects between two options.";
  }

  return 0;
}
```

If you enter **1**, the entire sentence

```
The switch statement provides a convenient means of selecting
between several options.
```

is output. However, if you enter **2**, then only

```
a convenient means of selecting between several options.
```

is displayed. If you enter **4**, then the sentence

```
The if statement selects between two options.
```

is output.

As you can see, once execution begins inside a **case**, it continues until a **break** statement or the end of the **switch** is encountered.

The statement sequence associated with a **case** may be empty. This allows two or more **case**s to share a common statement sequence without duplication of code. For example, here is a program that categorizes letters into vowels and consonants.

```cpp
#include <iostream.h>

main()
{
  char ch;

  cout << "Enter the letter: ";
  cin >> ch;

  switch(ch) {
    case 'a':
    case 'e':
    case 'i':
    case 'o':
    case 'u':
    case 'y':
      cout << "Vowel\n";
      break;
    default:
      cout << "Consonant";
  }

  return 0;
}
```

The for Loop

The **for** loop is one of C++'s three loop statements. It allows one or more statements to be repeated. Virtually all computer languages contain a **for**-style loop and you will be pleased to learn that the C++-style **for** behaves much like its equivalent in other languages.

The **for** loop is considered by many C++ programmers to be its most flexible loop. It allows a large number of variations, which makes it applicable to a much wider array of programming tasks than you might otherwise think. In its most common form, the **for** loop is used to repeat a statement or block of statements a specified number of times. Its general form is shown here.

for(*initialization; expression; increment*) *statement*;

The *initialization* section gives an initial value to the variable that controls the loop. This variable is usually referred to as the *loop-control variable*. The initialization section is executed only once, before the loop begins. The *expression* forms the conditional-test portion of the loop. It tests the loop-control variable against a target value each time the loop repeats. If the conditional test evaluates true, the loop repeats. If it is false, the loop stops, and program execution picks up with the next line of code that follows the loop. The conditional test is performed at the beginning of each iteration. (That is, the conditional expression is evaluated at the top of the loop.) The *increment* portion of the **for** is executed at the bottom of each loop. This means that the *increment* is executed after the body of the loop has been executed, but before the next conditional test. The purpose of the increment expression is to increase (or decrease) the loop-control value by a certain amount.

As a simple first example, this program uses a **for** loop to print the numbers 1 through 10 on the screen.

```
#include <iostream.h>

main()
{
  int num;

  for(num=1; num<11; num=num+1) cout << num << " ";

  return 0;
}
```

This program produces the following output:

```
1 2 3 4 5 6 7 8 9 10
```

The program works like this. First, the loop control variable **num** is initialized to 1. Next, the expression **num < 11** is evaluated. Since it is true, the **for** loop begins running. After the number is printed, **num** is incremented by one and the conditional test is evaluated again. This process continues until **num** equals 11. When this happens, the **for** loop stops and the program ends. Keep in mind that the initialization portion of the **for** loop is only executed once, when the loop is first entered.

As stated, the conditional test is performed at the start of each iteration. This means that if the test is false to begin with, the loop will not execute even once. For example, this program only displays **Program Terminating** because **num** is initialized to 11, causing the conditional test to fail.

2

```
#include <iostream.h>

main()
{
  int num;

  // This loop will not execute even once.
  for(num=11; num<11; num=num+1) cout << num << " ";
  cout << "Program Terminating";

  return 0;
}
```

To repeat several statements, use a block of code as the target of the **for** loop. For example, this program computes the product and sum of the numbers from 1 to 10.

```
#include <iostream.h>

main()
{
  int num, sum, prod;

  sum = 0;
  prod = 1;
  for(num=1; num<11; num=num+1) {
    sum = sum + num;
    prod = prod * num;
  }
  cout << "product and sum: " << prod << " " << sum;

  return 0;
}
```

A **for** loop can run negatively. For example, this fragment decrements the loop-control variable.

```
for(num=20; num>0; num = num-1) . . .
```

Further, the loop-control variable may be incremented or decremented by more than one. For example, this program prints leap years, beginning with 1996.

```cpp
#include <iostream.h>

main()
{
  int i;

  for(i=0; i<60; i=i+4) cout << 1996 + i << "\n";

  return 0;
}
```

Here is an interesting example that uses a **for** loop. It determines if a number is prime.

```cpp
// Prime number tester.
#include <iostream.h>

main()
{
  int num, i, is_prime;

  cout << "Enter the number to test: ";
  cin >> num;

  // now test for factors
  is_prime = 1;
  for(i=2; i<=num/2; i=i+1)
    if(!(num%i)) is_prime = 0;

  // If is_prime is not zero, then number is prime.
  if(is_prime) cout << "The number is prime.";
  else cout << "The number is not prime.";

  return 0;
}
```

Notice the use of the modulus operator (**%**) to determine whether a number is evenly divisible by another. The **%** operator obtains the remainder of an integer division. Therefore, in the program if **num % i** is zero, then **num** can be evenly divided by **i**.

Using the Increment and Decrement Operators

Before moving on, there are two additional operators that you need to know about because they are frequently used inside a **for** loop. In the previous section, you saw loops that looked more or less like the one shown here.

```
for(num=0; num<some_value; num=num+1) . . .
```

Although not incorrect, you will almost never see a statement like **num = num + 1** in professionally written C++ programs because C++ provides a special operator that increments a variable by one. The increment operator is **++** (two plus signs with no intervening space). Using the increment operator, you can change this line of code

```
i = i + 1;
```

into

```
i++;
```

Therefore, the **for** shown earlier will normally be written like this:

```
for(num=0; num<some_value; num++) . . .
```

In a similar fashion, to decrease a variable by one, you can use C++'s decrement operator: --. (There must be no space between the two minus signs.) Therefore,

```
count = count - 1;
```

can be rewritten as

```
count--;
```

Aside from saving you a little typing effort, you will want to use the increment and decrement operators because they will often be faster than the equivalent assignment statements. The reason for this difference is that the C++ compiler can often avoid separate load-and-store machine-language instructions and substitute a single increment or decrement instruction in the executable version of a program.

The increment and decrement operators do not need to follow the variable; they can precede it. Although the effect on the variable is the same, the position of the operator does affect when the operation is performed. To see how, examine this program.

```cpp
#include <iostream.h>

main()
{
  int i, j;

  i = 10;
  j = i++;

  // this will print 11 10
  cout << "i and j: " << i << " " << j;

  return 0;
}
```

Don't let the **j = i++** statement trouble you. The increment operator may be used as part of any valid C++ expression. This statement works like this. First, the current value of **i** is assigned to **j**. Then **i** is incremented. This is why **j** has the value 10, not 11. When the increment or decrement operator follows the variable, the operation is performed after its value has been obtained for use in the expression. Therefore, assuming that **max** has the value 1, an expression such as this

```cpp
count = 10 * max++;
```

assigns the value 10 to **count** and increases **max** by one.

If the variable is preceded by the increment or decrement operator, the operation is performed first, and then the value of the variable is obtained for use in the expression. For example, rewriting the previous program as follows causes **j** to be 11.

```cpp
#include <iostream.h>

main()
{
  int i, j;

  i = 10;
  j = ++i;
```

```
// this will print 11 11
cout << "i and j: " <<  i << " " << j;

return 0;
}
```

If you are simply using the increment or decrement operators to replace equivalent assignment statements, it doesn't matter if the operator precedes or follows the variable. This is a matter of your own personal style. However, if they will be used as part of a larger expression, then you must be careful about whether the prefix or postfix forms of these operators are used.

2

for Loop Variations

The **for** loop is extremely flexible and allows many variations. The reason for this is that the expressions previously referred to as the initialization, conditional expression, and increment portions of the loop are not limited to these narrow roles. The C++ **for** loop places no restrictions on the types of expressions that occur inside it. For example, you do not have to use the initialization section to initialize a loop-control variable. Further, there does not need to be any loop-control variable at all because the conditional test expression may use some other means of stopping the loop. Conversely, there may be two or more loop control variables. Also, the increment portion is technically just an expression that is evaluated each time the loop iterates. It does not have to increment or decrement a variable. Finally, one or more of the expressions inside the **for** may be empty. For example, if the loop control variable has already been initialized outside the **for**, there is no need for an initialization expression.

In this section, we will look at several variations on the **for** loop.

Using Multiple Loop Control Variables

More than one loop control variable can be used to control a **for** loop. Consider the following fragment:

```
for(x=0, y=10; x<=y; x++, y--)
  cout << x << ' ' << y << '\n';
```

Here, **x** increases while **y** decreases. Notice that commas separate the two initialization statements and the two increment expressions. This is necessary in order for the compiler to understand that there are two initialization and two increment statements. In C++, the comma is an operator that essentially means "do this and this." We will look at other uses for the comma operator later in this book. But its most common use is in the **for** loop. You can have any number of initialization and increment statements, but in practice more than two or three make the **for** unwieldy.

Freeing the Conditional Expression

The condition controlling the loop may be any valid C++ expression. It does not need to involve the loop control variable. For example, here is a program that computes the proper tip for a given amount. It prints amounts in $1.00 increments and assumes a 15% tip. Each pass through the loop, it asks if you want to continue. If you press any key other than **N**, the program prints another amount. If you press **N**, the program terminates.

```
// A simple tip calculator.
#include <iostream.h>

main()
{
   float amount;
   char more;

   for(amount = 1.0; more != 'N'; amount = amount + 1)
   {
     cout << "For $" << amount << " The tip is $";
     cout << amount * 0.15 << "    ";
     cout << "More? (Y/N): ";
     cin >> more;
   }

   return 0;
}
```

As you can see, the conditional portion of the loop has nothing to do with the loop control variable.

Missing Pieces

Another aspect of the **for** loop that is different in C++ than in many computer languages is that pieces of the loop definition need not be there. For example, here is one way to write a loop that runs until the user enters the number **1000**.

```
#include <iostream.h>

main()
{
```

2

```
int x;

for(x=0; x != 1000; ) {
  cout << "Enter a number: ";
  cin >> x;
}

return 0;
}
```

The increment portion of the **for** definition is blank. This means that each time the loop repeats, **x** is tested to see if it equals 1000, but no further action takes place. If, however, you type **1000** at the keyboard the condition becomes false and the loop exits. The **for** loop will not modify the loop control variable if no increment portion of the loop is present.

Another variation on the **for** is to move the initialization section outside the loop, as this fragment shows.

```
x = 0;

for( ; x<10; )
{
  cout << x << ' ';
  ++x;
}
```

Here, the initialization section has been left blank and **x** is initialized before the loop is entered. Placing the initialization outside the loop is generally done only when the initial value is derived through a complex process that does not lend itself to containment inside the **for** statement. This example also moves the increment portion of the **for** to inside the loop body.

The Infinite Loop

You can create an *infinite loop* (a loop that never terminates) using this **for** construct.

```
for(;;)
{
  // ...
}
```

This loop will run forever. Although there are some programming tasks, such as operating system command processors, that require an infinite loop, most "infinite loops" are really just loops with special termination requirements.

Near the end of this chapter you will see how to halt a loop of this type. (Hint: It's done using the **break** statement.)

Loops with No Targets

The target of a **for** loop (or any other C++ loop) may be empty. For example, the following loop runs from 0 to 999. It is simply a time-delay loop and performs no other function.

```
for(x=0; x<1000; x++) ;
```

The semicolon that terminates the line is necessary because the **for** expects a statement, which can be empty.

The while Loop

Another of C++'s loops is **while**. It has this general form:

> while(*expression*) *statement*;

Of course, the target of **while** may also be a block of code. The **while** loop works by repeating its target as long as the expression is true. When it becomes false, the loop stops. The following fragment prints the numbers between 1 and 10.

```
num = 1;
while(num <= 10) {
   cout << num << " ";
   num++;
}
```

The value of the expression is checked at the top of the loop. This means that if the expression is false to begin with, the loop will not execute even once. For example, the following program inputs an integer and then uses a **while** loop to print the odd numbers between that number and zero. If you enter zero, the body of the **while** never executes.

```
#include <iostream.h>

main()
{
   int num;

   cout << "Enter an integer: ";
   cin >> num;
```

```
  // Print the odd numbers between num and 0.
  while(num) {
    if(num%2) cout << num << " ";
    num--;
  }

  return 0;
}
```

2

The do Loop

C++'s final loop is **do**, which has this general form:

> do {
>   *statements*
> } while(*expression*);

If only one statement is being repeated, the curly braces are not necessary. Most programmers include them, however, so that they can easily recognize that the **while** that ends the **do** is part of a **do** loop, not the beginning of a **while** loop.

The **do** loop repeats the statement or statements while the expression is true. It stops when the expression becomes false. The **do** loop is unique—it will always execute the code within the loop at least once because the expression controlling the loop is tested at the bottom of the loop. For example, the following loop prints the numbers 1 through 10.

```
x = 1;
do {
  cout << x << " ";
  x++;
} while (x <= 10);
```

The fact that **do** will always execute the body of its loop at least once makes it perfect for checking menu input. For example, this version of the arithmetic program reprompts the user until a valid response is entered.

```
#include <iostream.h>

main()
{
  float a, b;
  char ch;
```

```
cout << "Do you want to:\n";
cout << "Add, Subtract, Multiply, or Divide?\n";

// force user to enter a valid response
do {
  cout << "Enter letter (A, S, M or D): ";
  cin >> ch;
} while(ch!='A' && ch!='S' && ch!='M' && ch!='D');

cout << "Enter first number: ";
cin >> a;
cout << "Enter second number: ";
cin >> b;

switch(ch) {
  case 'A':
    cout << a+b;
    break;
  case 'S':
    cout << a-b;
    break;
  case 'M':
    cout << a*b;
    break;
  case 'D':
    if(b!=0) cout << a/b;
}

  return 0;
}
```

Nested Loops

When the body of one loop contains another, the second is said to be nested inside the first. Any of C++'s loops may be nested within any other loop. At least 256 levels of nesting are guaranteed. However, most compilers allow nesting to virtually any level. As a simple example of nested **for**s, this fragment prints the numbers 1 to 10 on the screen ten times.

```
for(i=0; i<10; i++) {
  for(j=1; j<11; j++) cout << j << " ";
  cout << "\n";
}
```

Using break to Exit a Loop

The **break** statement allows you to exit a loop from any point within its body, bypassing its normal termination expression. The **break** statement can be used with all three loops. When the **break** statement is encountered inside a loop, the loop is immediately terminated, and program execution resumes at the next statement following the loop. For example, this loop prints only the numbers 1 to 10.

```
#include <iostream.h>

main()
{
  int i;

  for(i=i; i<100; i++) {
    cout << i << " ";
    if(i==10) break; // exit the loop
  }

  return 0;
}
```

2

For nested loops a break will cause an exit from only the innermost loop.

The continue Statement

The **continue** statement is somewhat the opposite of the **break** statement. It forces the next iteration of the loop to take place, skipping any remaining code. For example, this program never displays any output.

```
#include <iostream.h>

main()
{
  int x;

  for(x=0; x<100; x++) {
    continue;
    cout << x; // this is never executed
  }

  return 0;
}
```

Each time the **continue** statement is reached, it causes the loop to repeat, skipping the **cout** statement.

In **while** and **do-while** loops, a **continue** statement will cause control to go directly to the test condition and then continue the looping process. In the case of **for**, the increment part of the loop is performed, the conditional test is executed, and the loop continues.

Frankly, **continue** is seldom used, not because it is poor practice to use it, but simply because good applications for it are not common.

The goto Statement

C++ supports a nonconditional jump statement, called the **goto**. Because C++ is designed to be a full-featured, professional programming language, the inclusion of **goto** is necessary. However, most programmers do not use **goto** because it destructures a program and, if frequently used, can render the program virtually impossible to understand later. Also, there is no algorithm that requires a **goto**. For these reasons, it is not used in this book outside of this section.

The **goto** statement can perform a jump within a function. It cannot jump between functions. It works with a label. In C++, a *label* is a valid identifier name followed by a colon. For example, the following **goto** jumps around the **cout** statement.

```
goto mylabel;
 cout << "this will not print";
mylabel: cout << "this will print";
```

The following program uses **goto** to create the equivalent of a **for** loop running from 1 to 10. (This is just an example of **goto**. In actual practice, you should use a real **for** loop when one is needed.)

```
#include <iostream.h>

main()
{
  int i;

  i = 1;
  again:
    cout << i << " ";
    i++;
    if(i<10) goto again;

  return 0;
}
```

Perhaps the only good use for **goto** is to jump out of a deeply nested routine when a catastrophic error occurs.

2

Generating Random Numbers

Many programming tasks require the generation of a series of random values. For example, random number series are frequently used in simulations. Like most other computer languages, C++ provides a means of generating random numbers. It does so through one of its standard library functions, called **rand( ),** whose prototype is shown here.

    int rand( );

This function returns a randomly generated integer that will be between zero and (at least) 32,767. To use this function, your program must include the standard header file STDLIB.H.

The following program demonstrates **rand( )** by simulating the rolling of dice. Each time through the loop, one die is rolled and its value (1 through 6) is displayed.

```cpp
// A Computerized Dice Thrower.
#include <iostream.h>
#include <stdlib.h>

main()
{
  int dice;
  char more;

  do {
    dice = rand(); // randomly generate a value
    cout << "Value: " << (dice % 6) + 1;
    cout << "\nAgain? (Y/N): ";
    cin >> more;
  } while (more != 'N');

  return 0;
}
```

It is important to understand that the random number series generated by **rand( )** will always start at the same point. Thus, each time you run the dice program, it will generate the same series of values. However, you can randomize the random number generator using another library function called **srand( ).** You may want to examine **srand( )** on your own.

CHAPTER 3

A Closer Look at Data Types, Variables, and Expressions

This chapter examines more fully several concepts presented in Chapter 1. It covers C++'s data-type modifiers, global and local variables, and constants. It also discusses how C++ handles various type conversions.

Type Modifiers

In Chapter 1 you learned that C++ has seven basic data types: **void**, **char**, **int**, **float**, **double**, **bool**, and **wchar_t**. Of these, **char**, **int**, **float**, and **double** can be modified using C++'s *type modifiers*. Using a modifier, you can create a type that will more precisely fit your specific need. The type modifiers are

    signed
    unsigned
    long
    short

The type modifier precedes the type name. For example, this declares a **long** integer.

```
long int i;
```

Let's take a look at each modifier, now.

The **signed** modifier can be used on **char** and **int**. However, the use of **signed** on integers is redundant because the default integer declaration assumes a signed number. (A signed number means that it can be positive or negative.) The case with **char** is different. Whether a **char** is signed or unsigned is implementation dependent. In some implementations, **char** is unsigned. In others, it is signed. If you wish to ensure that a variable of type **char** can hold signed values, modify it with the **signed** modifier. An unsigned **char** variable can hold the positive numbers between 0 and 255. Specified as **signed**, it can hold numbers in the range –128 to 127. Since most implementations use **signed char**s, by default, this book assumes that characters are signed.

The **long** modifier may be applied to **int** or **double**. When applied to **int**, it usually doubles the length, in bits, of an integer. For example, in many environments an integer is 16 bits. Therefore, a **long int** is 32 bits in length. When **long** is applied to **double** it roughly doubles the magnitude. The **short** modifier applies only to **int.** In general, it halves the size of an **int.** Therefore, if your compiler uses 32-bit integers, a **short int** will usually be 16 bits long.

Although the preceding paragraph is generally correct, keep in mind that **short** and **long** may have no effect in your environment. Here is why. According to the proposed C++ standard, an **int** must simply provide "at least as much storage" as a **short int**. Further, a **long int** must provide "at least as much storage" as an **int**. Therefore, it is permissible (although rare) for a compiler to use the same size for **int**, **short int**, and **long int**. For this reason, you will want to check your compiler manual for details on the exact size of each integer type.

The **unsigned** modifier can be applied to **char** and **int**. It may also be used in combination with **long** or **short**. It is used to create an unsigned integer. The difference between signed and unsigned integers is in the way the high-order bit of the integer is interpreted. Unsigned integers use all bits (including the high-order bit) to store a value and all values are positive. If a signed integer is specified, then the compiler will generate code that assumes that the high-order bit of an integer is used as a sign flag. If the sign flag is 0, the number is positive; if it is 1, the number is negative. Negative numbers are generally represented using *two's complement* format. The following program demonstrates the differences in the way that signed and unsigned integers are interpreted.

3

```
#include <iostream.h>

main()
{
  int i;  // a signed integer
  unsigned int u; // an unsigned integer

  u = 33000;
  i = u; // copies bit pattern in u into i
  cout << i << " " << u;

  return 0;
}
```

When this program is run, the output is **–32536 33000**. The reason for this is that the bit pattern that 33000 represents as an **unsigned int** is interpreted as –32536 as a **signed int**.

C++ allows a shorthand notation for declaring **unsigned**, **short**, or **long** integers. You may simply use the keyword **unsigned**, **short**, or **long** without the **int**. The **int** is implied. For example,

```
unsigned count;
unsigned int num;
```

both declare **unsigned int** variables.

Table 3-1 shows all allowed combinations of the basic types and the type modifiers. The table also shows the most common size and range for each type.

Type	Common Bit Width	Common Range
char	8	–128 to 127
unsigned char	8	0 to 255
signed char	8	–128 to 127
int	16	–32,768 to 32,767
unsigned int	16	0 to 65535
signed int	16	–32,768 to 32,767
short int	16	same as int
unsigned short int	16	same as unsigned int
signed short int	16	same as short int
long int	32	–2,147,483,648 to 2,147,483,647
unsigned long int	32	0 to 4,294,967,295
signed long int	32	–2,147,483,648 to 2,147,483,647
float	32	3.4E–38 to 3.4E+38
double	64	1.7E–308 to 1.7E+308
long double	80	3.4E–4932 to 1.1E+4932

All Possible Combinations of C++'s Basic Types and Modifiers with Common Bit Lengths and Ranges
Table 3-1.

Using Character Types as Small Integers

It is important to understand that variables of type **char** may be used to hold values other than just the ASCII character set. C++ makes little distinction between a character and an integer, except for the magnitudes of the values each may hold. Therefore, as mentioned earlier, a **char** variable can also be used as a "small" integer with the range –128 through 127 and can be used in place of an integer when the situation does not require larger numbers. For example, the following program uses a **char** variable to control the loop that is summing the numbers between 1 and 100. For many computers, it takes the computer less time to access a single byte (one character) than it does to access two bytes. Therefore, many programmers use a character variable rather than an integer one when the range permits.

```
#include <iostream.h>

main()
{
  int i;
  char j;
```

```
  i = 0;
  for(j=1; j<101; j++) i = j + i;
    cout << "Total is: " << i;

  return 0;
}
```

The bool Data Type

C++ has recently added the **bool** data type. Expressions of type **bool** can have only one of two values: **true** or **false**. As mentioned earlier, **true** and **false** are keywords defined by C++. Both represent integer values. **false** is zero. **true** is nonzero. Technically, there is no need for the **bool** data type. However, due to numerous requests, the ANSI C++ standardization committee decided to add it. Whether you will need (or want) to use it is up to you.

Because **bool** is a new addition to C++, your compiler may not accept it. However, all future compilers will.

3

The Scope of Variables

The *scope* of a variable determines what parts of your program have access to it. A variable's scope depends on where that variable is declared. In C++, there are three places where variables will be declared: inside a block, in the definition of function parameters, and outside of all functions. These variables are called *local variables*, *formal parameters*, and *global variables*, respectively. Although the issue of scope will recur later in this book, the fundamental scopes relating to variables are discussed here.

Local Variables

Variables that are declared inside a block are local variables. Local variables may be accessed only by statements that are also inside the block in which they are declared. Thus, their scope is limited to the block in which they are declared. By far the most common block in which variables are declared is the function. In fact, all local variables occur within a function. A function's block begins with its opening curly brace and ends with its closing curly brace. Any variable declared within a function is local to that function.

Local variables are not known to code outside the block in which they are declared or to other functions outside their own. Consider:

```
#include <iostream.h>
```

```
void func();

main()
{
  int x; // local to main()

  x = 10;
  func();
  cout << "\n";
  cout << x; // displays 10

  return 0;
}

void func()
{
  int x; // local to func()

  x = -199;
  cout << x; // displays -199
}
```

The integer variable **x** is declared twice, once in **main( )** and once in **func( )**. The **x** in **main( )** has no bearing on, or relationship to, the **x** in **func( )**. Specifically, changes to **x** inside **func( )** will not affect the **x** inside **main( )**. Therefore, this program will print **–199** and **10** on the screen.

In C++, local variables are created when their block is entered and destroyed when their block is left. Correspondingly, the storage for these local variables is created and destroyed dynamically. Since all local variables reside within functions, this means that local variables are created when the function is called and destroyed when the function returns. For these reasons, local variables do not maintain their values between function calls. (That is, a local variable's value is lost each time its function returns.) Although called a *dynamic variable* or *automatic variable* in some other C++ literature, this book will continue to use the term *local variable* when referring to variables of this sort because it is the more common term.

Remember, local variables do not maintain their values between function calls. For example, the following program will not work correctly.

```
#include <iostream.h>

int series();

main()
{
```

```
    int i;

    for(i=0; i<10; i++) cout << series() << " ";

    return 0;
}

// This is incorrect.
series()
{
  int total;

  total = (total + 1423) % 1422;
  return total;
}
```

3

This program attempts to use **series( )** to generate a number series in which each number is based upon the value of the preceding one. However, the value of **total** will not be maintained between function calls, and the function fails to carry out its intended task.

Although all local variables are defined within a function, local variables are actually localized to the block in which they are declared. For example, in the following program, **difference** is known only inside its block.

```
#include <iostream.h>

main()
{
  int min, max;

  for(min=0, max=10; min < max; min++, max--)
  {
    int difference; // difference is local to this block

    difference = max - min;
    cout << difference << " ";
  }

   // cout << difference; // This statement is invalid here.

  return 0;
}
```

Here, **difference** is declared inside the block of code associated with the **for**. Thus, it is known to, and may be used by, that block. However, outside that block, **difference** is unknown. To prove this, remove the comments in front of the final **cout** statement and then try compiling the program. As you will see, an error will be reported.

In C++, a local variable may be declared anywhere within a block. This differs from C (C++'s predecessor), which requires that local variables be declared at the start of a block.

Formal Parameters

As you saw in Chapter 1, if a function has arguments, then parameters must be declared that receive those arguments. These are called the formal parameters of the function. As shown in the following fragment, this declaration occurs after the function name, inside the parentheses.

```
void ProcessTrans(int Start, int Finish, char Index)
{
    .
    .
    .
}
```

The **ProcessTrans( )** function has three arguments called **Start, Finish,** and **Index**. You must tell C++ what type of variables these are by declaring them as shown above. Once this has been done, they receive information passed to the function. They may also be used inside the function as normal local variables. For example, you may make assignments to a function's formal parameters or use them in any allowable C++ expression. Even though these variables perform the special task of receiving the value of the arguments passed to the function, they can be used like any other local variable. Like other local variables, their value is lost once the function terminates. The scope of formal parameters is limited to their function.

Global Variables

Since local variables and parameters come into and go out of existence, you may have been wondering how to make a variable and its data stay in existence throughout the entire execution of your program. You can do this in C++ by using global variables. Unlike local variables, global variables will hold their value throughout the lifetime of your program. Global variables are created by declaring them outside of any function. A global variable may be accessed by any function. That is, a global variable is available for use throughout your entire program. In fact, the scope of a global variable is the entire program. (Technically, the scope of a global variable can be partially restricted, as you will see later in this book.)

In the following program, you can see that the variable **count** has been declared outside of all functions. Its declaration is before the **main( )** function. However, it could have been placed anywhere, as long as it was not in a function. Remember, though, that since you must declare a variable before you use it, it is usually best to declare global variables at the top of the program.

```cpp
#include <iostream.h>

void func1();
void func2();

int count; // this is a global variable

main()
{
  int i; // this is a local variable

  for(i=0; i<10; i++) {
    count = i * 2; // access global count
    func1();
  }

  return 0;
}

void func1()
{
  cout << "count: " << count; // access global count
  cout << '\n';
  func2();
}

void func2()
{
  int count; // this is a local variable

  for(count=0; count<3; count++) cout << '.';
}
```

3

Looking closely at this program, it should be clear that although neither **main( )** nor **func1( )** has declared the variable **count**, both may use it. In **func2( )**, however, a local variable called **count** is declared. When **func2( )** references **count**, it will be accessing only its local variable, not the global one. It is important to remember that if a global variable and a local variable have the same name, all references to that variable name inside the function in which the local variable is declared will refer to that local variable and have no effect on the global variable.

Here is another program that demonstrates global variables.

```
#include <iostream.h>

int max; // this is a global variable

void f1();

main()
{
  max = 10;
  f1();

  return 0;
}

void f1()
{
  int i;

  for(i=0; i<max; i++) cout << i << " ";
}
```

Here, both **main( )** and **f1( )** reference the global variable max. The **main( )** function sets the value of **max** to 10, and **f1( )** uses this value to control its **for** loop.

Using Global Variables Correctly

If you have never programmed in a language that supports both local and global variables, you might be wondering when you should use each type. The rule is this: Global variables should be employed only when the same data is used by many functions in your program. Otherwise, you should use local variables. This rule is important. The excessive or unnecessary use of global variables has some negative consequences. First, global variables use memory the entire time your program is executing, not just when they are needed. In situations where memory is in short supply, this could be a problem. Second, using a global where a local variable will do makes a function less general, because it relies on something that must be defined outside itself. For example, here is a program in which global variables are being used for no reason.

```cpp
#include <iostream.h>

int power();
int m, e;

main()
{
  m = 2;
  e = 3;

  cout << m << " raised to the " << e;
  cout << " power is " << power();

  return 0;
}

// Non-general version of power.
power()
{
 int temp, temp2;

  temp = 1;
  temp2 = e;
  for( ; temp2 > 0; temp2--) temp = temp * m;
  return temp;
}
```

Here, the function **power( )** is created to compute the value of **m** raised to the **e**th power. Since **m** and **e** are global, the function cannot be used to compute the power of other values. However, if the program is rewritten like this, **power( )** can be used with any two values.

```cpp
#include <iostream.h>

int power(int m, int e);

main()
{
  int a, b, c, d;

  a = 2;
```

3

```
   b = 3;
   cout << a << " raised to the " << b;
   cout << " power is " << power(a, b);
   cout << "\n";

   c = 4;
   d = 3;
   cout << c << " raised to the " << d;
   cout << " power is " << power(c, d);

   return 0;
}

// Parameterized version of power.
power(int m, int e)
{
   int temp;

   temp = 1;
   for( ; e > 0; e--) temp = temp * m;
   return temp;
}
```

By parameterizing **power( )**, you can now use it to return the result of any value raised to some power, as the program shows.

The important point is that in the nongeneralized version, any program that uses **power( )** must always declare **m** and **e** as global variables and then load them with the desired values each time **power( )** is called. In the parameterized form, the function is complete within itself—no extra baggage need be carried about when it is used.

One last point, using a large number of global variables can lead to program errors because of unknown and unwanted side effects. A major problem in developing large programs is the accidental modification of a variable's value because it was used elsewhere in the program. This can happen in C++ if you use too many global variables in your programs.

Constants

Constants refer to fixed values that may not be altered by the program. For example, the number 100 is a constant. We have been using constants in the preceding sample programs without much fanfare because, in most cases, their use is intuitive. However, the time has come to cover them formally.

Integer constants are specified as numbers without fractional components. For example, 10 and –100 are integer constants. Floating-point constants require the use of the decimal point followed by the number's fractional component. For example 11.123 is a floating-point constant. C++ also allows you to use scientific notation for floating-point numbers. Constants using scientific notation must follow this general form.

number E *sign exponent*

The *sign* is optional. Although the general form is shown with spaces between the component parts for clarity, there may be no spaces between the parts in an actual number. For example, the following defines the value 1234.56 using scientific notation.

```
123.456E1
```

Character constants are enclosed between single quotes. For example 'a' and '%' are both character constants. This means that if you wish to assign a character to a variable of type **char**, you will use a statement similar to

```
ch = 'Z';
```

However, there is nothing in C++ that prevents you from assigning a character variable a value using a numeric constant. For example, the ASCII code for 'A' is 65. Therefore, these two assignment statements are equivalent.

```
char ch;

ch = 'A';
ch = 65;
```

When you enter numeric constants into your program, the compiler must decide what type of constant they are. For example, is 1000 an **int**, an **unsigned**, or a **short**? The reason we haven't worried about this earlier is that C++ automatically converts the type of the right side of an assignment statement to the type of the variable on the left. (We will examine this process more fully later in this chapter.) So, for many situations it doesn't matter what the compiler thinks 1000 is. However, this can be important when you use a constant as an argument to a function. In such a situation, the compiler must pass the correctly sized value to the function.

By default, the compiler fits a numeric constant into the smallest compatible data type that will hold it. Therefore, (assuming 16-bit integers) 10 is an **int** by default, but 64000 is **unsigned** and 100001 is a **long**. Even though the value 10 could be fit into a **char**, the compiler will not do this because it means crossing type boundaries. The only exceptions to the smallest-type rule are floating-point constants, which are assumed to be **double**s. For virtually all programs you will write as a beginner, the compiler defaults are perfectly adequate. However, as you will see later in this book, there will come a point when you will need to specify precisely the type of constant you want.

In cases where the default assumption that C++ makes about a numeric constant is not what you want, you can specify the exact type of numeric constant by using a suffix. For floating-point types, if you follow the number with an 'F', the number is treated as a **float**. If you follow it with an 'L', the number becomes a **long double**. For integer types, the 'U' suffix stands for **unsigned** and the 'L' for **long**. For example, the following fragment assigns an unsigned integer to **max.**

```
max = 103U; // explicitly declare 103 as unsigned.
```

As you may know, in programming it is sometimes easier to use a number system based on 8 or 16 instead of 10. The number system based on 8 is called *octal* and it uses the digits 0 through 7. The base-16 number system is called *hexadecimal* and uses the digits 0 through 9 plus the letters 'A' through 'F', which stand for 10 through 15. C++ allows you to specify integer constants as hexadecimal or octal instead of decimal if you prefer. A hexadecimal constant must begin with 0x (a zero followed by an x) then the constant in hexadecimal form. An octal constant begins with a zero. For example, **0xAB** is a hexadecimal constant, and **024** is an octal constant. You may use either upper- or lowercase letters when entering hexadecimal constants.

C++ supports one other type of constant in addition to those of the predefined data types: the string. A string is a set of characters enclosed by double quotes. You have been working with strings since Chapter 1. Keep in mind one important fact: Although C++ allows you to define string constants, it does not formally have a built-in string data type. (It does define a string class library which your program may use, but this is separate from the data types built into C++.) Instead, as you will see a little later in this book, strings are supported in C++ as character arrays.

Backslash Character Constants

Enclosing character constants in single quotes works for most printing characters, but a few, such as the carriage return, pose a special problem when a text editor is used. For this reason, C++ has created the special backslash character constants.

You have already learned that **\n** stands for newline. C++ supports several additional backslash codes (listed in Table 3-2) so that you may easily enter these special characters as constants.

For example, the following program outputs a newline, a backslash, and a backspace.

```
#include <iostream.h>

main()
{
  cout << "\n\\\b";

  return 0;
}
```

3

Code	Meaning
\b	backspace
\f	form feed
\n	newline
\r	carriage return
\t	horizontal tab
\"	double quote
\'	single quote character
\0	null
\\	backslash
\v	vertical tab
\a	alert
\?	?
\N	octal constant (where N is an octal constant)
\xN	hexadecimal constant (where N is a hexadecimal constant)

Backslash
Character
Constants

Table 3-2.

FAST TRACK TIP

Wide Character Constants

Although English (and many other languages) has relatively few characters in its alphabet, some languages have many. For example, Chinese uses many different symbols. To handle large character sets, C++ supports *wide characters,* of type **wchar_t.** Wide characters are typically 16 bits long. However, this is implementation dependent. You can specify a wide-character constant using the following format:

L'*xy*'

where *x* and *y* are characters that form the wide-character constant. In environments where the length of a wide character is more than 16 bits, more than two characters are specified.

The following fragment declares a wide-character variable and assigns it a value.

```
wchar_t c;

c = L'ab';
```

Here, 'a' is put into the low-order byte of **c** and 'b' is put into the high-order byte.

If you will be programming for multilingual markets, then wide characters will be of interest to you. You will want to see what features your compiler has to support them.

Variable Initialization

A variable may be given an initial value when it is declared. This is called *variable initialization.* The general form of variable initialization is shown here.

type var-name = value;

For example, this statement declares **count** as an **int** and gives it an initial value of 100.

```
int count = 100;
```

The main advantage of using an initialization rather than a separate assignment statement is that the compiler may be able to produce faster code. Also, this saves some typing effort on your part.

The expression used to initialize a variable may be of any type as long as it is valid at the time the variable is being declared. That is, it may include other variables or calls to functions.

Global variables are initialized only once, at the start of program execution. Local variables are initialized each time their block is entered. Local variables that are not initialized contain unknown values. Although some C++ compilers automatically initialize noninitialized local variables to zero, you should not count on this. However, all uninitialized global variables are given the value zero by default.

3

Here is an example that uses a variable initialization. This program gives **i** the initial value of –1 and then displays its value.

```
#include <iostream.h>

main()
{
  int i = -1;

  cout << "i is initialized to " << i;

  return 0;
}
```

When you declare a list of variables, you may initialize one or more of them. For example, this fragment initializes **min** to 0 and **max** to 100. It does not initialize **count**.

```
int min=0, count, max=100;
```

As stated, local variables are initialized each time their block is entered. For this reason, this program prints **10** three times.

```
#include <iostream.h>

void f();

main()
{
  f();
  f();
  f();
```

```
  return 0;
}

void f()
{
  int i = 10;

  cout << i << " ";
  i++; // This has no lasting effect
}
```

Type Conversions in Expressions

Unlike many other computer languages, C++ lets you mix different types of data together in one expression. For example, this is perfectly valid C++ code.

```
char ch;
int i;
float f;
double outcome;

ch = '0';
i = 10;
f = 10.2;

outcome = ch*i/f;
```

C++ allows the mixing of types within an expression because it has a strict set of conversion rules that dictate how type differences are resolved. Let's look closely at them in this section.

One portion of C++'s conversion rules is called *type promotions*. In C++, whenever a **char** or a **short int** is used in an expression, its value is automatically elevated to **int** during the evaluation of that expression. Keep in mind that the type promotion is only in effect during the evaluation of an expression. The variable does not become physically larger. In essence, the compiler just uses a temporary copy of its value.

After the automatic type promotions have been applied, the compiler will convert all operands "up" to the type of the largest operand. This is done on an operation-by-operation basis, as described in the following type-conversion algorithm.

> IF an operand is a **long double**
> THEN the second is converted to **long double**
> ELSE IF an operand is a **double**

THEN the second is converted to **double**
ELSE IF an operand is a **float**
THEN the second is converted to **float**
ELSE IF an operand is an **unsigned long**
THEN the second is converted to **unsigned long**
ELSE IF an operand is **long**
THEN the second is converted to **long** (or **unsigned long**, if necessary)
ELSE IF an operand is **unsigned**
THEN the second is converted to **unsigned**

Once these conversion rules have been applied, each pair of operands will be of the same type and the result of each operation will be the same as the type of both operands.

For example, in this program, **i** is elevated to a **float** and the outcome is of type **float**. Thus, the program prints **232.3**.

```
#include <iostream.h>

main()
{
  int i;
  float f;

  i = 10;
  f = 23.23;

  cout << i*f;   // displays 232.3

  return 0;
}
```

Even though the final outcome of an expression will be of the largest type, the type conversion rules are applied on an operation-by-operation basis. For example, in this expression

```
100.0/(10/3)
```

the division of 10 by 3 produces an integer result, since both are integers. Then this value is elevated to 3.0 to divide 100.0.

Type Conversions in Assignments

In an assignment statement in which the type of the right side differs from that of the left, the type of the right side is converted into that of the left.

When the type of the left side is larger than the type of the right side, this process causes no problems. However, when the type of the left side is smaller than the type of the right, data loss may occur. For example, consider this program. It displays the value **–24**.

```
#include <iostream.h>

main()
{
  char ch;
  int i;

  i = 1000;
  ch = i; // high order bits are lost
  i = ch; // now, i only contains the value of ch

  cout << i;

  return 0;
}
```

The reason that the value **–24** is displayed is that only the low-order eight bits of **i** are copied into **ch**. These eight bits are then assigned to **i,** leaving the high-order eight bits of **i** zero.

Although the assignments in the preceding program may seem strange, they are not in error and you will receive no error message. Remember, one reason C++ was created was to replace assembly language, so it must allow all sorts of type conversions. For example, in some instances you may only want the low-order eight bits of **i**, and this sort of assignment is an easy way to obtain them.

When there is an integer-to-character or a longer-integer-to-shorter-integer type conversion across an assignment, the basic rule is that the appropriate number of high-order bits will be removed. For example, in many environments, this means 8 bits will be lost when going from an **int** to a **char**, and 16 bits will be lost when going from a **long** to an **int**.

When converting from a **long double** to a **double** or from a **double** to a **float**, precision may be lost. When converting from a floating-point value to an integer value, the fractional part is lost, and if the number is too large to fit in the target type, a garbage value will result.

Remember two important points. First, the conversion of an **int** to a **float** or a **float** to **double**, and so on, will not add any precision or accuracy. These kinds of conversions will only change the form in which the value is represented. Second, some C++ compilers will always treat a **char** variable as an **unsigned** value. Others will treat it as a **signed** value. Thus, what will happen when a character variable holds a value greater than 127 is implementation-dependent. If this is important in a program that you write, it is best to declare the variable explicitly as either **signed** or **unsigned**.

As stated, when converting from a floating-point value to an integer value, the fractional portion of the number is lost. The following program illustrates this fact. It prints **1234.98 1234**

```cpp
#include <iostream.h>

main()
{
  int i;
  float f;

  f = 1234.98;
  i = f; // convert to int
  cout << f << " " << i;

  return 0;
}
```

3

When converting from a larger integer type to a smaller one, it is possible to generate a garbage value, as this program illustrates.

```cpp
#include <iostream.h>

main()
{
  int i;
  long int x;

  x = 100000;
  i = x; // convert to int

  cout << i;

  return 0;
}
```

Since the largest value that a 16-bit integer can hold is 32,767, it cannot hold 100,000. What the compiler does, however, is copy the lower order half of **x** into **i**. This produces the meaningless value of **–31072** on the screen.

Type Casts

Sometimes you may want to transform the type of a variable temporarily. For example, you may want to use a floating-point value for one computation, but wish to apply the modulus operator to it elsewhere. Since the modulus operator can only be used on integer values, you have a problem. One solution is to create an integer variable for use in the modulus operation and assign the value of the floating-point variable to it when the time comes. This is a somewhat inelegant solution, however. A better way around this problem is to use a *type cast*, which causes a temporary type change.

A type cast takes this general form:

(type) expression

where *type* is the name of a valid C++ data type to which the expression is being converted. For example,

```
float f;

f = 100.2;

// print f as an integer
cout << (int) f;
```

Here, the type cast causes the value of **f** to be temporarily converted to an **int** for use in the **cout** statement.

Here is a program that uses a cast. It displays the result of **i/3** as an integer expression and as a floating-point expression.

```
#include <iostream.h>

main()
{
  int i;

  i = 10;

  // print integer outcome
  cout << i/3 << "\n";

  // print floating point outcome
  cout << (float) i/3 << "\n";

  return 0;
}
```

You cannot cast a variable that is on the left side of an assignment statement. For example, this is an invalid statement in C++.

```
int num;

(float) num = 123.23; // this is incorrect
```

In addition to the cast operator described here, C++ defines several other ones. These other casting operators are designed to support run time type identification (RTTI). RTTI applies mostly to class types and is an advanced feature that is beyond the scope of this book.

3

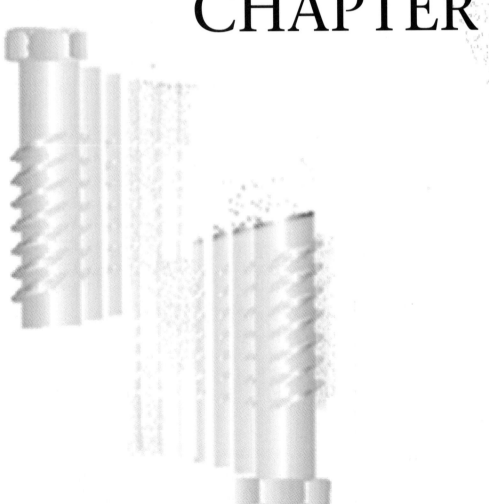

CHAPTER 4

Arrays and Strings

This chapter discusses the array. An *array* is a collection of related variables which are referred to by a common name. In the language of C++, an array is called an *aggregate* data type. Arrays may have from one to several dimensions. As you probably know from your previous programming experience, arrays are useful in a variety of situations.

In C++, strings are implemented as arrays of characters. Therefore, this chapter also discusses the string and several of C++'s standard string functions.

One-Dimensional Arrays

A one-dimensional array is a list of variables that are all of the same type and are referenced through a common name. An individual variable in the array is called an array *element*. Arrays form a convenient way to handle groups of related data.

To declare a one-dimensional array, use the general form

> *type var_name[size];*

where *type* is a valid C++ data type, *var_name* is the name of the array, and *size* specifies the number of elements in the array. For example, to declare an integer array with 20 elements called **myarray**, use this statement.

```
int myarray[20];
```

An array element is accessed by indexing the array using the number of the element. In C++, all arrays begin at zero. This means that if you want to access the first element in an array, use zero for the index. To index an array, specify the index of the element you want inside square brackets. For example, the following statement assigns **i** the value of the second element of **myarray**:

```
i = myarray[1];
```

Remember, arrays start at zero, so an index of 1 refers to the second element.

To assign an array element a value, put the array on the left side of an assignment statement. For example, this gives the first element in **myarray** the value 100.

```
myarray[0] = 100;
```

C++ stores one-dimensional arrays in one contiguous memory location with the first element at the lowest address. Thus, **myarray[0]** is adjacent to **myarray[1]**, which is adjacent to **myarray[2]**, and so on.

You may use the value of an array element anywhere you would use a simple variable or constant. For example, the following program loads the **sqrs** array with the squares of the numbers 1 through 10 and then displays them.

```
#include <iostream.h>

main()
{
  int sqrs[10];
```

```
  int i;

  for(i=1; i<11; i++) sqrs[i-1] = i*i;
  for(i=0; i<10; i++) cout << sqrs[i] << " ";

  return 0;
}
```

C++ does not perform any bounds checking on array indexes. This means that it is possible to overrun the end of an array. For example, if an array called **a** is declared as having five elements, the compiler will still let you access the (nonexistent) tenth element with a statement like **a[9]**. Of course, attempting to access nonexistent elements will generally have disastrous results, often causing the program—even the computer—to crash. It is up to you, the programmer, to make sure that the ends of arrays are never overrun.

In C++, you may not assign one entire array to another. For example, this fragment is incorrect.

4

```
char a1[10], a2[10];
.
.
.
a2 = a1; // this is wrong
```

If you wish to copy the values of all the elements of one array to another, you must do so by copying each element separately. For example, this program loads **a1** with the numbers 1 through 10 and then copies them into **a2**.

```
#include <iostream.h>

main()
{
  int a1[10], a2[10];
  int i;

  // initialize a1
  for(i=1; i<11; i++) a1[i-1] = i;

  // copy a1 into a2
  for(i=0; i<10; i++) a2[i] = a1[i];

  // display a2
  for(i=0; i<10; i++) cout << a2[i] << " ";
```

```
  return 0;
}
```

Arrays are very useful when lists of information need to be managed. For example, this program reads the noonday temperature for each day of a month and then reports the month's average temperature, as well as its hottest and coolest days.

```
#include <iostream.h>

main()
{
  int temp[31], i, min, max, avg;
  int days;

  cout << "How many days in the month? ";
  cin >> days;

  for(i=0; i<days; i++) {
    cout << "Enter noonday temperature for day " << i+1 << ": ";
    cin >> temp[i];
  }

  // find average
  avg = 0;
  for(i=0; i<days; i++) avg = avg + temp[i];
  cout << "Average temperature: " << avg/days << "\n";

  // find min and max
  min = 200;   // initialize min and max
  max = 0;
  for(i=0; i<days; i++) {
    if(min>temp[i]) min = temp[i];
    if(max<temp[i]) max = temp[i];
  }
  cout << "Minimum temperature: " << min << "\n";
  cout << "Maximum temperature: " <<  max << "\n";

  return 0;
}
```

Arrays are especially useful when you want to sort information. For example, this program lets the user enter up to 100 numbers and then sorts them. The sorting algorithm is the bubble sort. The bubble sort algorithm is not the best sorting algorithm, but it is simple to understand and easy to code. The general concept behind the bubble sort, indeed how it got its name, is the repeated comparisons and, if necessary, exchanges of adjacent elements.

This is a little like bubbles in a tank of water with each bubble, in turn, seeking its own level.

```cpp
#include <iostream.h>

main()
{
  int item[100];
  int a, b, t;
  int count;

  // read in numbers
  cout << "How many numbers? (2 to 100): ";
  cin >> count;
  cout << "Enter numbers now: ";
  for(a=0; a<count; a++) cin >> item[a];

  // now, sort them using a bubble sort
  for(a=1; a<count; ++a)
    for(b=count-1; b>=a; --b) {
      // compare adjacent elements
      if(item[b-1] > item[b]) {
        // exchange elements
        t = item[b-1];
        item[b-1] = item[b];
        item[b] = t;
      }
    }

  // display sorted list
  for(t=0; t<count; t++) cout << item[t] << " ";

  return 0;
}
```

4

Strings

The most common use of the one-dimensional array in C++ is the string. Unlike most other computer languages, C++ has no built-in string data type. Instead, C++ supports strings using one-dimensional character arrays. A string is defined as a null-terminated character array. In C++, a null is zero. The fact that the string must be terminated by a null means that you must define an array that is going to hold a string one byte larger than the largest string it will be required to hold, to make room for the null. For example, the following array can hold a string that is up to 10 characters long.

```
char name[11];
```

The reason that **name** has a size of 11 is to allow room for the null terminator.

You have already been using string constants (which are character sequences enclosed by double quotes). A string constant is also a null-terminated character array. The null-terminator is added automatically by the compiler.

Reading and Writing Strings from the Console

To read a string from the keyboard you can simply put the name of the array receiving the string on the right side of a **cin** statement. For example:

```
#include <iostream.h>

main()
{
  char str[80];
  int i;

  cout << "Enter a string (less than 80 chars): ";
  cin >> str; // input a string

  // display string one character at a time
  for(i=0; str[i]; i++) cout << str[i] << " ";

  return 0;
}
```

The **cin** statement performs no bounds checking, so it is possible for the user to enter more characters than the string can hold. Therefore, be sure to use an array large enough to hold the expected input. One other point: Notice how the program uses the fact that a null is false to control the loop that outputs the string one character at a time.

In the previous program, the string that was entered by the user was output to the screen a character at a time. There is however, a much easier way to display a string, using **cout**. Here is the previous program rewritten.

```
#include <iostream.h>

main()
{
  char str[80];

  cout << "Enter a string (less than 80 chars): ";
  cin >> str; // input a string
```

```
  cout << str; // output the string

  return 0;
}
```

As this program shows, using **cout,** you can output a string contained in a character array in just the same way that you have been outputting string constants. Simply use the name of the array without an index. For reasons that will be clear after you have learned more about C++, the name of a character array that holds a string can be used any place that a string constant can be used.

A Problem Inputting Strings Using cin

If you tried the preceding program, you may have noticed a problem. To see what it is, run the program and try entering the string "This is a test". As you will see, when the program redisplays your string, it will only show the word "This" and not the entire sentence. The reason for this is that the C++ I/O system stops reading a string when the first *whitespace* character is encountered. Whitespace characters include spaces, tabs, and newlines. Thus, the space after the "This" causes the **cin** statement to terminate.

4

There are various ways to solve the preceding problem. Some solutions use C++'s object-oriented I/O system, which will be discussed later in this book. However, there is one solution that you can use now. It uses another of C++'s library functions called **gets( )**. The general form of a **gets( )** call is:

    gets(*array-name*);

gets( ) will read a string from the keyboard until you press ENTER. This means that it will read a string containing spaces. To use **gets( )**, call it with the name of the array receiving the string as an argument. Do not specify any index. Upon return from **gets( )** the array will hold the string input at the keyboard. The header file used by **gets( )** is STDIO.H.

This version of the preceding program uses **gets( )** to allow strings containing spaces to be entered.

```
#include <iostream.h>
#include <stdio.h>

main()
{
  char str[80];

  cout << "Enter a string (less than 80 chars): ";
```

```
gets(str);
cout << str; // output the string

return 0;
}
```

Keep in mind that neither **cin** nor **gets( )** performs any bounds checking on the array. Therefore, if the user enters a string longer than the size of the array, the array will be overrun.

Remember: C++ also has some object-oriented functions that let you read strings from the keyboard, which you will learn about later in this book.

Some Standard String Functions

The C++ standard library supplies many string-related functions. The four most important are **strcpy( )**, **strcat( )**, **strcmp( )**, and **strlen( )**. These functions require the header file STRING.H. Let's look at each now.

The **strcpy( )** function has this general form.

strcpy(*to, from*);

It copies the string contained in *from* to *to*. The contents of *from* are unchanged. For example, this fragment copies the string "hello" into **str** and displays it on the screen.

```
char str[80];

strcpy(str, "hello");
cout << str;
```

The **strcpy( )** function performs no bounds checking, so you must make sure that the array on the receiving end is large enough to hold what is being copied, including the null terminator.

You can create a string of zero length using a **strcpy( )** statement like this:

```
strcpy(str, "");
```

Such a string is called a *null string*. It contains only one element: the null terminator.

The **strcat( )** function adds the contents of one string to the end of another. As you probably know, this process is called *concatenation*. Its general form is

strcat(*to, from*);

It appends the contents of *from* to the contents of *to*. It performs no bounds checking, so you must make sure that *to* is large enough to hold its current contents plus what it will be receiving. This fragment displays **hello there**.

```
char str[80];

strcpy(str, "hello");
strcat(str, " there");
cout << str;
```

The **strcmp( )** function compares two strings. It takes this general form.

strcmp(*s1, s2*);

It returns zero if the strings are the same. It returns less than zero if *s1* is less than *s2* and greater than zero if *s1* is greater than *s2*. The strings are compared lexicographically, that is, in dictionary order. Therefore, a string is less than another when it would appear before the other in a dictionary. A string is greater than another when it would appear after the other. The comparison is not based upon the length of the string. Also, the comparison is case-sensitive, lowercase characters being greater than uppercase. This fragment prints zero, because the strings are the same.

4

```
cout << strcmp("one", "one");
```

The **strlen( )** function returns the length, in characters, of a string. Its general form is

strlen(*str*);

The **strlen( )** function does not count the null terminator. This means that if **strlen( )** is called using the string "test", it will return 4.

The following program demonstrates the four string functions.

```
#include <string.h>
#include <iostream.h>

main()
{
  char str1[80], str2[80];
```

```
    int i;

    cout << "Enter the first string: ";
    cin >> str1;
    cout << "Enter the second string: ";
    cin >> str2;

    // see how long the strings are
    cout << str1 << " is " << strlen(str1) << " chars long.\n";
    cout << str2 << " is " << strlen(str2) << " chars long.\n";

    // compare the strings
    i = strcmp(str1, str2);
    if(!i) cout << "The strings are equal.\n";
    else if(i<0) cout << str1 << " is less than " << str2 << ".\n";
    else cout << str1 << " is greater than " << str2 << ".\n";

    /* concatenate str2 to end of str1 if
       there is enough room */
    if(strlen(str1) + strlen(str2) < 80) {
      strcat(str1, str2);
      cout << str1 << "\n";
    }

    // copy str2 to str1
    strcpy(str1, str2);
    cout << str1 << " " << str2 << "\n";

    return 0;
}
```

Here is another example that illustrates strings. One common use of strings is to support a command-based interface. Unlike a menu, which allows the user to make a selection, a command-based interface displays a prompting message, waits for the user to enter a command, and then does what the command requests. Many operating systems use command-line interfaces, for example. The following program is similar to a program developed earlier in this book. It allows the user to add, subtract, multiply, or divide, but does not use a menu. Instead, it uses a command-based interface.

```
#include <iostream.h>
#include <string.h>

main()
{
  char command[80];
  int i, j;
```

```
for( ; ; ) {
  cout << "Operation? ";
  cin >> command;
  // see if user wants to stop
  if(!strcmp(command, "quit")) break;

  cout << "Enter first number: ";
  cin >> i;

  cout << "Enter second number: ";
  cin >> j;

  //  now, perform the operation
  if(!strcmp(command, "add"))
    cout << i+j << "\n";
  else if(!strcmp(command, "subtract")) {
    if(j) cout << i-j << "\n";
  }
  else if(!strcmp(command, "divide")) {
    if(j) cout << i/j << "\n";
  }
  else if(!strcmp(command, "multiply"))
    cout << i*j << "\n";
  else cout << "Unknown command. \n";
}

  return 0;
}
```

You might use a variation on this example to implement a command-driven interface to programs that you write.

Using toupper( ) and tolower( )

The C++ standard library contains two functions that are quite useful when working with characters and strings: **toupper( )** and **tolower( )**. These functions have the following prototypes:

> int toupper(int *ch*);
> int tolower(int *ch*);

The **toupper( )** function returns the uppercase equivalent of the character passed in *ch*. **tolower( )** returns the lowercase equivalent of *ch*. If *ch* does not specify a letter of the alphabet, then *ch* is returned, unaltered. Although *ch* is specified as an integer and both functions return an integer value, don't worry. You can pass a normal character (**char**) value to them. You can also assign their return values to a character variable. (The use of **int** rather than **char** is, essentially, an historical quirk.) For example, the following fragment assigns a lowercase 'x' to **ch**.

```
char ch;

ch = tolower('X');
```

Both **toupper( )** and **tolower( )** require the header file CTYPE.H.

The reason that **toupper( )** and **tolower( )** are so useful is that they let your program ignore the case of a character or characters. This is especially useful where user input is concerned. For example, in the command-driven arithmetic program shown in the text, you need to enter the commands in lowercase so that they can be matched using **strcmp( )**. That is, if you enter **ADD**, it will *not* match the string "add." However, the following version of the program automatically converts your command to lowercase, allowing you to use upper- or lowercase, as you desire.

```
#include <iostream.h>
#include <string.h>
#include <ctype.h>

main()
{
  char command[80];
  int i, j;

  for( ; ; ) {
    cout << "Operation? ";
    cin >> command;

    // convert to lowercase
    for(i=0; i<strlen(command); i++)
      command[i] = tolower(command[i]);

    // see if user wants to stop
    if(!strcmp(command, "quit")) break;

    cout << "Enter first number: ";
    cin >> i;

    cout << "Enter second number: ";
    cin >> j;
```

```
    //  now, perform the operation
    if(!strcmp(command, "add"))
      cout << i+j << "\n";
    else if(!strcmp(command, "subtract")) {
      if(j) cout << i-j << "\n";
    }
    else if(!strcmp(command, "divide")) {
      if(j) cout << i/j << "\n";
    }
    else if(!strcmp(command, "multiply"))
      cout << i*j << "\n";
    else cout << "Unknown command. \n";
  }

  return 0;
}
```

Notice one other thing about this program. When converting your command to lowercase, it obtains the length of the string using **strlen( ).** This value can then be used as the upper limit when indexing **command**. As you can see, the string functions are designed to be fully integrated with the way C++ implements strings.

4

Multidimensional Arrays

In addition to one-dimensional arrays, you can create arrays of two or more dimensions. For example, to create a 10x12 two-dimensional integer array called **count**, you would use this statement;

```
int count[10][12];
```

As you can see in the example, to add a dimension, you simply specify its size inside square brackets.

A two-dimensional array is essentially an array of one-dimensional arrays and is most easily thought of in a row, column format. For example, given a 4x5 integer array called **two_d**, you can think of it looking like that shown in Figure 4-1. Assuming this conceptual view, a two-dimensional array is accessed a row at a time, from left to right. This means that the rightmost index will change most quickly when the array is accessed sequentially from the lowest to highest memory address.

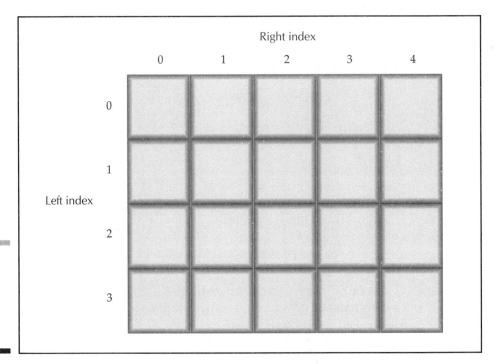

Right index

Left index

A conceptual
view of a
4X5 two-
dimensional
array
Figure 4-1.

Two-dimensional arrays are used like one-dimensional ones. For example, this program loads a 4x5 array with the products of the indices, then displays the array in row, column format.

```
#include <iostream.h>

main()
{
  int two_d[4][5];
  int i, j;

  for(i=0; i<4; i++)
    for(j=0; j<5; j++)
      two_d[i][j] = i*j;

  for(i=0; i<4; i++) {
    for(j=0; j<5; j++)
      cout << two_d[i][j] << " ";
    cout << "\n";
  }
}
```

```
    return 0;
}
```

The program output looks like this:

```
0 0 0 0 0
0 1 2 3 4
0 2 4 6 8
0 3 6 9 12
```

To create arrays of three dimensions and greater, simply add the size of the additional dimension. For example, the following statement creates a 10x12x8 three-dimensional array.

```
float values[10][12][8];
```

A three-dimensional array is essentially an array of two-dimensional arrays.

You may create arrays of more than three dimensions, but this is seldom done because the amount of memory they consume increases exponentially with each additional dimension. For example, a 100-character one-dimensional array requires 100 bytes of memory. A 100x100 character array requires 10,000 bytes, and a 100x100x100 array requires 1,000,000. A 100x100x100x100 four-dimensional array would require 100,000,000 bytes of storage—large even by today's standards.

4

A good use of a two-dimensional array is to manage lists of numbers. For example, you could use this two-dimensional array to hold the noontime temperature for each day of the year, grouped by month.

```
float yeartemp[12][31];
```

In the same vein, the following program can be used to keep track of the number of points scored per quarter by each member of a basketball team.

```
#include <iostream.h>

main()
{
  int bball[5][4];
  int i, j;

  for(i=0; i<4; i++)
```

```
    for(j=0; j<5; j++) {
      cout << "Quarter " << i+1 << ", player " << j+1;
      cout << " Enter number of points: ";
      cin >> bball[i][j];
    }

  // display results
  for(i=0; i<4; i++)
    for(j=0; j<5; j++) {
      cout << "Quarter " << i+1 << " player " << j+1;
      cout << ": " << bball[i][j] << "\n";
    }

  return 0;
}
```

Array Initialization

Like other types of variables, you can give the elements of an array initial values. This is accomplished by specifying a list of values the array elements will have. The general form of array initialization for one-dimensional arrays is shown here:

type array-name[size] = {*value-list* };

The *value-list* is a comma-separated list of values that are type compatible with the base type of the array. The first constant will be placed in the first position of the array, the second constant in the second position, and so on. Note that a semicolon follows the }. In the following example, a five-element integer array is initialized with the squares of the numbers 1 through 5.

```
int i[5] = {1, 4, 9, 16, 25};
```

This means that **i[0]** will have the value 1 and **i[4]** will have the value 25.

You can initialize character arrays two ways. First, if the array is not holding a null-terminated string, you simply specify each character using a comma-separated list. For example, this initializes **letters** with the letters 'A', 'B', and 'C'.

```
char letters[3] = {'A', 'B', 'C'};
```

If the character array is going to hold a string, you can initialize the array using a quoted string, as shown here.

```
char name[4] = "ABC";
```

Notice that no curly braces surround the string. They are not used in this form of initialization. Because strings in C++ end with a null, you must make sure that the array you declare is long enough to include the null. This is why **name** is 4 characters long, even though "ABC" is only 3. When a string constant is used, the compiler automatically supplies the null terminator.

Multidimensional arrays are initialized in the same way as one-dimensional ones. For example, here the array **sqr** is initialized with the values 1 through 9, using row order.

```
int  sqr[3][3] = {
  1, 2, 3,
  4, 5, 6,
  7, 8, 9
};
```

This initialization causes **sqr[0][0]** to have the value 1, **sqr[0][1]** to contain 2, **sqr[0][2]** to hold 3, and so forth.

A common use of an initialized array is to create a lookup table. For example, in the following program a 5x2 two-dimensional array is initialized so that the first element in each row specifies an angle in degrees and the second element contains the equivalent angle in radians. The program allows a user to enter the number of degrees in an angle and converts it to radians.

4

```
// A lookup table for radians.
#include <iostream.h>

double radians[5][2] = {
  // degrees, radians
  1.0, 0.0175,
  2.0, 0.0349,
  3.0, 0.0524,
  4.0, 0.0698,
  5.0, 0.0873
};

main()
{
  double degrees;
  int i;

  cout << "Enter number of degrees (1 to 5): ";
  cin >> degrees;

  // look up radians in table
```

```
for(i=0; i<5; i++)
  if(radians[i][0] == degrees) {
    cout << radians[i][1] << " Radians\n";
    break;
  }

// Report error if degrees not found in table
if(i==5) cout << "Degrees not found.\n";

return 0;
}
```

Even though an array has been given an initial value, its contents may be changed. For example, this program prints "hello" on the screen.

```
#include <iostream.h>
#include <string.h>

main()
{
  char str[80] = "I like C++";

  strcpy(str, "hello");
  cout << str;

  return 0;
}
```

As this program illustrates, in no way does an initialization fix the contents of an array.

Unsized Arrays

If you are initializing a one-dimensional array, you need not specify the size of the array—simply put nothing inside the square brackets. If you don't specify the size, the compiler automatically counts the number of initialization constants and uses that value as the size of the array. For example,

```
int pwr[] = {1, 2, 4, 8, 16, 32, 64, 128};
```

causes the compiler to create an initialized array eight elements long. Arrays that don't have their dimensions explicitly specified are called *unsized arrays*. An unsized array is useful because it is easier for you to change the size of the initialization list without having to count it and then change the array dimension. This helps avoid counting errors on long lists, which is especially important when initializing strings. Here, an unsized array is used to hold a prompting message.

```
char prompt[] = "Enter your name: ";
```

If, at a later date, you wanted to change the prompt to "Enter your last name:", you would not have to count the characters and then change the array size.

Unsized array initializations are not restricted to only singly dimensioned arrays. However, for multidimensional arrays you must specify all but the leftmost dimension. (The other dimensions are needed to allow C++ to index the array properly.) By leaving the leftmost dimension empty, you may build tables of varying lengths with the compiler allocating enough storage for them automatically. For example, the declaration of **sqr** as an unsized array is shown here.

```
int sqr[][3] = {
   1, 2, 3,
   4, 5, 6,
   7, 8, 9
};
```

4

The advantage to this declaration over the sized version is that tables may be lengthened or shortened without changing the array dimensions.

String Tables

Arrays of strings, often called *string tables*, are common in C++ programming. A two-dimensional string table is created like any other two-dimensional array. However, the way you think about it will be slightly different. For example, here is a small string table. What do you think it defines?

```
char names[10][40];
```

This statement specifies a table that can contain 10 strings, each up to 40 characters long (including the null terminator). To access a string within this table, specify only the first index. For example, to read a string from the keyboard into the third string in **names**, use this statement.

```
cin >> names[2];
```

By the same token, to output the first string, use this **cout** statement.

```
cout << names[0];
```

The declaration that follows creates a three-dimensional table with three lists of strings. Each list is five strings long, and each string can hold 80 characters.

```
char animals[3][5][80];
```

To access a specific string in this situation, you must specify the first two dimensions. For example, to access the second string in the third list, specify **animals[2][1]**.

Here is an example that uses a string table. It inputs ten strings, putting each into the **text** string table. The program then lets you display each string, one at a time, in any order you choose. To stop the program, enter a negative number.

```cpp
#include <iostream.h>

main()
{
  char text[10][80]; // string table
  int i;

  for(i=0; i<10; i++) {
    cout << i+1 << ": ", i+1;
    cin >> text[i];
  }
  do {
    cout << "Enter number of string (1 - 10) : ";
    cin >> i;
    i--;  // adjust value to match array index
    if(i>=0 && i<10) cout << text[i] << "\n";
  } while(i>=0);

  return 0;
}
```

You can initialize a string table as you would any other type of array. For example, the following program uses an initialized string table to translate between German and English. Notice that curly braces are needed to surround the list.

```cpp
// A very limited English-to-German translator.
#include <iostream.h>
```

```
#include <string.h>

char words[][2][40] = {
  "dog", "Hund",
  "no", "nein",
  "year", "Jahr",
  "child", "Kind",
  "I",   "Ich",
  "drive", "fahren",
  "house", "Haus",
  "to", "zu",
  "",""
};

main()
{
  char english[80];
  int i;

  cout << "Enter English word: ";
  cin >> english;

  // look up the word
  i = 0;
  // search while null string not yet encountered
  while(strcmp(words[i][0], "")) {
    if(!strcmp(english, words[i][0])) {
      cout << "German translation: " << words[i][1];
      break;
    }
    i++;
  }
  if(!strcmp(words[i][0], ""))
    cout << "Not in dictionary\n";

  return 0;
}
```

You can access the individual characters that comprise a string within a string table by using the rightmost index. For example, the following program prints the strings in the table one character at a time.

```
#include <iostream.h>

char text[][80] = {
  "When", "in", "the",
  "course", "of", "human",
```

4

```
  "events", ""
};

main()
{
  int i, j;

  // now, display them
  for(i=0; text[i][0]; i++) {
    for(j=0; text[i][j]; j++)
      cout << text[i][j];
    cout << " ";
  }

  return 0;
}
```

FAST TRACK TIP

The is... Character Functions

The C++ standard library contains several useful functions that allow you to categorize characters. These functions all begin with **is.** All the functions take a character argument and return either a true or false result. The character-testing functions are shown here.

Function	Purpose
isalnum(ch)	Returns true if *ch* is a letter of the alphabet or a digit
islapha(ch)	Returns true if *ch* is a letter of the alphabet
iscntrl(ch)	Returns true if *ch* is a control character
isdigit(ch)	Returns true if *ch* is a digit
isgraph(ch)	Returns true if *ch* is a printing character (except a space)
islower(ch)	Returns true if *ch* is a lowercase letter
isprint(ch)	Returns true if *ch* is a printing character (including a space)
ispunct(ch)	Returns true if *ch* is a punctuation character
isspace(ch)	Returns true if *ch* is a whitespace character
isupper(ch)	Returns true if *ch* is an uppercase letter
isxdigit(ch)	Returns true if *ch* is a hexadecimal digit

These functions require the header file CTYPE.H.

The character-testing functions are especially useful when your program must perform various types of lexical analysis. For example, the following program counts the number of spaces contained in the string **str**.

```
#include <ctype.h>
#include <iostream.h>
#include <string.h>

main()
{
  char str[] = "This is a test.";
  int i, spaces;

 spaces = 0;
  for(i=0; i<strlen(str); i++) if(isspace(str[i])) spaces++;

  cout << spaces; // displays 3

  return 0;
}
```

4

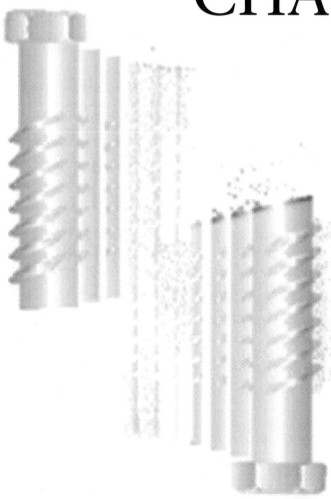

CHAPTER 5

Pointers

This chapter covers one of C++'s most important (and most troublesome) features: the *pointer*. A pointer is, essentially, the address of another object. One reason that pointers are so important is that much of the power of the C++ language is derived from the unique way in which they are implemented. This chapter discusses pointers, pointer operators, pointer arithmetic, and the relationship between pointers and arrays. You will want to pay close attention to the material in this chapter because pointers are used to support several advanced OOP features (such as run-time polymorphism) discussed later in this book.

Pointer Basics

A pointer is a variable that holds the memory address of another object. For example, if a variable called **p** contains the address of another variable called **q**, then **p** is said to *point to* **q**. Therefore if **q** is at location 100 in memory, then **p** would have the value 100 (**q**'s address).

To declare a pointer variable, use this general form.

> *type *var-name;*

Here, *type* is the *base type* of the pointer. The base type specifies the type of the object that the pointer will point to. Notice that the variable name is preceded by an asterisk. This tells the compiler that a pointer variable is being created. For example, the following statement creates a pointer to an integer.

```
int *p;
```

C++ contains two special pointer operators: * and **&**. The **&** operator returns the address of the variable it precedes. The * operator returns the value stored at the address that it precedes. (The * pointer operator has no relationship to the multiplication operator, which uses the same symbol.) To see how these operators are used, examine this short program.

```
#include <iostream.h>

main()
{
  int *p, q;

  q = 144; // assign q 144

  p = &q; // assign p the address of q

  cout << *p; // display q's value using pointer

  return 0;
}
```

This program prints **144** on the screen. Let's see why. First, the line

```
int *p, q;
```

defines two variables: **p**, which is declared as an integer pointer, and **q**, which is an integer. Then, **q** is assigned the value 144. In the next line, **p** is assigned the *address of* **q**. You can verbalize the **&** operator as "address of." Therefore, this line can be read as "assign **p** the address of **q**." Finally, the value is displayed using the ***** operator applied to **p**. The ***** operator can be verbalized as "at address." Therefore, the **cout** statement can be read as "print the value at address **p**," which is 144. When a variable's value is referenced through a pointer, the process is called *indirection*.

It is possible to use the ***** operator on the left side of an assignment statement in order to assign a variable a new value using a pointer to it. For example, this program assigns **q** a value indirectly using the pointer **p**.

```
#include <iostream.h>

main()
{
  int *p, q;

  p = &q; // get q's address

  *p = 199; // assign q a value using a pointer

  cout << "q's value is " << q;

  return 0;
}
```

In the two simple example programs just shown, there is no reason to use a pointer. However, as you learn more about C++, you will understand why pointers are important.

Before moving on, let's graphically work through one more example. To begin, assume these declarations.

```
int *p, q, r;
```

Further assume that **p** is located at memory address 100, **q** at address 102, and **r** at location 104. After this statement

```
p = &q;
```

the pointer **p** contains the value 102. Therefore, after this assignment, memory looks like this:

5

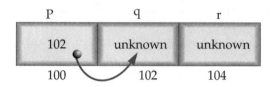

After the statement

```
*p = 1000;
```

executes, memory looks like this:

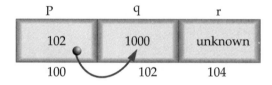

After this statement

```
r = *p;
```

memory now looks like this:

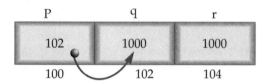

Remember, the value of **p** has nothing to do with the *value* of **q**. It simply holds **q**'s *address*, to which the indirection operators may be applied.

Declaring a pointer variable simply creates a variable capable of holding a memory address. It does not give it any meaningful initial value. If you attempt to use a pointer before it has been assigned the address of a variable, your program will probably crash. This is why the following fragment is incorrect.

```
main()
{
   int *p;
```

```
*p = 10;   /* incorrect - p is not pointing to
                anything */
```

As the comment notes, the pointer **p** is not pointing to any known object. Hence, trying to indirectly assign a value using **p** is meaningless and dangerous.

Understanding the Null Pointer

If you examine professionally written C++ code, you will find that the *null pointer* appears frequently. As pointers are defined in C++, a pointer that contains a null value (i.e., zero) is assumed to be unused and pointing at nothing. In C++, null is, by convention, assumed to be an invalid memory address. This convention is used to simplify and improve the efficiency of many algorithms in which pointers are involved. However, you must keep in mind that the null-pointer convention is simply a voluntary device which virtually all C++ programs adhere to. The compiler, however, will still let you use a null pointer, usually with disastrous results. It is simply by common usage that a null pointer is assumed to be unused.

To create a null pointer, assign it the value zero. One way to do this is to use the predefined constant **NULL**. (**NULL** is defined by including IOSTREAM.H or other header files.) For example, the following initializes **ptr** to null.

```
int *ptr = NULL;
```

By definition a null pointer is false. Therefore, you can legally write a statement such as this:

```
if(p) cout << "p is not null";
```

As you will see, the null-pointer convention is used frequently in C++ as a terminating condition for loops and in **if** statements like the one just shown.

The Base Type Matters

The base type of a pointer is important for two reasons. First, the base type of a pointer has significant implications relative to several of C++'s object-oriented features. Second, it determines the size of an object to which the pointer is assumed to be pointing. In this section, the importance of the second reason is discussed.

C++ allows any type of pointer to point anywhere in memory. That is, a pointer can point to any valid address that is within the program's address space. However, it is the pointer's base type that determines how the

5

contents of the memory pointed to by the pointer will be interpreted. For example, whatever is pointed to by an integer pointer will be interpreted as an integer—whether it actually is one or not! Therefore, it doesn't matter whether the target address actually holds an object of the pointer's base type. The compiler will act as though it does when it evaluates an expression involving that pointer. To understand the importance of this, consider the following fragment.

```
int q;
float *fp;

fp = (float *) &q; // technically correct, but ...

// this causes an error at runtime
*fp = 100.23;
```

Although syntactically correct, consider what would occur if such a fragment were executed. The **float** pointer **fp** is assigned the address of an integer. This address is then used on the left side of an assignment statement to assign a floating-point value. However, (assuming 2-byte integers and 4-byte **float**s) **int**s are shorter than **float**s, and this assignment statement causes memory adjacent to **q** to be overwritten. That is, the assignment statement uses the 2 bytes allocated to **q** as well as 2 adjacent bytes, which might be where **fp** is stored, thus causing an error.

In the preceding fragment, notice the use of the cast to **float *.** It is used to override the type incompatibilities between the pointer type (**float ***) and the integer pointer that is generated by **&q**. The cast is necessary. In C++, you cannot assign one type of pointer to another unless the two types of pointers are compatible (that is, essentially the same). However, it is possible to override this safety feature using a cast (as the foregoing example shows).

Notice the way the cast to **float *** is formed in the preceding example. This specific case can be generalized. To cast to a pointer type, simply specify the base type followed by an ***** inside the parentheses.

Here is a complete program that further illustrates why you must make sure that the base type of a pointer is the same as the object it points to. In this example, the errors generated by the invalid pointer operations are benign and no harm is done. However, in real world programs, invalid pointer operations are generally disastrous. (Some compilers may generate a warning message when you compile the following example, but none will issue an actual error message and stop compilation.)

```
// This program is wrong, but harmless.

#include <iostream.h>

main()
{
  int *p;
  double q, temp;

  temp = 1234.34;

  p = (int *) &temp; // Attempt to assign q a value using
  q = *p;            // indirection through an integer pointer.

  cout << q; // this will not print 1234.34

  return 0;
}
```

Even though **p** points to **temp**, which does, indeed, hold the value 1234.34, the assignment

```
q = *p;
```

fails to copy the number because only 2 bytes (assuming 2-byte integers) will be transferred. Since **p** is an integer pointer, it cannot be used to transfer an 8-byte quantity (assuming 8-byte **double**s). Remember, it is the base type of the pointer that determines the size of the target object.

As you can probably already guess, it is seldom a good idea to cast pointers because the compiler uses the base type to determine how many bytes are in the object pointed to by the pointer. This is how C++ knows how many bytes to copy when an indirect assignment is made, or how many bytes to compare if an indirect comparison is made. Therefore, unless you are doing something unusual, never use a pointer of one type to point to an object of a different type.

void * Pointers

There is one special type of pointer defined by C++: the *void pointer*. A void pointer is declared using **void ***. A void pointer may point to any type of object. As mentioned in the previous section, normally, you may only assign one pointer to another if their types are compatible. However, a void pointer

5

can be assigned any type of pointer without the use of a type cast. For example, the following is valid C++ code.

```
int *p;
void *v;

v = p; // assign int * to void *
```

The most common use of **void *** is as a function return type.

Pointer Expressions

In general, pointers may be used like other variables in any valid C++ expression. However, a few rules and restrictions apply.

Pointer Arithmetic

There are only four arithmetic operators that may be applied to pointer variables: **+, ++, -,** and **--.** Further, you may add or subtract only integer quantities. You cannot, for example, add a floating-point number to a pointer.

Pointer arithmetic differs from "normal" arithmetic in one very important way: it is performed relative to the base type of the pointer. Each time a pointer is incremented, it will point to the next item, as defined by its base type, beyond the one currently pointed to. For example, assume that an integer pointer called **p** contains the address 200. After the statement

```
p++;
```

executes, **p** will have the value 202, assuming integers are two bytes long. By the same token, if **p** had been a **float** pointer (assuming 4-byte **float**s), then the resultant value contained in **p** would have been 204.

The only pointer arithmetic that appears as "normal" occurs when **char** pointers are used. Because characters are one byte long, an increment increases the pointer's value by one, and a decrement decreases its value by one.

You may add or subtract an integer quantity to or from a pointer. For example, the following is a valid fragment.

```
int *p
.
.
```

```
   .
p = p + 200;
```

This statement causes **p** to point to the 200th integer past the one to which **p** is currently pointing.

The following program demonstrates the effects of pointer arithmetic for a variety of pointer types. When a pointer is used in a **cout** statement, the address it points to is displayed. The program uses this capability to illustrate the effects of pointer arithmetic.

```cpp
#include <iostream.h>

main()
{
  int   *ip, i;
  float *fp, f;
  double *dp, d;

  ip = &i;
  fp = &f;
  dp = &d;

  // print the current values
  cout << ip << " " << fp << " " << dp;

  cout << "\n";

  // now increment them by one
  ip++;
  fp++;
  dp++;

  // print their new values
  cout << ip << " " << fp << " " << dp;

  return 0;
}
```

Here is sample output from this program.

```
0xfff4 0xfff0 0xffe6
0xfff6 0xfff4 0xffee
```

Remember, the values displayed by this program will vary widely among compilers and even among versions of the same compiler. (You will most likely see different values.) However, in all cases, the pointers will be incremented by the number of bytes in their base types, typically 2 for **int**s, 4 for **float**s, and 8 for **double**s.

Aside from addition and subtraction, you may not perform any other type of arithmetic operations—you may not multiply, divide, or take the modulus of a pointer. However, you may subtract one pointer from another in order to find the number of elements separating them. This is useful when both pointers point to a common object, such as an array. The result of subtracting one pointer from the other yields the number of elements in the array that separate the elements pointed to by the pointers.

Incrementing Pointers Vs. Incrementing Objects

It is possible to apply the increment and decrement operators to either a pointer variable or to the object to which it points. However, you must be careful when attempting to increment the object pointed to by a pointer. For example, assume that **p** points to an integer that contains the value 1. What do you think the following statement will do?

```
*p++;
```

Contrary to what you might think, this statement first increments **p** and then obtains the value at the new location. To increment the object pointed to by a **p**, you must use a form like this:

```
(*p)++;
```

The parentheses cause the * to associate with **p,** allowing the value pointed to by **p** to be incremented.

If you want to confirm the preceding discussion for yourself, try the following program.

```
#include <iostream.h>

main()
{
  int *p, q;

  p = &q;

  q = 1;
  cout << p << " ";

  *p++; // this will not increment q
```

```
      cout << q << " " << p;

      return 0;
}
```

After this program has executed, **q** still has the value 1, but **p** has been incremented.

However, if you change the increment line to the following

```
(*p)++; // now q is incremented and p is unchanged
```

then **q** is incremented to 2 and **p** is unchanged.

Comparing Pointers

You may compare two pointers using the relational operators. However, pointer comparisons make sense in only two cases. First, you can compare two pointers to see if they both are null. Second, you can compare pointers if the pointers relate to each other—if they both point to the same object, for example. If the two pointers point to different objects, then (excepting the most unusual circumstances) there can be no meaningful comparison of the two. The main reason for this is that C++ does not guarantee where in memory two different objects will be located. In fact, it is possible that the relative location of two different objects will be different each time your program is executed. However, if two pointers point to a common object (such as an array), then the comparison between them will be valid.

5

Pointers and Arrays

In C++, pointers and arrays are closely related. In fact, they are often interchangeable. It is this relationship between the two that makes their implementation both unique and powerful.

Access an Array Using a Pointer

When you use an array name without an index, you are generating a pointer to the start of the array. For example, consider the following fragment.

```
int nums[3] = { 1, 2, 3};
int *p;
```

```
p = nums;      // These two lines do the same thing.
p = &nums[0];
```

Here, both of the assignments perform the same action: they assign to **p** the address of the first element in the **nums** array.

Since an array name used by itself (without any index) generates a pointer to the start of the array, it stands to reason that you can access the array using this pointer. And, in fact, this is exactly what you can do. Consider this program.

```
#include <iostream.h>

int nums[10] = {1, 2, 3, 4, 5, 6, 7, 8, 9, 10};

main()
{
  int *p;

  p = nums; // assign p the beginning address of nums

  // this prints nums' first, second and third elements
  cout << *p << " " << *(p+1) << " " << *(p+2) << "\n";

  // this does the same thing by indexing nums
  cout << nums[0] << " " <<  nums[1] << " " << nums[2];

  return 0;
}
```

Here, both **cout** statements display the same thing. They both display the first 3 elements of **nums**. In both statements, the pointer operations parallel the array indexes. For example, **nums[2]** is the same as ***(p+2)**. The parentheses in expressions such as ***(p+2)** are necessary because the ***** has a higher precedence than the **+** operator. As this example illustrates, because pointer arithmetic is done relative to the base type, it allows arrays and pointers to relate to each other.

Here is another example. The following program uses a pointer to copy the contents of one string into another in reverse order.

```
#include <iostream.h>
#include <string.h>

char str1[] = "Pointers are fun to use";

main()
```

```
{
  char str2[80], *p1, *p2;

  // make p1 point to end of str1
  p1 = str1 + strlen(str1) - 1;

  p2 = str2;

  while(p1 >= str1) {
    *p2 = *p1;
    p1--;
    p2++;
  }

  // null terminate str2
  *p2 = '\0';

  cout << str1 << " " << str2;

  return 0;
}
```

This program works by setting **p1** to point to the end of **str1**, and **p2** to the start of **str2**. It copies the contents of **str1** into **str2** in reverse order. Notice the pointer comparison in the **while** loop. It is used to stop the copying process when **p1** points to the start of **str1**.

To use a pointer to access multidimensional arrays, you must manually do what the compiler does automatically. For example, in this array

```
float balance[10][5];
```

each row is five elements long. Therefore, to access **balance[3][1]** using a pointer (assume **p** is a **float** pointer), you must use a fragment like this:

```
*(p + (3*5) + 1)
```

To reach the desired element, you must multiply the row number by the number of elements in the row and then add the number of the element within the row. Generally, with multidimensional arrays it is easier to use array indexing than it is to use pointer arithmetic.

Although an array name (without an index) generates a pointer to the start of the array, it is not, itself, a pointer variable. Specifically, you may not modify it. For example, the following fragment is invalid:

5

```
char str[80];

str++; // wrong

str = str + 2; // wrong
```

The pointer that is generated by **str** is a constant that always points to the start of the array. Therefore, it is invalid to modify it and the compiler will report an error.

Indexing a Pointer

As you have seen, you can access an array via a pointer. What you might find surprising is that the reverse is also true: you can index a pointer as if it were an array. The following program, for example, is perfectly valid.

```
#include <iostream.h>

char str[] = "Pointers are fun";

main()
{
  char *p;
  int i;

  p = str;

  // display str one character at a time
  for(i=0; p[i]; i++) // loop until null is found
    cout << p[i];

  return 0;
}
```

Here, **p** is set to the start of **str** and then indexed as if it were an array. As stated, this is completely valid in C++.

Keep one point firmly in mind: you should only index a pointer when that pointer points to an array. While the following fragment is syntactically correct, it is wrong; if you tried to execute it, you would probably crash your computer.

```
char *p, ch;
int i;

p = &ch;
for(i=0; i<10; i++) p[i] = 'A'+i; // wrong
```

Since **ch** is not an array, it cannot be meaningfully indexed.

Although you can index a pointer as if it were an array, you will seldom want to do this. The reason is that, in general, using pointer arithmetic is faster than using array indexing. For somewhat complex reasons, a C++ compiler often generates faster executable code for an expression such as

```
*(p+3)
```

than it will for the comparable array index:

```
p[3]
```

Pointer Techniques

In professionally written C++ code, pointers often take the place of array indexing. For example, consider the following fragment, which converts a string to uppercase.

```
char str[] = "this is a test";
int i;

for(i=0; str[i]; i++)
  str[i] = toupper(str[i]);
```

While there is nothing technically wrong with this code, the following version is more likely to be the way that you will see it coded in C++.

```
char str[] = "this is a test";
char *p;

p = str;
while(*p) {
  *p = toupper(*p);
  p++;
}
```

Here, pointer arithmetic has been substituted for array indexing. However, even this version can be improved and will generally be written like this by experienced C++ programmers.

```
char str[] = "this is a test";
char *p;

p = str;
```

5

```
while(*p)
  *p++ = toupper(*p);
```

Because the **++** follows the **p**, the value pointed to by **p** is first obtained and then **p** is incremented to point to the next element. Since this is the way C++ code is often written, this book will use the more compact form from time to time when it seems appropriate.

Here is another example. This **while** loop (from an earlier program)

```
while(p1 >= str1) {
    *p2 = *p1;
    p1--;
    p2++;
  }
```

will almost always be written like this by professional C++ programmers.

```
while(p1 >= str1)
    *p2++ = *p1--;
```

Pointers to String Constants

As you know, C++ allows string constants enclosed between double quotes to be used in a program. When the compiler encounters such a string, it stores it in the program's string table and generates a pointer to the string. For this reason, the following program is correct and prints **one two three** on the screen.

```
#include <iostream.h>

main()
{
  char *p;

  p = "one two three";

  cout << p;

  return 0;
}
```

Here, **p** is declared as a character pointer. This means that it may point to an array of characters. When the compiler compiles the line

```
p = "one two three";
```

it stores the string in the program's string table and assigns to **p** the address of the string in the table. Therefore, when **p** is used in the **cout** statement, **one two three** is displayed on the screen.

As a point of interest, you can initialize **p** when it is declared, eliminating the separate assignment statement, as this version of the program shows.

```
#include <iostream.h>

main()
{
  char *p = "one two three";

  cout << p;

  return 0;
}
```

Here, **p** is initialized to point to the string, which (as stated) is the address at which the string is stored in the program's string table.

Using pointers to string constants can be very helpful when those constants are quite long. For example, suppose that you had a program that at various points would prompt the user to insert a diskette into drive A. To save yourself some typing, you might elect to initialize a pointer to the string and then simply use the pointer when the message needed to be displayed. For example:

```
char *message = "Insert disk into drive A, then press ENTER";
  .
  .
  .
cout << message;
  .
  .
  .
cout << message;
```

Another advantage to this approach is that to change the prompt, you only need to change it once, and all references to it will reflect the change.

5

Arrays of Pointers

Pointers may be arrayed like any other data type. For example, the following statement declares an integer pointer array that has 20 elements.

```
int *pa[20];
```

The address of an integer variable called **myvar** is assigned to the ninth element of the array as follows:

```
pa[8] = &myvar;
```

Because **pa** is an array of pointers, the only values that the array elements may hold are the addresses of integer variables. To assign a *value* to one of the integers pointed to by an element of the array, precede the array with an *****. For example, to assign the integer pointed to by the third element of **pa** the value 100, use the statement:

```
*pa[2] = 100;
```

Probably the single most common use of arrays of pointers is to create string tables in much the same way that unsized arrays were used in the previous chapter. For example, the **error ( )** function shown in the following program displays an error message based upon the value of its parameter **err_num**.

```
#include <iostream.h>

char *p[] = {
  "Input exceeds field width\n",
  "Out of range\n",
  "Printer not turned on\n",
  "Paper out\n",
  "Disk full\n",
  "Disk write error\n"
};

void error(int err_num);

main()
{
  int i;

  // display all error messages
  for(i=0; i<6; i++) error(i);

  return 0;
```

```
}

void error(int err_num)
{
  cout << p[err_num];
}
```

Of course, you may have multidimensional arrays of pointers. For example, the following program uses a two-dimensional array of pointers to create a string table that links apple varieties with their colors. To use the program, enter the name of the apple, and the program will tell you its color.

```
#include <iostream.h>
#include <string.h>
#include <stdio.h>

char *p[][2] = {
  "Red Delicious", "red",
  "Golden Delicious", "yellow",
  "Winesap", "red",
  "Gala", "reddish orange",
  "Lodi", "green",
  "Mutsu", "yellow",
  "Cortland", "red",
  "Jonathan", "red",
  "", "" // terminate the table with null strings
};

main()
{
  int i;
  char apple[80];

  cout << "Enter name of apple: ";
  gets(apple);

  for(i=0; *p[i][0]; i++) {
    if(!strcmp(apple, p[i][0]))
      cout << apple << " is " << p[i][1] << "\n";
  }

  return 0;
}
```

Look carefully at the condition controlling the **for** loop. The expression ***p[i][0]** gets the value of the first byte of the **i**th string. Since the list is terminated by null strings, this value will be zero (false) when the end of the table is reached. In all other cases it will be non-zero, and the loop will repeat.

Multiple Indirection

It is possible in C++ to have a pointer point to another pointer. This is called *multiple indirection*. Figure 5-1 illustrates the difference between single and multiple indirection. When a pointer points to another pointer, the first pointer contains the address of the second pointer, which points to the location containing the object.

To declare a pointer to a pointer an additional asterisk is placed in front of the pointer's name. For example, this declaration tells the compiler that **mp** is a pointer to a character pointer.

```
char **mp;
```

It is important to understand that **mp** is not a pointer to a character, but rather a pointer to a character pointer.

Accessing the target value indirectly pointed to by a pointer to a pointer requires that the asterisk operator be applied twice. For example,

```
char **mp, *p, ch;

p = &ch; // get address of ch
mp = &p; // get address of p
```

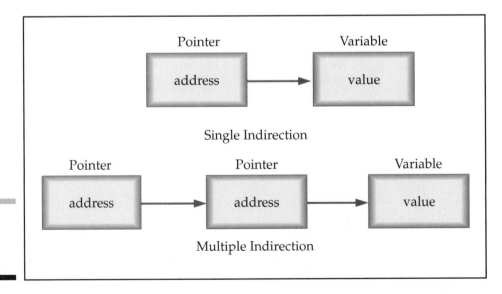

```
**mp = 'A'; // assign ch the value A using multiple indirection
```

As the comments suggest, **ch** is assigned a value indirectly using two pointers.

Multiple indirection is not limited to merely "a pointer to a pointer." You can apply the ***** as often as needed. However, multiple indirection beyond a pointer to a pointer is very difficult to follow and is not recommended.

You may not see the need for multiple indirection at this time, but as you learn more about C++, you will see some examples in which it is very valuable. If you are a little confused, don't worry. Over time, you will develop a clearer understanding of pointers to pointers.

Pointer Parameters

Pointers may be passed to functions. For example, when you call a function like **strlen( )** with the name of a string, you are actually passing a pointer to the function. When you pass a pointer to a function, the function must be declared as receiving a pointer of the same type. In the case of **strlen( )**, this is a character pointer. A complete discussion of using pointers as parameters is presented in the next chapter. However, some basic concepts are discussed here.

When you pass a pointer to a function, the code inside that function has access to the variable pointed to by the parameter. This means that the function can change the variable used to call the function. This is why functions like **strcpy( )**, for example, can work. Because it is passed pointers, the function is able to modify the array that receives the string.

5

To illustrate passing pointers to functions, the following program shows one way to implement the **strcpy( )** function, called **mystrcpy( )**.

```cpp
#include <iostream.h>

void mystrcpy(char *to, char *from);

main()
{
  char str[80];

  mystrcpy(str, "this is a test");
  cout << str;

  return 0;
}


void mystrcpy(char *to, char *from)
```

```
{
  while(*from) *to++ = *from++;
    *to = '\0'; // null terminates the string
}
```

In the next chapter, the topic of pointers as parameters is resumed.

Common Pointer Problems

Pointers are without a doubt the most error-prone of all C++ features. Further, bugs involving pointers are usually the most difficult to track down. Often, an error caused by an invalid pointer operation will not manifest itself until some time after the offending operation took place. Indeed, "wild pointers" have caused C++ programmers to spend untold hours of frustrating debugging. Even experienced programmers will encounter a pointer bug at some point. They simply "come with the territory" when programming in C++.

Pointer bugs are most often caused by the following three programming errors:

1. Using an uninitialized pointer
2. Performing an invalid pointer comparison
3. Failing to reset a pointer variable (that is, to re-initialize it) after it has been altered

Let's look at each of these, now.

Here is a fragment that uses an uninitialized pointer.

```
int *p;

*p = 100;  // where is p pointing???
```

In this case, **p** has not been initialized. That is, it has not been assigned a memory address. Therefore, you have no idea where **p** is pointing. When your program is small, the odds that **p** is pointing to something important are also small and the program may, in fact, run correctly. However, as your program grows, the odds increase that **p** will point to something used by your program (to another variable or function, for example). When this happens, your program will malfunction.

In most instances, it is conceptually invalid to compare two pointers that do not point to the same object. For example, the following fragment is fundamentally flawed.

```
int *p1, *p2;
int a1[3], a2[4];
// ...
p1 = a1;
p2 = a2;
// ...
if(p1 < p2) ...
```

Since **p1** and **p2** do not point to the same object, there is no meaningful information obtained by comparing the two. Further, the relative placement of **a1** and **a2** may change when compiled using a different compiler.

The third frequently encountered pointer error often occurs when a pointer is used to access array elements. For example, consider the following fragment.

```
char *p, str[] = "this is a test";

p = str;
while(p) cout << *p++;  // output str using p
// ...
while(p) cout << *p++;  // this won't work
```

Here, the first **while** loop succeeds because **p** is set to the start of **str** and the string is output one character at a time. However, **p** has not been reset when the second loop executes. Thus, when the loop begins, **p** is pointing to the null terminator at the end of the string and nothing is displayed.

If your previous programming experience was in a language that did not include pointer types, then you may be thinking that pointers are more trouble than they are worth. However, this is wrong. Pointers are crucial to successful C++ programming and they enable highly efficient code to be written. You simply must be very careful when using them.

5

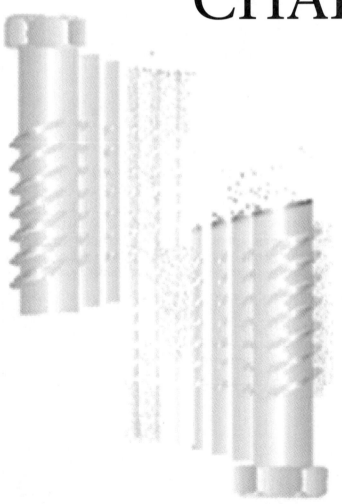

CHAPTER 6

Functions, Part I

This chapter begins an in-depth discussion of the function and associated issues. (The discussion of functions concludes in Chapter 7.) Functions are the building blocks of a C++ program and their importance cannot be understated. They are the place in which all program activity occurs. Also, functions in C++ have capabilities not found in other languages and their role has expanded importance.

This chapter covers the following topics: function prototypes, the **return** statement, recursion, passing pointers and arrays to a function, and passing arguments to **main( )**.

Function Prototypes

Function prototypes were introduced in Chapter 1. Here, they are examined more closely. As you know, in C++ all functions must be prototyped prior to their first use. A *function prototype* is used to declare a function prior to its definition. A prototype tells the compiler three things about a function:

- Its return type
- The number of its parameters
- The type of each parameter

Prototypes allow the compiler to perform these three operations:

- They allow the compiler to generate the correct type of code when a function is called. Different return types must be handled differently by the compiler.
- They allow the compiler to find and report any illegal type conversions between the type of arguments used to call a function and the type definition of its parameters.
- They allow the compiler to detect differences between the number of arguments used to call a function and the number of parameters in the function.

The general form of a function prototype definition is shown here.

> *type function-name(type parameter-name1,*
> > *type parameter-name2, ...*
> > *type parameter-nameN);*

Technically, the use of the parameter names is optional in a prototype. However, most programmers include them.

To fully understand the reason for function prototypes, let's look at two examples. First, consider this program. If you try to compile it, an error message will be issued because there is an attempt to call **cube_it( )** with an integer argument instead of the integer pointer required. (In C++ it is illegal to transform an integer into a pointer.)

```
#include <iostream.h>

void cube_it(int *i); // prototype

main()
{
```

```
   int x;

   x = 10;
   cube_it(x); // error, type mismatch
   cout << x;

   return 0;
}

void cube_it(int *i)
{
  *i = *i * *i * *i;
}
```

The compiler can catch the type mismatch error because the function prototype has identified the type of **cube_it( )**'s parameter. Therefore, when the attempt is made to invoke the function using an invalid type of parameter, the error will be found.

It is important to understand that C++ will automatically convert the type of an argument into the type of the parameter when possible. This is part of C++'s standard type conversions. For example, if a function declares a parameter to be of type **int**, that function can still be called with an argument of type **char**. C++ automatically converts the character value into an integer. However, as the preceding example shows, not all conversions are legal. And, illegal conversions will be caught by the compiler.

In the following program, the function prototype allows the compiler to catch the fact that **volume( )** is being called with the improper number of arguments.

```
#include <iostream.h>

double volume(double s1, double s2, double s3);

main()
{
  double vol;

  vol = volume(12.2, 5.67, 9.03, 10.2); // error, too many args
  cout << "Volume: " << vol;

  return 0;
}

// Compute the volume of a cube.
double volume(double s1, double s2, double s3)
```

6

```
{
  return s1 * s2 * s3;
}
```

This program will not compile because the compiler knows that **volume( )** is declared as having only three parameters, but the program is attempting to call it with four parameters.

One last point: In C++, it is also legal to fully define a function prior to its first use, thus eliminating the need for a separate prototype. However, this only works in very small programs. In real-world programs, this option is not feasible. Therefore, for all practical purposes, function prototypes must exist for all functions.

 FAST TRACK TIP

C Code Versus Prototypes

In C (C++'s predecessor), prototypes are optional. The reason for this is that when C was originally created, it did not support the full prototype syntax. Specifically, it was not possible to specify the parameter list in a prototype. Only the return type could be specified. When C was standardized, full function prototypes were added. However, because of the need to support existing, non-prototyped code, prototypes were made an optional (but recommended) feature. As you can guess, the possible lack of full prototyping in older C programs can cause problems for the C++ programmer—especially when updating such code to C++. Since C++ requires full prototyping, you will need to add all the necessary prototypes when porting older C code.

There is, however, a nuance to the C versus C++ prototyping issue. In C++, the prototype

```
int f();
```

declares the function **f( )** as returning an integer and having no parameters. However, in C, the same prototype has a slightly different meaning. In C, when a prototype specifies nothing within the function's parameter list, then the prototype simply says *nothing* about the parameters. That is, the function may have one or more parameters, or it may not. The reason for this odd situation is to provide compatibility with older C code. In C, to prototype a function that has no parameters, you must put the keyword **void** inside the function's parameter list. For example, here is the way **f( )** would be prototyped in C.

```
int f(void);
```

You can also use this form in C++, it is just that the **void** is redundant.

There is another issue that may occur when converting C to C++ that relates to prototypes. Since C does not require prototypes, some programmers elected to ignore the fundamental type differences between such things as pointers and integers. That is, you might see code like the following in C programs:

```
convert(0x1243); // call convert with an "integer" argument
// ...
float *convert(int *p) // but, convert expects a pointer
{
   // ...
}
```

Because of the lack of prototyping, the preceding fragment would compile without error in older C programs. And, in some environments where the size of a pointer equaled the size of an integer, it would work. However, such sloppiness is not allowed in a C++ program. You will need to correct such "bad grammar" when you find it.

Frankly, there is a great deal of older C code still in use that does not contain proper prototypes. Be prepared for problems when you attempt to convert it to C++.

The return Statement

As you know, the **return** statement performs two important operations. First, it causes a function to immediately return to its calling routine. Second, it may be used to return a value. You were introduced to the **return** statement in Chapter 1. In this section, it is discussed more formally.

6

Returning from a Function

A function returns to its calling routine one of two ways: either when the function's closing curly brace is encountered or when a **return** statement is executed. The **return** statement can be used with or without a value associated with it. However, functions that are declared as returning a value (that is, that have a non-**void** return type) must return a value. Only functions declared as **void** may use **return** without a value.

For **void** functions, the **return** statement is mostly used as a program control mechanism. For example, in the following program, the function **reverse( )** reverses in place the contents of the string with which it is called.

However, if called with a null string, the function returns immediately, bypassing the **for** loop.

```cpp
#include <iostream.h>
#include <string.h>

void reverse(char *str);

main()
{
  char message[] = "Hello There";

  reverse(message);
  cout << message;

  return 0;
}

void reverse(char *str)
{
  int i, j;
  char t;

  if(!*str) return; // return if string is null

  for(i=0, j=strlen(str)-1; i<j; i++, j--) {
    t = str[i];
    str[i] = str[j];
    str[j] = t;
  }
}
```

A function may contain several **return** statements. As soon as one is encountered the function returns. For example, the following fragment is perfectly valid.

```cpp
void f()
{
  // ...
  switch(err_code) {
    case 1: return;
    case 2: // ...
    case 3: return;
    case 4: return;
    default:
      cout << "Error undefined.\n";
```

```
      return;
   }
   // ...
   if(count<100) return;
   // ...
}
```

Be aware, however, that having too many **return**s can muddy the operation of a routine and confuse its meaning. The best advice is to use multiple **return**s only when they help clarify a function or simplify an algorithm.

Returning Values

All functions, except those declared to be of type **void**, return a value. This value is explicitly specified by the **return** statement. This means that as long as a function is not declared as **void** it may be used as an operand in any valid C++ expression. Therefore, each of the following expressions is valid in C++.

```
x = sin(y);
if(min(x, y)) < 0) cout << "Minimum value less than zero.";
switch(abs(x)) { //...
```

Although all functions, except those of type **void**, return values, you don't necessarily have to use these values for anything. A very common question concerning function return values is, "Don't I have to use the return value in some way?" The answer is "No." If there is no assignment specified, then the return value is simply discarded. Consider the following program that uses the standard library function **abs( )**.

```
#include <iostream.h>
#include <stdlib.h>

main()
{
  int i;

  i = abs(-10);      // line 1
  cout << abs(-23);  // line 2
  abs(100);          // line 3

  return 0;
}
```

The **abs( )** function returns the absolute value of its integer argument. It uses the STDLIB.H header file. In line 1, the return value of **abs( )** is assigned

6

to **i**. In line 2, the return value is not actually assigned, but it is used by the **cout** statement. Finally, in line 3, the return value is lost because it is neither assigned to another variable nor used as part of an expression.

If a non-**void** function returns because its closing curly brace is encountered, an undefined (that is, unknown) value is returned. Because of a quirk in the formal C++ syntax, a non-**void** function need not actually execute a **return** statement. However, because the function is declared as returning a value, a value will be returned—even if it is just a garbage value. Generally, non-**void** functions that you create should return a value via an explicit **return** statement.

Functions can be declared to return any valid C++ data type. The method of declaration is similar to that of variables: the type specifier precedes the function name. The type specifier tells the compiler what type of data the function is to return. This return type must be compatible with the type of data used in the **return** statement. If it isn't, a compile-time error will result.

As mentioned early in this book, if no type specifier is present, then the return type of a function is assumed to be integer, by default. Therefore, the following two function declarations are equivalent.

```
int f(int i);

f(int i);
```

Even though C++ defaults a function's return type to **int**, some programmers still like to explicitly specify the **int.** Whether you include the **int** specifier or not is a matter of taste.

void Functions

As you have seen, functions that don't return values may be declared as **void**. Doing so prevents their use in any expression and helps head off accidental misuse. For example, the function **DisplayUpper( )**, shown here, displays a string in uppercase. Since it returns no value it is declared as **void**.

```
void DisplayUpper(char *str)
{
  while(*str) cout << (char) toupper(*str++);
}
```

Since **DisplayUpper( )** is declared as **void**, it cannot be used in an expression. For example, the following statement is wrong and would not compile.

```
x = DisplayUpper("hello"); // error
```

Note: Early versions of C (C++'s predecessor) did not allow the **void** return type. Thus, in old C programs, functions that did not return values were simply allowed to default to type **int**. You may still encounter this situation when updating older C programs to C++. If you do, then convert them to **void** functions.

Functions Returning Pointers

Functions can return pointers. Pointers are returned like any other data type and pose no special problem. However, because pointers are one of C++'s more confusing features, a short discussion of pointer return types is warranted.

To return a pointer, a function must declare its return type to be a pointer. For example, this declares the return type of **f( )** to be a character pointer.

```
char *f();
```

If a function's return type is a pointer, then the value used in its **return** statement must also be a pointer. (As with all functions, the return value must be compatible with the return type.)

The following program illustrates a pointer return type. In it, the function **FindDelimiter( )** searches a string for the first occurrence of a delimiter. If found, it returns a pointer to that character. It returns null if the delimiter is not part of the string.

```
#include <iostream.h>

char *FindDelimiter(char delim, char *str);

main()
{
  char *p;

  // find first space
  p = FindDelimiter(' ', "This is a test.");

  if(p) cout << p; // displays "is a test"

  return 0;
}
```

6

```
char *FindDelimiter(char delim, char *str)
{
  while(delim != *str && *str) str++;

  return str;
}
```

Many of the string-related library functions return character pointers. For example, the **strcpy( )** function returns a pointer to the first argument.

FAST TRACK TIP

The C++ Standard Mathematics Functions

If you will be writing mathematical programs, you will be happy to know that the C++ standard library contains a comprehensive set of mathematical functions. To use the mathematical functions, you must include MATH.H in your program. The mathematical functions are listed in here.

Function	Purpose
double acos(double *arg*)	Returns the arc cosine of *arg*
double asin(double *arg*)	Returns the arc sine of *arg*
double atan(double *arg*)	Returns the arc tangent of *arg*
double atan2(double *x*, double *y*)	Returns the arc tangent of *x/y*
double ceil(double *arg*)	Returns the ceiling of *arg*
double cos(double *arg*)	Returns the cosine of *arg*
double cosh(double *arg*)	Returns the hyperbolic cosine of *arg*
double exp(double *arg*)	Returns e^{arg}
double fabs(double *arg*)	Returns the absolute value of *arg*
double floor(double *arg*)	Returns the floor of *arg*
double fmod(double *x*, double *y*)	Returns the remainder of *x/y*
double frexp(double *num*, int *exp*)	Decomposes *num* into a mantissa and an exponent
double ldexp(double *num*, int *exp*)	Returns $num*2^{exp}$
double log(double *arg*)	Returns the natural logarithm of *arg*
double log10(double *arg*)	Returns the base 10 logarithm of *arg*
double modf(double *arg*, double *i*)	Decomposes *arg* into its integer and fractional parts
double pow(double *base*, double *exp*)	Returns $base^{exp}$
double sin(double *arg*)	Returns the sine of *arg*

double sinh(double *arg*)	Returns the hyberbolic sine of *arg*
double sqrt(double *arg*)	Returns the square root of *arg*
double tan(double *arg*)	Returns the tangent of *arg*
double tanh(double *arg*)	Returns the hyberbolic tangent of *arg*

In addition to these standard functions, your compiler may contain other, specialized, mathematical functions that you can use.

Recursion

Recursion is the process by which something is defined in terms of itself. When applied to computer languages, recursion means that a function can call itself. Not all computer languages support recursive functions, but C++ does. A very simple example of recursion is shown in this program.

```
#include <iostream.h>

void recurse(int i);

main()
{
  recurse(0);

  return 0;
}

void recurse(int i)
{
  if(i<10) {
    recurse(i+1);
    cout << i << " ";
  }
}
```

This program prints

```
9 8 7 6 5 4 3 2 1 0
```

on the screen. Let's see why.

The **recurse( )** function is first called with 0. This is **recurse( )**'s first activation. Since 0 is less than 10, **recurse( )** then calls itself with the value

6

of **i** (in this case 0) plus 1. This is the second activation of **recurse( )**, and **i** equals 1. This causes **recurse( )** to be called again using the value 2. This process repeats until **recurse( )** is called with the value 10. This causes **recurse( )** to return. Since it returns to the point of its call, it will execute the **cout** statement in its previous activation, print **9**, and return. This, then, causes the function to return to the point of its call in the previous activation, which causes **8** to be displayed. The process continues until all the calls return, and the program terminates.

It is important to understand that there are not multiple copies of a recursive function. Instead, only one copy exists. When a function is called, storage for its parameters and local data are allocated on the stack. Thus, when a function is called recursively, the function begins executing with a new set of parameters and local variables, but the code that constitutes the function remains the same.

If you think about the preceding program, you may note that recursion is essentially a new type of program control mechanism. This is why every recursive function you write will have a statement that controls whether the function will call itself again or return. Without such a statement, a recursive function will simply run wild, using up all the memory allocated to the stack and then crashing the program.

Recursion is generally employed sparingly. However, it can be quite useful in simplifying certain algorithms. For example, the Quicksort sorting algorithm is difficult to implement without the use of recursion. If you have not used recursion before, you might find yourself uncomfortable with it. Don't worry; as you become more experienced, the use of recursive functions will become more natural.

One point to understand about recursive algorithms is that the placement of the recursive call is critical. For example, the recursive program described above can be altered to print the numbers **0** through **9** on the screen in ascending order quite easily. To accomplish this, the recursive call to **recurse( )** need only be moved one line down, so that it follows (rather than precedes) the **cout** statement. This change is shown here.

```
#include <iostream.h>

void recurse(int i);

main()
{
  recurse(0);

  return 0;
```

```
  }

void recurse(int i)
{
  if(i<10) {
    cout << i << " ";
    recurse(i+1);
  }
}
```

Because the **cout** statement now precedes the recursive call to **recurse( )**, the numbers are printed in ascending order rather than descending order.

Mutual Recursion

It is possible to have a program in which two or more functions are *mutually recursive*. Mutual recursion occurs when one function calls another, which in turn calls the first. For example, study this short program.

```
#include <iostream.h>

void f2(int b);
void f1(int a);

main()
{
  f1(30);

  return 0;
}

void f1(int a)
{
  if(a) f2(a-1);
  cout << " " << a;
}

void f2(int b)
{
  cout << ".";
  if(b) f1(b-1);
}
```

This program displays

```
...............0 2 4 6 8 10 12 14 16 18 20 22 24 26 28 30
```

6

on the screen. Its output is caused by the way the two functions **f1( )** and **f2( )** call each other. Each time **f1( )** is called, it checks to see if **a** is 0. If not, it calls **f2( )** with **a–1**. The **f2( )** function first prints a period and then checks to see if **b** is 0. If not, it calls **f1( )** with **b–1**, and the process repeats. Eventually, **b** is 0 and the function calls start unraveling, causing **f1( )** to display the numbers **0** to **30** counting by twos.

Passing Pointers to Functions

You have already seen several examples in which a pointer is passed to a function. However, since pointers are fundamental to C++, let's take a closer look at this feature. To pass a pointer to a function involves two steps. First, declare the parameter as a pointer type. Second, when you call the function, pass an address (i.e., pointer) rather than a value as the argument. For example, consider the following program.

```cpp
#include <iostream.h>

void sqr(double *arg);

main()
{
  double x = 12.2;

  cout << "Here is x: " << x << "\n";

  sqr(&x); // call sqr with address of x

  cout << "Here is x squared: " << x << "\n";

  return 0;
}

void sqr(double *arg)
{
  *arg = *arg * *arg;
}
```

The output from this program is shown here.

```
Here is x: 12.2
Here is x squared: 148.84
```

In the program, the function **sqr( )** receives a pointer to a **double** variable called **x**. It then squares **x**'s value. This means that **sqr( )** operates directly on the variable pointed to by **arg,** which in this case is **x.** Thus, after the call, **x** contains the square of its original value.

It is important to understand the difference between standard parameters and pointer parameters. Normally, a parameter receives a copy of its argument. This means that changes to the parameter do not affect the calling argument. Thus, what occurs inside a function cannot alter objects outside the function. However, when you pass a pointer, whatever that pointer is pointing to is capable of being altered by the function. For this reason, you must be careful when operating upon pointer parameters. It is easy to create unintended side effects. In the next chapter, C++'s parameter passing mechanism is examined in detail. As you will see, C++ defines a special type of parameter, called a *reference parameter*, which operates somewhat similarly to a pointer parameter.

Passing Arrays to Functions

As you know from the preceding chapter, when an array name is used by itself (without an index), a pointer to the start of the array is generated. Therefore, when an array is used as an argument to a function, only the address of the array is passed, not a copy of the entire array. This means that the parameter declaration must be of a compatible pointer type. There are three ways to declare a parameter that is to receive a pointer to an array. First, the parameter may be declared as an array of the same type and size as that used to call the function. Second, it may be specified as an unsized array. Finally, and most commonly, it may be specified as a pointer to the base type of the array. The following program demonstrates all three methods.

6

```
#include <iostream.h>

void f1(int num[5]);
void f2(int num[]);
void f3(int *num);

main()
{
  int count[5] = {1, 2, 3, 4, 5};

  f1(count);
  f2(count);
  f3(count);

  return 0;
}
```

```
// sized array
void f1(int num[5])
{
  int i;

  for(i=0; i<5; i++) cout << num[i] << " ";
}

// unsized array
void f2(int num[])
{
  int i;

  for(i=0; i<5; i++) cout << num[i] << " ";
}

// pointer
void f3(int *num)
{
  int i;

  for(i=0; i<5; i++) cout << num[i] << " ";
}
```

Even though each of the three methods of declaring a parameter that will receive a pointer to an array look different, they all result in a pointer parameter being created.

Arguments to main( )

Many programs allow command-line arguments to be specified when they are run. A *command-line argument* is the information that follows the program's name on the command line of the operating system. Command line arguments are used to pass information to the program. For example, when you use a text editor, you probably specify the name of the file you want to edit after the name of the word processing program. For example, if you use a word processor called WP, then this line causes the file TEST to be edited.

```
WP TEST
```

Here, TEST is a command-line argument.

Your C++ programs may also utilize command-line arguments. These are passed to a C++ program through two arguments to the **main( )** function. The parameters are called **argc** and **argv**. As you probably guessed, these parameters are optional and are not present when no command-line arguments are being used. Let's look at **argc** and **argv** more closely.

Note: Command-line arguments apply mostly to nonwindowed environments.

The **argc** parameter holds the number of arguments on the command line and is an integer. It will always be at least 1 because the name of the program qualifies as the first argument.

The **argv** parameter is an array of string pointers. The most common method for declaring **argv** is shown here.

```
char *argv[];
```

The empty brackets indicate that it is an array of undetermined length. All command-line arguments are passed to **main( )** as strings. To access an individual string, index **argv**. For example, **argv[0]** points to the program's name and **argv[1]** points to the first argument. This program displays all the command-line arguments with which it is called.

```
#include <iostream.h>

main(int argc, char *argv[])
{
  int i;

  for(i=1; i<argc; i++) cout << argv[i] << "\n";

  return 0;
}
```

C++ does not specify what constitutes a command-line argument, because operating systems vary considerably on this point. However, the most common convention is as follows: Each command-line argument must be separated by a space or a tab character. Commas, semicolons, and the like are not considered separators. For example,

```
This is a test
```

is made up of four strings, but

```
this,that,and,another
```

6

is one string.

If you need to pass a command-line argument that does, in fact, contain spaces, you must place it between quotes, as shown in this example.

```
"this is a test"
```

The names of **argv** and **argc** are arbitrary—you can use any names you like. However, **argc** and **argv** are the traditional names. It is a good idea to use these names so that anyone reading your program can quickly identify them as the command-line parameters. Also, while C++ only defines the **argc** and **argv** parameters, your compiler may allow additional parameters to **main( )**. For example, most compilers allow access to the operating system's environmental information. Check your compiler's user manual.

When you need to pass numeric data to a program, that data will be received in its string form. Your program will need to convert it into the proper internal format using one or another of C++'s standard library functions. The most common conversion functions are shown here, using their prototypes.

```
int atoi(char *str);
double atof(char *str);
long atol(char *str);
```

These functions use the STDLIB.H header file. The **atoi( )** function returns the **int** equivalent of its string argument. The **atof( )** returns the **double** equivalent of its string argument, and the **atol( )** returns the **long** equivalent of its string argument. If you call one of these functions with a string that is not a valid number, zero will be returned. The following program demonstrates these functions. To use it, enter an integer, a long integer, and a floating-point number on the command line. It will then redisplay them on the screen.

```
#include <iostream.h>
#include <stdlib.h>

main(int argc, char *argv[])
{
  int i;
  double d;
  long l;

  i = atoi(argv[1]);
  l = atol(argv[2]);
  d = atof(argv[3]);
```

```
   cout << i << " " <<  l << " " << d;

   return 0;
}
```

Although the examples up to this point haven't done so, you should verify that the right number of command-line arguments have been supplied by the user. The way to do this is to test the value of **argc**. For example, here is a program that converts ounces to pounds. The program informs the user when an incorrect number of command-line arguments are specified.

```
#include <iostream.h>
#include <stdlib.h>

main(int argc, char *argv[])
{
  double pounds;

  if(argc!=2) {
    cout << "Usage: CONVERT <ounces>\n";
    cout << "Try again.";
  }
  else {
    pounds = atof(argv[1]) / 16.0;
    cout << pounds << " pounds\n";
  }

  return 0;
}
```

By testing the value of **argc**, the program will only perform a conversion if a command-line argument is present. Of course, you may prompt the user for any missing information, if you choose.

A Restriction on main( )

While **main( )** is a function that is more or less like other functions that you create, it does have one important restriction: Your program *cannot* call it. That is, **main( )** may not be called recursively, either directly or indirectly. In this regard, C++ differs from C. In C, your program may call **main( ).** You will want to watch for this difference when converting C programs to C++.

6

Using exit( ) and abort( )

Sometimes you will want to stop the execution of a program immediately. For example, you may have a program that can only execute if one or more necessary conditions have been met. If the conditions are not met, program execution must be terminated. When some condition necessary for a program's execution has not been satisfied, most C++ programmers call the standard library function **exit( )** to terminate the program. The **exit( )** function has this prototype

> void exit(int *exit-code*);

and uses the STDLIB.H header file. When **exit( )** terminates the program, it returns the value of *exit-code* to the operating system. By convention, most operating systems use a return code of zero to mean that a program has terminated normally. Nonzero values indicate abnormal termination. No matter what value of *exit-code* is used, **exit( )** causes normal program termination. This means that all normal program shutdown activities will occur. In fact, calling **exit( )** is the same as returning from **main( )**.

Using **exit( )**, the ounces-to-pounds program can be rewritten like this.

```
#include <iostream.h>
#include <stdlib.h>

main(int argc, char *argv[ ])
{
  double pounds;

  if(argc!=2) {
    cout << "Usage: CONVERT <ounces>\n";
    cout << "Try again.";
    exit(1); // stop the program
  }

  pounds = atof(argv[1]) / 16.0;
  cout << pounds << " pounds\n";

  return 0;
}
```

C++ includes another program termination function called **abort( )**. It has the following prototype.

> void abort( );
>
> **abort( )** is C++'s equivalent of an emergency stop signal. Calling **abort( )** causes immediate, but abnormal, program termination. Generally, this means that no program shutdown activities are performed. Your program should only call **abort( )** in the most dire of circumstances when only the fastest possible termination of the program is required.

Classic Versus Modern Function Declarations

If you have examined older C code, you may have noticed that the function parameter declarations look different. When C was first invented it used a fundamentally different parameter declaration method. This older method, sometimes called the *classic* form, is outdated but is still commonly found in older code. The declaration approach used by C++ (and newer C code) is called the *modern* form. Because you may need to work on older C programs, especially if you are updating them to C++, it is useful to understand the classic parameter declaration form.

The classic function parameter declaration consists of two parts: a parameter list, which goes inside the parentheses that follow the function name; and the actual parameter declarations, which go between the closing parenthesis and the function's opening curly brace. For example, this modern declaration:

```
float f(int a, int b, char ch)
{ ...
```

will look like this in its classic form:

```
float f(a, b, ch)
int a, b;
char ch;
{ ...
```

Notice that in classic form more than one parameter can be in a list after the type name. To convert the classic form into the modern (C++-style) form, simply move the parameter declarations to inside the function's parentheses.

One last point: While C++ currently accepts the classic function definition syntax, it is considered obsolete and its usage in new programs is strongly discouraged. This means that you should convert any older C code to the modern format.

6

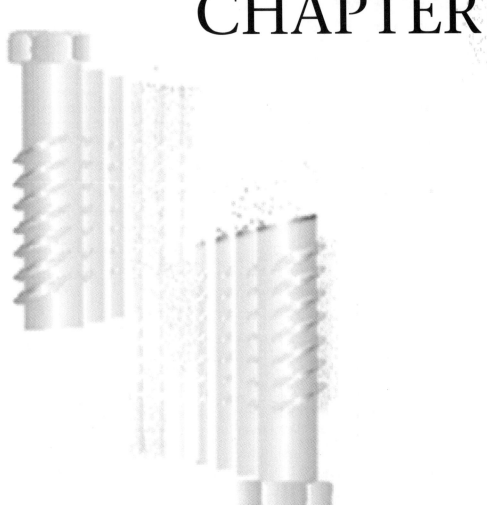

CHAPTER 7

Functions, Part II

This chapter concludes our examination of the
function. It begins with a formal examination of
C++'s parameter passing mechanism. It then
discusses references, function overloading, default
arguments, and function pointers. These features
greatly expand the capabilities of the function and
are not found in many other computer languages.
As you will see, a reference is an implicit pointer.
Function overloading is the quality that allows one
function to be implemented two or more different
ways, each performing a separate task. Function
overloading is one way that C++ supports
polymorphism. Using a default argument, it is
possible to specify a value for a parameter that will
be automatically used when no corresponding

argument is specified. Finally, using a function pointer it is possible to call a function, indirectly, through that pointer.

To understand how C++ passes arguments to functions, you must understand the two general methods by which argument passing may be accomplished. Therefore, this chapter begins with a brief definition of call-by-value and call-by-reference.

Call-by-Value Versus Call-by-Reference

There are two ways that a computer language can pass an argument to a subroutine. If your previous programming experience includes languages such as Pascal, then you will already be familiar with the two types of parameter passing. If you are not, then pay close attention to following definitions.

The first way that an argument can be passed to a subroutine is called *call-by-value*. This method copies the *value* of an argument into the formal parameter of the subroutine. Therefore, changes made to the parameters of the subroutine have no effect on the arguments used to call it.

Call-by-reference is the second way a subroutine can be passed arguments. In this method, the *address* of an argument (not its value) is copied into the parameter. Inside the subroutine, this address is used to access the actual argument specified in the call. This means that changes made to the parameter will affect the argument used to call the subroutine.

C++ supports both call-by-value and call-by-reference parameter passing. As you will see, it actually supports two versions of call-by-reference. However, before exploring C++'s approach to call-by-reference, let's review the normal C++ parameter passing approach: call-by-value.

Passing Arguments by Value

By default, C++ uses *call-by-value* to pass arguments. All of the programs up to this point have made use of this fact. As just stated, call-by-value means that a copy of the argument is passed to the parameter of the function. Therefore, in general, code inside a function cannot alter an argument used to call the function. Consider the following function.

```
#include <iostream.h>

double AreaOfCircle(double radius);

main()
{
```

```
    double r = 10.0;
    double a;

    a = AreaOfCircle(r);

    cout << "The area of a circle with radius " << r;
    cout << " is " << a << ".\n";

    return 0;
}

double AreaOfCircle(double radius)
{
    radius = 3.14 * radius * radius; // no lasting effect
    return radius;
}
```

In this example, the value of the argument to **AreaOfCircle( )**, 10.0, is copied into the parameter **radius**. When the assignment **radius = 3.14 * radius * radius** takes place, the only thing modified is the local variable **radius**. The variable **r**, used to call **AreaOfCircle( )**, will still have the value 10.0 and is unaffected by the operations inside the function. Hence, the output will be:

```
The area of a circle with radius 10 is 314.
```

As this example illustrates, by default, a copy of an argument is passed into a function. What occurs inside the function will have no effect on the variable used in the call.

Using Pointers to Create a Call-by-Reference

Even though C++'s default parameter passing convention is call-by-value, it is possible to manually create a call-by-reference by passing the address of an argument (i.e., a pointer to the argument) to a function. It will then be possible to change the value of the argument outside the function. You saw an example of this in the preceding chapter when the passing of pointers was discussed. Keep in mind that when you pass a pointer, you are still using C++'s normal, call-by-value parameter passing mechanism. That is, a copy of the pointer is passed to the function. It's just that what you are passing to the function is the address of another object.

7

To see how passing pointers allows you to manually create a call-by-reference, consider this version of **swap( )**. It exchanges the value of the two variables pointed to by its arguments.

```
void swap(int *x, int *y)
{
  int temp;

  temp = *x; // save the value at address x
  *x = *y;   // put y into x
  *y = temp; // put x into y
}
```

The ***x** and the ***y** reference the variables pointed to by **x** and **y**, which are the addresses of the arguments used to call the function. Hence, the contents of the variables used to call the function will be swapped.

Since **swap( )** expects to receive two pointers, you must remember to call **swap( )** with the *addresses* of the variables you wish to exchange. The program below shows the correct method.

```
#include <iostream.h>

// Declare swap() using pointers.
void swap(int *x, int *y);

main()
{
  int i, j;

  i = 10;
  j = 20;

  cout << "Initial values of i and j: ";
  cout << i << ' ' << j << "\n";

  swap(&j, &i); // call swap() with addresses of i and j

  cout << "Swapped values of i and j: ";
  cout << i << ' ' << j << "\n";

  return 0;
}

// Exchange arguments.
void swap(int *x, int *y)
{
  int temp;

  temp = *x; // save the value at address x
  *x = *y;   // put y into x
```

```
  *y = temp; // put x into y
}
```

In this example, the variable **i** is assigned the value 10 and **j** the value 20. Then **swap( )** is called with the addresses of **i** and **j**. The unary operator **&** is used to produce the address of the variables. Therefore, the addresses of **i** and **j**, not their values, are passed into the function **swap( )**. In the next section, you will learn how to automate this process.

Reference Parameters

As the preceding section shows, it is possible to achieve a call-by-reference by manual means using the pointer operators. However, for some applications, this approach is rather clumsy. First, it causes you to perform all operations through pointers. Second, it requires that you remember to pass the addresses (rather than the values) of the arguments when calling the function. Fortunately, in C++, it is possible to tell the compiler to automatically use call-by-reference rather than call-by-value for one or more parameters of a particular function. This is accomplished using a *reference parameter*. When using a reference parameter, the address (not the value) of an argument is automatically passed to the function. Within the function, operations on the reference parameter are automatically dereferenced, so there is no need to use the pointer operators.

A reference parameter is declared by preceding the parameter name in the function's declaration with the **&**. Operations performed on a reference parameter affect the argument used to call the function, not the reference parameter itself.

To understand reference parameters, let's begin with a simple example. In the program shown here, the function called **reciprocal( )** takes one reference parameter of type **double**.

```
// Using a reference parameter.
#include <iostream.h>

void reciprocal(double &num);

main()
{
  double val = 100.0;

  cout << "Original value for val: " << val << "\n";

  reciprocal(val); // pass address of val to reciprocal()
```

7

```
  cout << "Reciprocal of val: " << val << "\n";

  return 0;
}

void reciprocal(double &num)
{
  num = 1.0 / num; // this modifies calling argument
}
```

This program displays the following output.

```
Original value for val: 100

Reciprocal of val: 0.01
```

Pay special attention to the definition of **reciprocal( )**. Notice the declaration of **num**. It is preceded by the **&** which causes it to become a reference parameter. (This declaration is also used in the function's prototype.) Inside the function, the statement

```
num = 1.0 / num;
```

does *not* cause **num** to be given a new value. Instead, it causes the variable *referenced* by **num** (in this case, **val**) to be assigned the value. Notice that it does not use the ***** pointer operator. When using a reference parameter, the C++ compiler automatically knows that it is an address (i.e., a pointer) and dereferences it for you. In fact, using the ***** would be an error.

Since **num** has been declared as a reference parameter, the compiler will automatically pass **reciprocal( )** the *address* of any argument it is called with. Thus, in **main( )**, the statement

```
reciprocal(val); // pass address of val to reciprocal()
```

passes the address of **val** (not its value) to **reciprocal( )**. There is no need to precede **val** with the **&** operator. (In fact, doing so would be an error.) Since **reciprocal( )** receives the address of **val** in the form of a reference, it may modify its value.

Note: If you are familiar with Pascal, it may help to know that a reference parameter in C++ is similar to a **VAR** parameter in Pascal.

To see reference parameters in actual use—and to fully appreciate their benefits—the **swap( )** function is rewritten using references. Look carefully at how **swap( )** is declared and called.

```
#include <iostream.h>

// Declare swap() using reference parameters.
void swap(int &x, int &y);

main()
{
  int i, j;

  i = 10;
  j = 20;

  cout << "Initial values of i and j: ";
  cout << i << ' ' << j << "\n";

  swap(j, i);

  cout << "Swapped values of i and j: ";
  cout << i << ' ' << j << "\n";

  return 0;
}

/* Here, swap() is defined as using call-by-reference,
   not call-by-value.  Thus, it can exchange the two
   arguments it is called with.
*/
void swap(int &x, int &y)
{
  int temp;

  temp = x; // save the value at address x
  x = y;    // put y into x
  y = temp; // put x into y
}
```

7

Notice again, that by making **x** and **y** reference parameters, there is no need to use the **&** or the ***** operator. In fact, it would be an error to do so. Remember, the compiler automatically generates the addresses of the arguments used to call **swap( )** and automatically dereferences **x** and **y**.

Let's review. When you create a reference parameter, that parameter automatically refers to (implicitly points to) the argument used to call the function. Further, there is no need to apply the **&** operator to an argument. Also, inside the function, the reference parameter is used directly without need to apply the ***** operator. All operations involving the reference parameter automatically refer to the argument used in the call to the function.

Note: C does not support references. Thus, the only way to create a call-by-reference is to use pointers, as shown in the first version of **swap( )**. When converting C code to C++, you will want to convert these types of parameters to references where feasible.

FAST TRACK TIP

Declaring Reference Parameters

When Bjarne Stroustrup wrote *The C++ Programming Language* (in which he first described the C++ language) in 1986, he introduced a style of declaring reference parameters which some other programmers have adopted. In this approach, the **&** is associated with the type name rather than the variable name. For example, here is another way to write the prototype to **swap( )**:

```
void swap(int& x, int& y);
```

As you can see, the **&** is immediately adjacent to **int** and not to **x**.

Further, some programmers also specify pointers by associating the ***** with the type rather the variable, as shown here:

```
float* p;
```

These types of declarations reflect the desire by some programmers for C++ to contain a separate reference or pointer type. However, the trouble with associating the **&** or ***** with the type rather than the variable is that, according to the formal C++ syntax, neither the **&** nor the ***** is distributive over a list of variables and this can lead to confusing declarations. For example, the following declaration creates one, *not* two, integer pointers. Here, **b** is declared as an integer (not an integer pointer) because, as specified by the C++ syntax, when used in a declaration the ***** and **&** are linked to the individual variable that they precede, not to the type that they follow.

```
int* a, b; // a is a pointer, b is not
```

It is important to understand that as far as the C++ compiler is concerned it doesn't matter whether you write **int *p** or **int* p**. Thus, if you prefer to associate the ***** or **&** with the type rather than the variable, feel free to do so. However, to avoid confusion, this book will continue to associate the ***** and the **&** with the variable names that they modify rather than the type name.

Returning References

A function may return a reference. There are several uses in C++ programming for a reference return value. You will see some of these uses later in this book when you learn about operator overloading. However, reference return values have other important applications which you can use now.

When a function returns a reference, it returns an implicit pointer to its return value. When returning a reference, a rather startling possibility occurs: the function can be used on the left side of an assignment statement! For example, consider this simple program.

```
// Returning a reference.
#include <iostream.h>

double &f();

double val = 98.6;

main()
{
  double newval;

  cout << f() << "\n"; // display val's value

  newval = f(); // assign value of val to newval
  cout << newval << "\n"; // display newval's value

  f() = 101.2; // change val's value
  cout << f() << "\n"; // display val's new value

  return 0;
}

double &f()
{
```

7

```
  return val; // return reference to val
}
```

The output of this program is shown here.

```
98.6
98.6
101.2
```

Let's examine this program closely. At the beginning, **f( )** is declared as returning a reference to a **double** and the global variable **val** is initialized to 98.6. Next, the original value of **val** is displayed using this statement:

```
cout << f() << "\n"; // display val's value
```

When **f( )** is called, it returns a reference to **val**. Because **f( )** is declared as returning a reference, the line:

```
return val; // return reference to val
```

automatically returns a reference to **val**. This reference is then used by the **cout** statement to display **val**'s value.

In the line

```
newval = f(); // assign value of val to newval
```

the reference to **val** returned by **f( )** is used to assign the value of **val** to **newval**.

The most interesting line in the program is shown here.

```
f() = 101.2; // change val's value
```

This line causes the value of **val** to be changed to 101.2. Here is why. Since **f( )** returns a reference to **val**, this reference becomes the target of the assignment statement. Thus, the value of 101.2 is assigned to **val** indirectly through the reference to it returned by **f( )**.

Creating a Bounded Array

One good use for a reference return type is to create a bounded array. As you know, in C++ there is no run-time boundary checking on array indexing. This means that arrays may be overrun. That is, an array index may be specified that exceeds the size of the array. However, it is possible to prevent array overruns by creating a *bounded* or *safe array*. When a bounded array is created, an out-of-bounds index is not allowed to index the array. The following program illlustrates one way to accomplish this.

```cpp
#include <iostream.h>

int &put (int 1) ; // put value into the array
int get (int 1) ; // obtain a value from the array

int vals [10] ;
int error = <->1;

main ( )
 {

  int i;

  put (0) = 10; // put values into the array
  put (1) = 20;
  put (9) = 30;

  cout << get (0) << ' ' ;
  cout << get (1) << ' ' ;
  cout << get (9) << ' ' ;

  // now, intentionally generate an error
  put (12) = 1; / / Out of Bounds

  return 0;
}

// Put a value into the array.
int &put (int 1)
 {
```

7

```
    if (i>=0 && i<10)
      return vals[i]; // return a reference to the ith element
    else {
      cout << "Bounds Error!\n";
      return error; // return a reference to error
    }
}


// Get a value from the array.
int get (int i)
{
  if( i>=0 && i<10 )
    return vals[i]; // return the value of the ith element
  else {
    cout << "Bounds Error!\n";
    return error; // return an error
  }
}
```

This program creates a safe array of 10 integers. To put a value into the array, use the **put( )** function. To retrieve a value, call **get( )**. For both functions, the index of the desired element is specified as an argument. As the program shows, both **get( )** and **put( )** prevent an array overrun. Notice that **put( )** returns a reference to the specified element and can be used on the left side of an assignment statement.

While the approach to implementing a bounded array just shown is correct, an even better implementation is possible. As you will see when you learn about operator overloading later in this book, it is possible to create your own custom, bounded arrays that also use the standard array notation.

Independent References

Even though references are included in C++ primarily for supporting call-by-reference parameter passing and for use as a function return type, it is possible to declare a stand-alone reference variable. This is called an *independent reference*. It must be stated at the outset, however, that nonparameter reference variables are seldom used because they tend to confuse and destructure your program. With these reservations in mind, we will take a short look at them, here.

An independent reference must point to some object. Thus, an independent reference must be initialized when it is declared. Generally, this means that it will be assigned the address of a previously declared variable. Once this is done, the name of the reference variable may be used anywhere that the variable it references may. In fact, there is virtually no distinction between the two. For example, consider this program.

```cpp
#include <iostream.h>

main()
{
  int j, k;
  int &i = j; // independent reference

  // Here, i is just another name for j, therefore
  j = 10; // these two statements are
  i = 10; // functionally equivalent.

  cout << j << " " << i; // outputs 10 10

  k = 1001;
  i = k; /* copies k's value into j
            not k's address */

  cout << "\n" << j << "\n";  // outputs 1001

  cout << i << "\n"; // also outputs 1001

  return 0;
}
```

This program displays this output:

```
10 10
1001
1001
```

The address pointed to by a reference variable is fixed and cannot be changed. Thus, when the statement **i = k** is evaluated, it is **k**'s value that is copied into **j** (referenced to by **i**), not its address. For another example, **i++** does *not* cause **i** to point to a new address. Instead, **k** is increased by one. (Remember, references are not pointers.)

7

Restrictions When Using References

There are some restrictions that apply to reference variables. First, you cannot reference a reference variable. Second, you cannot create arrays of references. Third, you cannot create a pointer to a reference. That is, you cannot apply the **&** operator to a reference. Finally, references are not allowed on bit-fields. (Bit-fields are discussed later in this book.)

Function Overloading

In this section you will learn about one of C++'s most exciting features: function overloading. It is also the first C++ feature that exhibits an object-oriented attribute: polymorphism. In C++, two or more functions can share the same name as long as their parameter declarations are different. In this situation, the functions which share the same name are said to be *overloaded* and the process is referred to as *function overloading*. Function overloading is one way that C++ achieves polymorphism.

Let's begin with a short example. Consider the following program.

```
// Overload a function three times.
#include <iostream.h>

void f(int i); // integer parameter
void f(int i, int j); // two integer parameters
void f(double k); // one double parameter

main()
{
  f(10); // call f(int)

  f(10, 20); // call f(int, int)

  f(12.23); // call f(double)

  return 0;
}

void f(int i)
{
  cout << "In f(int), i is " << i << "\n";
}

void f(int i, int j)
{
  cout << "In f(int, int), i is " << i;
  cout << ", j is " << j << "\n";
}

void f(double k)
{
  cout << "In f(double), k is " << k << "\n";
}
```

This program produces the following output.

```
In f(int), i is 10
In f(int, int), i is 10, j is 20
In f(double), k is 12.23
```

As you can see, **f( )** is overloaded three times. The first version takes one integer parameter, the second version requires two integer parameters, and the third version has one **double** parameter. Because the parameter list for each version is different, the compiler is able to call the correct version of the function based upon the arguments used in each specific invocation.

In general, to overload a function, you simply declare different versions of it. The compiler uses the type and/or number of arguments as its guide to determining which version of an overloaded function to call. Thus, overloaded functions must differ in the type and/or number of their parameters. While overloaded functions may have different return types, the return type alone is not sufficient to distinguish two versions of a function. (Return types do not provide sufficient information in all cases for the compiler to correctly decide which function to use.)

To better understand the benefit of function overloading, consider these three functions found in the standard library: **abs( )**, **labs( )**, and **fabs( )**. These functions were first defined by C and, for compatibility, are also included in C++. The **abs( )** function returns the absolute value of an integer, **labs( )** returns the absolute value of a **long**, and **fabs( )** returns the absolute value of a **double**. In C (which does not support function overloading), three slightly different names must be used to represent these essentially similar tasks. This makes the situation more complex, conceptually, than it actually is. Even though the underlying concept of each function is the same, the programmer has three names to remember, not just one. However, in C++, it is possible to use just one name for all three functions, as this program illustrates.

```
// Overloading abs().
#include <iostream.h>

// abs() is overloaded three ways.
int abs(int i);
double abs(double d);
long abs(long l);

main()
{
  cout << abs(-10) << "\n";

  cout << abs(-11.0) << "\n";
```

7

```
  cout << abs(-9L) << "\n";

  return 0;
}

int abs(int i)
{
  cout << "Using integer abs()\n";
  if(i<0) return -i;
  else return i;
}

double abs(double d)
{
  cout << "Using double abs()\n";
  if(d<0.0) return -d;
  else return d;
}

long abs(long l)
{
  cout << "Using long abs()\n";
  if(l<0) return -l;
  else return l;
}
```

This program creates three similar but different functions called **abs**, each of which returns the absolute value of its argument. The compiler knows which function to use in each given situation because of the type of the argument. The value of overloading is that it allows related sets of functions to be accessed using a common name. Thus, the name **abs** represents the *general action* which is being performed. It is left to the compiler to choose the right *specific* version for a particular circumstance. Therefore, by applying polymorphism, three things to remember have been reduced to one. Although this example is fairly simple, if you expand the concept, you can see how overloading can help you manage complexity.

Here is one more example that uses function overloading. In this case, the function **date( )** is overloaded to accept a date either as a string or as three integers. In both cases, the function displays the date passed to it.

```
#include <iostream.h>

void date(char *date); // date as a string
void date(int month, int day, int year); // date as integers
```

```
main()
{
  date("6/25/96");
  date(2, 28, 97);

  return 0;
}

// Date as string.
void date(char *date)
{
  cout << "Date: " << date << "\n";
}

// Date as integers.
void date(int month, int day, int year)
{
  cout << "Date: " << month << "/";
  cout << day << "/" << year << "\n";
}
```

This example illustrates how function overloading can provide the most natural interface to a function. Since it is very common for the date to be represented as either a string or as three integers containing the month, day, and year, you are free to select the version most convenient to the situation at hand.

When you overload a function, each version of that function may perform any activity you desire. That is, there is no rule that states that overloaded functions must relate to one another. However, from a stylistic point of view, function overloading implies a relationship. Thus, while you can use the same name to overload unrelated functions, you should not. For example, you could use the name **sqr( )** to create functions which return the *square* of an **int** and the *square root* of a **double**. However, these two operations are fundamentally different and applying function overloading in this manner defeats its original purpose. (In fact, programming in this manner is definitely considered to be extremely bad style!) In practice, you should only overload closely related operations.

7

Note: When C++ was created, overloaded functions had to be explicitly declared as such using the **overload** keyword. Although it is no longer required, you may still find **overload** used in some older C++ programs. While most C++ compilers still accept its use, **overload** is outmoded and you should remove it when updating older C++ programs.

Default Function Arguments

Another unique and innovative function-related feature in C++ is the *default argument*. In C++, you may give a parameter a default value that is automatically used when no argument corresponding to that parameter is specified in a call to that function. Default arguments can be used to simplify calls to complex functions. Also, they can sometimes be used as a "shorthand" form of function overloading.

To give a parameter a default argument, simply follow that parameter with an equal sign and the value you want it to default to if no corresponding argument is present when the function is called. For example, this function gives its two parameters default values of 0:

```
void f(int a=0, int b=0);
```

Notice that this syntax is similar to giving a variable an initialization.

This function can now be called three different ways. First, it can be called with both arguments specified. Second, it can be called with only the first argument specified. In this case, **b** will default to zero. Finally, **f( )** can be called with no arguments, causing both **a** and **b** to default to zero. That is, the following invocations of **f( )** are all valid:

```
f(); // a and b default to 0
f(10); // a is 10, b defaults to 0
f(10, 99) // a is 10, b is 99
```

In this example, it should be clear that there is no way to default **a** and specify **b**.

Here is a program that illustrates the example described in the preceding discussion:

```
#include <iostream.h>

void f(int a=0, int b=0);

main()
{
  f();
  f(10);
  f(10, 99);

  return 0;
}
```

```
void f(int a, int b)
{
  cout << "a: " << a << ", b: " << b;
  cout << "\n";
}
```

As you should expect, this program displays the following output:

```
a: 0, b: 0

a: 10, b: 0

a: 10, b: 99
```

One reason that default arguments are included in C++ is that they provide another method of enabling you, the programmer, to manage greater complexity. In order to handle the widest variety of situations, quite frequently a function contains more parameters than are required for its most common usage. Thus, when the default arguments apply, you need only remember and specify the arguments that are meaningful to the exact situation—not the most general case.

A good application of a default argument is found when a parameter is used to select an option or is used as a flag. For example, in the following program, the function **print( )** displays a string on the screen. If its **how** parameter is set to zero, the text is displayed as is. If **how** is 1, the text is displayed in uppercase. If **how** is –1, the text is displayed in lowercase. When **how** is not specified, it defaults to 0, which tells the function to display the text as is.

```
#include <iostream.h>
#include <ctype.h>

void print(char *s, int how = 0);

main()
{
  print("Hello There\n", 0); // as is explicitly specified
  print("Hello There\n", 1); // uppercase
  print("Hello There\n"); // as is by default
  print("Hello there\n", -1); // lowercase
  print("That's All!\n", -1);  // continue in lowercase

  return 0;
}
```

7

```
/* Print a string in the specified case. Use
   last case specified if none is given.
*/
void print(char *s, int how)
{
  while(*s) {
    switch(how) {
      case 1: cout << (char) toupper(*s);
        break;
      case -1: cout << (char) tolower(*s);
        break;
      case 0: cout << *s;
    }
    s++;
  }
}
```

This program displays the following output:

```
Hello There

HELLO THERE

Hello There

hello there

that's all!
```

One important point to remember about creating functions that have default argument values is that the default values must be specified only once and this must be the first time the function is declared within the file. In the preceding example, the default argument was specified in **print( )**'s prototype. If you try to specify new (or even the same) default values in **print( )**'s definition, the compiler will display an error and not compile your program.

Even though default arguments may not be redefined within a program, you can specify different default arguments for each version of an overloaded function. That is, each version of the overloaded function can have different default arguments.

It is important to understand that all parameters that take default values must appear to the right of those that do not. For example, the following prototype is invalid.

```
void f(int a = 1, int b); // wrong!
```

Once you begin to define parameters that take default values, you may not specify a nondefaulting parameter. That is, a declaration like this is also wrong and will not compile:

```
int myfunc(float f, char *str, int i=10, int j); // wrong!
```

Since **i** has been given a default value, **j** must be given one too.

Default Arguments Versus Overloading

As mentioned at the beginning of this section, one application of default arguments is as a shorthand form of function overloading. To see why this is the case, imagine that you want to create two customized versions of the standard **strcmp( )** function. The first version will operate like **strcmp( )** and compare the entire contents of one string with another. The second version takes two additional arguments that specify the beginning and ending indexes of the characters that you want to compare. That is, the second version of **strcmp( )** will compare substrings. Thus, assuming that you call your customized functions **mystrcmp( )**, they will have the following prototypes.

```
void mystrcmp(char *s1, char *s2, int start, int end);
void mystrcmp(char *s1, char *s2);
```

The first version will compare characters from **s1** to those in **s2** beginning at **start** and ending at **end**. The second version will compare the entire string pointed to by **s1** with the string pointed to by **s2** and would operate like **strcmp( )**.

While it would not be wrong to implement two overloaded versions of **mystrcmp( )** to create the two versions that you desire, there is an easier way. Using a default argument you can create only one version of **mystrcmp( )** that performs both functions. The following program demonstrates this.

```
// Customized versions of strcmp().
#include <iostream.h>
#include <string.h>

int mystrcmp(char *s1, char *s2, int start = 0, int end = 0);

main()
{
  int result;
```

7

```
  char str1[80] = "This is a test";
  char str2[80] = "This is also a test";

  result = mystrcmp(str1, str2, 1, 5); // compare chars 1 through 5
  if(!result) cout << "Substrings compare\n";
  else cout << "Substrings differ\n";

  result  = mystrcmp(str1, str2); // compare entire string
  if(!result) cout << "Strings compare\n";
  else cout << "Strings differ\n";

  return 0;
}

// A custom version of strcmp().
int mystrcmp(char *s1, char *s2, int start, int end)
{
  int i, j;

  j = end;
  if(!j) { // if end is zero
    if(strlen(s1) > strlen(s2)) j = strlen(s1);
    else j = strlen(s2);
  }

  for(i=start; i <= j; i++)
    if(s1[i] != s2[i]) return s1[i]-s2[i];

  return 0;
}
```

Here, **mystrcmp( )** compares characters from the string pointed to by **s1** with the string pointed to by **s2** beginning at **start** and ending at **end.** However, if **start** and **end** are zero, as they will be when they are allowed to default, **mystrcmp( )** compares the entire string pointed to by **s1** to **s2**. (Thus, when **start** and **end** are zero, the function operates like the standard **strcmp( )** function.) By using default arguments for **start** and **end**, it was possible to combine both operations into one function. In this way, default arguments sometimes provide a shorthand form of function overloading.

Using Default Arguments Correctly

Although default arguments can be a very powerful tool when used correctly, they can be misused. The point of default arguments is to allow a function to perform its job in an efficient and easy to use manner while still allowing considerable flexibility. Towards this end, all default arguments should represent the way a function is generally used or a reasonable alternate usage. When there is no single value that is normally associated with a parameter, then there is no reason for a default argument. In fact, declaring default arguments when there is insufficient basis destructures your code because it misleads and confuses anyone reading your program.

Ambiguity

Before leaving the topics of overloading and default arguments, it is necessary to discuss a type of error unique to C++: *ambiguity*. It is possible to create a situation in which the compiler is unable to choose between two (or more) overloaded functions. When this happens, the situation is said to be *ambiguous*. Ambiguous statements are errors and programs containing ambiguity will not compile.

By far the main cause of ambiguity involves C++'s automatic type conversions. C++ automatically attempts to convert the type of the arguments used to call a function into the type of the parameters defined by the function. In C++, very few type conversions are actually disallowed. When a function is called with an argument that is of a compatible (but not the same) type as the parameter it is being passed to, the type of the argument is automatically converted to the target type. While automatic type conversions are convenient, they are also a prime cause of ambiguity. For example, consider the following program.

```
// Overloading ambiguity caused by type conversions.
#include <iostream.h>

float myfunc(float i);
double myfunc(double i);

main()
{
  // unambiguous, calls myfunc(double)
  cout << myfunc(10.1) << " ";

  // unambiguous, calls myfunc(float)
  cout << myfunc(21.023F); // arg explicitly specified as float

  // ambiguous -- use myfunc(float) or myfunc(double)??
  cout << myfunc(10); // ERROR

  return 0;
}

float myfunc(float i)
{
```

7

```
   return i;
}

double myfunc(double i)
{
   return -i;
}
```

Here, **myfunc( )** is overloaded so that it can take arguments of either type **float** or type **double**. As the comments in **main( )** indicate, the compiler is able to select the correct version of **myfunc( )** when it is called with either a **float** or a **double** value. However, what happens when it is called with an integer? Does the compiler call **myfunc(float)** or **myfunc(double)**? (Both are valid conversions!) In either case, it is valid to promote an integer into either a **float** or a **double**. Thus, the ambiguous situation is created.

The central issue illustrated by the preceding example is that it is not the overloading of **myfunc( )** relative to **double** and **float** that causes the ambiguity. Rather, it is the specific call to **myfunc( )** using an indeterminate type of argument that causes the confusion. Put differently, it is not the overloading of **myfunc( )** that is in error, but the specific invocation.

Another way you can cause ambiguity is by using default arguments in overloaded functions. To see how, examine this fragment.

```
int myfunc(int i);
int myfunc(int i, int j=0);

// ...

cout << myfunc(1, 2) << " "; // unambiguous
cout << myfunc(99); // ambiguous
```

Here, in the first call to **myfunc( )** two arguments are specified and therefore no ambiguity is introduced and **myfunc(int i, int j)** is called. However, when the second call to **myfunc( )** is made, ambiguity occurs because the compiler does not know whether to call the version of **myfunc( )** that takes one argument, or to apply the default to the version that takes two arguments.

Another type of ambiguity is caused when you try to overload functions in which the only difference is the fact that one uses a reference parameter and the other uses the default call-by-value parameter. Given C++'s formal syntax, there is no way for the compiler to know which function to call. Remember, there is no syntactical difference between calling a function that takes a value parameter and calling a function that takes a reference parameter. For example:

```
// These two functions are inherently ambiguous.
int f(int a, int b);
int f(int a, int &b);

// ...

y = f(a, b); // which function is called?
```

Here, the overloading of **f( )** is ambiguous because there is no way to invoke it that differentiates between the two versions.

As you continue to write your own C++ programs, be prepared to see ambiguity errors. Unfortunately, they are fairly easy to create until you become more experienced.

Pointers to Functions

A particularly confusing yet powerful feature of C++ is the *function pointer*. Even though a function is not a variable, it still has a physical location in memory that can be assigned to a pointer. The address assigned to the pointer is the entry point of the function. This pointer can then be used in place of the function's name.

The address of a function is obtained by using the function's name without any parentheses or arguments. (This is similar to the way an array's address is obtained when only the array name, without indices, is used.) If you assign the address of a function to a pointer, then you can call that function using the pointer.

To create a variable that can point to a function, declare the pointer as having the same type as the return type of the function, followed by any parameters. For example, the following declares **p** as a pointer to a function that returns an integer and has two integer parameters, **a** and **b**.

```
int (*p) (int a, int b);
```

The parentheses surrounding ***p** are necessary because of C++'s precedence rules.

To assign the address of a function to a function pointer, simply use its name without any parentheses. For example, assuming that **sum( )** has the prototype

7

```
int sum(int a, int b);
```

the assignment statement

```
p = sum;
```

is correct. Once this has been done, you can call **sum( )** indirectly through **p** using a statement like

```
result = (*p) (10, 20);
```

Again, because of C++'s precedence rules, the parentheses are necessary around ***p**. However, you can also just use **p** directly, like this:

```
result = p(10, 20);
```

However, the **(*p)** form tips off anyone reading your code that a function pointer is being used to indirectly call a function, instead of calling a function named **p**.

The following program fills in the details and demonstrates the function pointer that was just described.

```
#include <iostream.h>

int sum(int a, int b);

main()
{
  int (*p) (int a, int b);
  int result;

  p = sum; // get address of sum()
  result = (*p) (10, 20);
  cout << result;

  return 0;
}

// sum two numbers
sum(int a, int b)
{
  return a+b;
}
```

The program prompts the user for two numbers, calls **sum( )** indirectly using **p**, and displays the result.

Although the preceding program illustrates the mechanics of using function pointers, it does not even hint at their power. One of the most important uses of function pointers occurs when a function-pointer array is created. Each element in the array can point to a different function. To call any specific function, the array is simply indexed. A function-pointer array allows very efficient code to be written when a variety of functions need to be called under differing circumstances. Function-pointer arrays are typically used when writing systems software, such as compilers, assemblers, and interpreters. However, they are not limited to these applications. Although meaningful, short examples of function-pointer arrays are difficult to find, the program shown next gives you an idea of their power. Like the preceding program, this program prompts the user for two numbers. Next, it asks the user to enter the number of the operation to perform. This number is then used directly to index the function-pointer array to execute the proper function. Finally, the result is displayed.

```cpp
#include <iostream.h>

int sum(int a, int b);
int subtract(int a, int b);
int mul(int a, int b);
int div(int a, int b);
int (*p[4]) (int a, int b);

main()
{
  int result;
  int i, j, op;

  p[0] = sum; // get address of sum()
  p[1] = subtract; // get address of subtract()
  p[2] = mul; // get address of mul()
  p[3] = div; // get address of div()

  cout << "Enter two numbers: ";
  cin >> i >> j;

  cout << "0: Add, 1: Subtract, 2: Multiply, 3: Divide\n";
  do {
    cout << "Enter number of operation: ";
    cin >> op;
  } while(op<0 || op>3);
```

7

```
   result = (*p[op]) (i, j);
   cout << result;

   return 0;
}

sum(int a, int b)
{
   return a+b;
}

subtract(int a, int b)
{
   return a-b;
}

mul(int a, int b)
{
   return a*b;
}

div(int a, int b)
{
   if(b) return a/b;
   else return 0;
}
```

When you study this code, it becomes clear that using a function-pointer array to call the appropriate function is more efficient than using a **switch** statement.

One last point: function-pointer arrays can be initialized, just like any other array. For example, you could initialize **p** in the preceding program, as shown here.

```
// initialize the pointer array
int (*p[4]) (int a, int b) = {
   sum, subtract, mul, div
} ;
```

Although function pointers may still be somewhat confusing to you, with a little practice and thought, you should have no trouble using them. There is one more aspect to function pointers, however, that you need to know about that concerns overloaded functions.

Finding the Address of an Overloaded Function

Finding the address of an overloaded function is a bit more complex than obtaining the address of a single function. Since there are two or more versions of an overloaded function, there must be some mechanism that determines which specific version's address is obtained. The solution provided by C++ is both elegant and effective. When obtaining the address of an overloaded function, it is *the way the pointer is declared* that determines which overloaded function's address will be obtained. In essence, the pointer's declaration is compared to those of the overloaded functions. The function whose declaration matches is the one whose address is obtained.

The following program shows how to obtain a pointer to an overloaded function. It contains two versions of a function called **fill( )**. The first version outputs **count** number of spaces to the screen. The second version outputs **count** number of whatever type of character is passed to **ch**. In **main( )**, two function pointers are declared. The first one is specified as a pointer to a function having only one integer parameter. The second is declared as a pointer to a function taking two parameters.

```cpp
// Illustrate assigning function pointers to overloaded functions.
#include <iostream.h>

void fill(int count);
void fill(int count, char ch);

main()
{
  /* Create a pointer to void function with
     one int parameter. */
  void (*fp1)(int);

  /* Create a pointer to void function with
     one int parameter and one character parameter. */
  void (*fp2)(int, char);

  fp1 = fill; // gets address of fill(int)
  fp2 = fill; // gets address of fill(int, char)

  fp1(22);   // output 22 spaces
  cout << "|\n";

  fp2(30, 'x'); // output 30 xs
  cout << "|\n";
```

7

```
    return 0;
}

// Output count number of spaces.
void fill(int count)
{
   for( ; count; count--) cout << ' ';
}

// Output count number of chars.
void fill(int count, char ch)
{
   for( ; count; count--) cout << ch;
}
```

As the comments illustrate, the compiler is able to determine which overloaded function's address to obtain based on how **fp1** and **fp2** are declared.

Remember: When you assign the address of an overloaded function to a function pointer, it is the declaration of the pointer that determines which function's address is assigned. Further, the declaration of the function pointer must exactly match one and only one of the overloaded functions. If it does not, ambiguity will be introduced, causing a compile-time error.

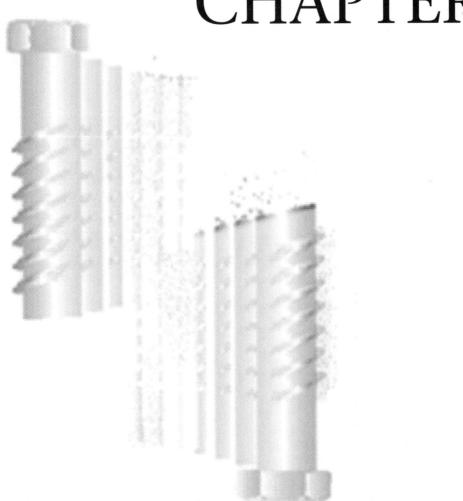

CHAPTER 8

Structures, Unions, and Enumerations

In addition to C++'s built-in data types, you may also define your own types of data. There are several ways to do this. The most common are the structure, the union, the enumeration, and the class. This chapter discusses the first three of these. (The class, which is primarily used to support C++'s object-oriented features, is deferred until later in this book.) Although the structure and the union fill different needs, they both provide a convenient means of managing groups of related variables. When you define an enumeration, you are creating an integer type and a list of named, integer constants that are its valid values.

Note: Both the structure and the union have object-oriented and nonobject-oriented attributes. This chapter is only concerned with their nonobject-oriented features. Their object-oriented aspects are described when the class is discussed.

Structure Basics

A structure is an *aggregate* (sometimes called *conglomerate*) data type. It is composed of two or more *members* that form a single logical unit. Unlike arrays (in which each element is of the same type), each member of a structure can have its own type, which may differ from the type of any other members.

To create a structure, you must first define its form. This is done using a structure declaration. The structure declaration determines what type of variables the structure contains. (That is, the declaration specifies the structure's members.) After the structure has been defined, variables (or *objects*) of that type of structure may be declared. Therefore, a structure declaration defines a logical entity, which is a new data type.

Structures are declared using this general form.

```
struct type-name {
  type member1;
  type member2;
  type member3;

    .

    .

    .

  type memberN;
} variable-list;
```

The keyword **struct** tells the compiler that a structure type is being defined. Here, each *type* is a valid C++ type. The types need not be the same. The *type-name* is the type name of the structure, and the *variable-list* is where actual variables of the structure are declared. Either the *type-name* or the *variable-list* is optional, but one must be present. (You will see why shortly.) The members of a structure are also commonly referred to as *fields* or *elements*. This book will use these terms interchangeably.

Generally, the information contained in a structure is logically related. For example, you might use a structure to hold a person's address. Another structure might be used to support an inventory program which stores each item's name, retail and wholesale cost, and number on hand. For example, the structure shown here holds card-catalog information for books.

```
struct catalog  {
  char name[40];    // author's name
  char title[40];   // book title
  char pub[40];      // publisher
  unsigned date;    // publication date
  int ed;            // edition number
} card, card1, card2;
```

Here, **catalog** is the type name of the structure. It is not the name of an object. The objects defined by this structure are **card**, **card1**, and **card2**. That is, the structure declaration defines only a logical entity (the new data type). In this case, the new type is called **catalog**. It is not until variables of that type are declared that an object of that type physically exists. Figure 8-1 shows how the **card** structure will appear in memory.

It is important to understand that each structure variable contains its own copy of the variables that make up the structure. For example, the **date** member of **card1** is separate and distinct from the **date** member of **card2**. In fact, the only relationship that **card**, **card1**, and **card2** have with one another is that they are all variables of the same type of structure. There is no other linkage between the three.

Once you have defined a structure type, you can create more variables of that type using this general form.

   type-name var-list;

Assuming, for example, that **catalog** has been defined as shown earlier, this statement declares three variables of type **catalog**.

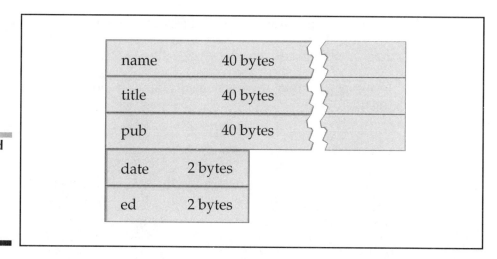

How the **card** structure variable appears in memory
Figure 8-1.

8

```
catalog var1, var2, var3;
```

This is why it is not necessary to declare any variables when the structure type is defined. You can declare them separately, as needed.

If you know you only need a fixed number of structure variables, you do not need to specify the type name. For example, the following creates two structure variables, but the structure is unnamed.

```
struct {
  int a;
  char ch;
} var1, var2;
```

In actual practice, however, you will seldom want to leave your structures nameless.

Accessing Structure Members

To access a member of a structure variable, you must specify both the variable name and the member name, separated by a period. For example, using **card**, the following statement assigns the **date** member the value 1997.

```
card.date = 1997;
```

C++ programmers generally refer to the period as the *dot operator*. To print the date of publication, you can use a statement such as

```
cout << "Publication date: " << card.date;
```

To input the publication date, use a **cin** statement such as:

```
cin >> card.date;
```

In a similar fashion, these statements input the author's name and output the title.

```
cin >> card.name;
cout << card.title;
```

To access an individual character in the title, simply index **title**. For example, the following statement prints the third letter.

```
cout <<  card.title[2];
```

The following program uses the **catalog** structure to demonstrate member access.

```
/* Here are some examples of accessing members
   of a structure.
*/
#include <iostream.h>
#include <string.h>

struct catalog  {
  char name[40];  // author's name
  char title[40]; // book title
  char pub[40];   // publisher
  unsigned date;  // publication date
  int ed;         // edition number
} card1, card2;

main()
{
  strcpy(card1.name, "Herbert Schildt");
  strcpy(card2.name, "P. J. Plauger");

  strcpy(card1.title, "C++: The Complete Reference");
  strcpy(card2.title, "The Standard C++ Library");

  strcpy(card1.pub, "Osborne/McGraw-Hill");
  strcpy(card2.pub, "Prentice Hall");

  card1.date = 1995;
  card2.date = 1995;

  card1.ed = 2;
  card2.ed = 1;

  cout << card1.name << "\n" << card1.title;
  cout << "\n" << card1.pub << "\n";
  cout << "Edition: " << card1.ed;
  cout << ", " << card1.date << "\n\n";

  cout << card2.name << "\n" << card2.title;
  cout << "\n" << card2.pub << "\n";
  cout << "Edition: " << card2.ed;
  cout << ", " << card2.date << "\n\n";

  return 0;
}
```

8

This program displays the following output.

```
Herbert Schildt
C++: The Complete Reference
Osborne/McGraw-Hill
Edition: 2, 1995

P. J. Plauger
The Standard C++ Library
Prentice Hall
Edition: 1, 1995
```

Assigning Structure Variables

You may assign the contents of one structure variable to another structure variable of the same type. For example, this fragment is perfectly valid.

```
struct s_type {
  int a;
  float f;
} var1, var2;

var1.a = 10;
var1.f = 100.23;

var2 = var1;
```

After this fragment executes, **var2** will contain exactly the same thing as **var1**. This example can be generalized: Whenever you assign one structure variable to another, an identical, bitwise copy is made. After the assignment, the two structures are physically identical.

As stated, you may assign one structure to another only if they are both of the same type. In C++, each structure declaration creates a new data type. Therefore, even if two structures are physically the same, they will only be able to be assigned to one another if their type names are the same. Otherwise, they will be judged incompatible by the compiler. For example, the following fragment is incorrect.

```
struct s_type1 {
  int a;
  float f;
} var1;
```

```
struct s_type2 { // same as s_type1, but with a different name
  int a;
  float f;
} var2;

// ...

var1 = var2; // ERROR! type mismatch
```

As the comment suggests, because the type name of **var1** is different than the type name of **var2**, the assignment is illegal.

The Scope of a Structure

Members of a structure are within the scope of that structure. That is, the names of members are local to the scope defined by the structure. This means that the name of a structure member, by itself, is not known outside the structure. Since a structure's member names are not known outside the structure, the name of a structure member will not conflict with another variable of the same name declared outside the structure. For example, consider this program.

```
#include <iostream.h>

main()
{
  struct s_type {
    int i; // this is i of s_type
    int j;
  } s;
  int i; // this is outside s_type

  // Because the scopes of i and s.i are distinct,
  i = 10;    // this statement does not conflict with
  s.i = 100; // this statement.

  s.j = 101;
  cout << i << " " << s.i << " " << s.j;

  return 0;
}
```

8

Because the **i** declared inside **s_type** is local to **s_type**, the variable **i** and the structure member **i** have no relationship to each other and do not conflict.

Arrays of Structures

Structures can be arrayed in the same fashion as other data types. For example, the following structure definition creates a 100-element array of structures of type **catalog** (defined earlier).

```
catalog cat[100];
```

To access an individual structure within the array, you must index the array name. For example, the following accesses the first structure of **cat**.

```
cat[0]
```

To access a member within a specified structure, follow the index with a period and the name of the member you want. For example, the following statement loads the **ed** field of structure 34 with the value of 2.

```
cat[33].ed = 2;
```

Passing Structures to Functions

Structures may be passed as parameters to functions just like any other type of value. For example, this program passes a structure of type **s_type** to a function.

```
#include <iostream.h>

struct s_type {
  int i;
  double d;
} var1;

void f(s_type temp);

main()
{
  var1.i = 99;
  var1.d = 98.6;
  f(var1);

  return 0;
}
```

```
void f(s_type temp)
{
  cout << temp.i << " " << temp.d;
}
```

When passing a structure to a function, the type of the parameter must be the same as the type of the argument. No automatic type conversion is supplied. Structures are passed to functions using the standard call-by-value parameter passing mechanism.

Structures as Return Values

A function may return a structure to the calling procedure. For example:

```
#include <iostream.h>

struct s_type {
  int i;
  double d;
} var1;

s_type f();

main()
{
  var1 = f();
  cout << var1.i << " " << var1.d;

  return 0;
}

s_type f()
{
  s_type temp;

  temp.i = 100;
  temp.d = 123.23;
  return temp;
}
```

Here, **f( )** creates a local structure called **temp**, assigns values to its members, and returns the structure. Inside **main( )**, the variable **var1** receives the return value. As expected, the output from this program is **100 123.23**.

8

Pointers to Structures

It is very common to access a structure through a pointer. You declare a pointer to a structure in the same way that you declare a pointer to any other type of variable. For example, the following fragment defines a structure called **s_type** and declares two variables. The first, **s**, is an actual structure variable. The second, **p**, is a pointer to structures of type **s_type**.

```
struct s_type {
  int i;
  char str[80];
} s, *p;
```

Given this definition, the following statement assigns to **p** the address of **s**.

```
p = &s:
```

Now that **p** points to **s** you can access **s** through **p**. However, to access an individual element of **s** using **p** you cannot use the dot operator. Instead, you must use the *arrow operator*, as shown in the following example.

```
p->i = 1;
```

This statement assigns the value 1 to **i** of **s** through **p**. The arrow operator is formed using a minus sign followed by a greater-than sign. There must be no spaces between the two.

The following program illustrates the preceding discussion.

```
#include <iostream.h>
#include <string.h>

struct s_type {
  int i;
  char str[80];
} s, *p;

main()
{
  p = &s;

  s.i = 0;   // this is functionally the same
  p->i = 10; // as this
```

```
strcpy(p->str, "I like structures");
cout << s.i << " " << p->i << " " << p->str;

return 0;
}
```

As you know, C++ passes structures to functions in their entirety. However, if the structure is very large, the passing of a structure can cause a considerable reduction in a program's execution speed. For this reason, when working with large structures, you might want to pass a pointer to a structure in situations that allow it instead of passing the structure itself.

Apply Structure Pointers

One useful application of structure pointers is found in C++'s time and date functions. Several of these functions use a pointer to the current time and date of the system. The time and date functions require the header file TIME.H, in which a structure called **tm** is defined. This structure can hold the date and time broken down into their elements. This is called the *broken-down* time. The **tm** structure is defined as

```
struct tm {
  int tm_sec;   // second, 0-59
  int tm_min;   // minutes, 0-59;
  int tm_hour;  // hours, 0-23
  int tm_mday;  // day of the month, 1-31;
  int tm_mon;   // months since Jan. 0-11
  int tm_year;  // years from 1900
  int tm_wday;  // days since Sunday, 0-6
  int tm_yday;  // days since Jan, , 0-356;
  int tm_isdst; // Daylight Saving Time indicator
};
```

The value of **tm_isdst** will be positive if Daylight Saving Time is in effect, 0 if it is not in effect, and negative if there is no information available. Also defined in TIME.H is the type **time_t**. It is essentially a long integer capable of representing the time and date of the system in an encoded implementation-specific internal format. This is referred to as the *calendar time*.

To obtain the calendar time of the system, you must use the **time( )** function, whose prototype is

8

time_t time(time_t *systime);

The **time( )** function returns the encoded calendar time of the system or −1 if no system time is available. It also places this encoded form of the time into the variable pointed to by *systime*. However, if *systime* is null, the argument is ignored.

Since the calendar time is represented using an implementation-specified internal format, you must use another of C++'s time and date functions to convert it into a form that is easier to use. One of these functions is called **localtime( )**. Its prototype is

tm *localtime(time_t *systime)

The **localtime( )** function returns a pointer to the broken-down form of time. The structure that holds the broken-down time is internally allocated by the compiler and will be overwritten by each subsequent call.

This program demonstrates **time( )** and **localtime( )** by displaying the current time of the system.

```cpp
// Display current time and date.
#include <iostream.h>
#include <time.h>

main()
{
  tm *systime;
  time_t t;

  t = time(NULL);
  systime = localtime(&t);

  cout << "Time is " << systime->tm_hour << ":";
  cout << systime-> tm_min << ":" << systime->tm_sec;
  cout << "\n";

  cout << "Date is " << systime->tm_mon+1 << "/";
  cout << systime->tm_mday << "/" <<  systime->tm_year;
  cout << "\n";

  return 0;
}
```

Remember: When accessing a structure member through a pointer, use the arrow operator. When accessing the member using a structure variable, use the dot operator.

References to Structures

Structures may be referenced. Specifically, a function may have a reference to a structure as a parameter or as a return type. When accessing members using a structure reference, use the dot operator. The arrow operator is explicitly reserved for accessing members through a pointer.

Since there is significant overhead incurred when passing a structure to a function or when returning a structure, many C++ programmers use references when performing these tasks.

Nested Structures

So far, we have been working with structures whose elements consist solely of C++'s basic types. However, structure members can also be other structures. These are referred to as *nested structures*. For example, here is an example that uses nested structures to hold information on the performance of two assembly lines, each with ten workers.

```
struct worker {
  char name[80];
  int avg_units_per_hour;
  int avg_errs_per_hour;
};

struct assembly_line {
  int product_code;
  double material_cost;
  worker wkers[10]; // nested structure
} line1, line2;
```

To assign the value 12 to the **avg_units_per_hour** of the second **wkers** structure of **line1**, use this statement.

```
line1.wkers[1].avg_units_per_hour = 12;
```

8

As you see, the structures are referenced from the outer to the inner. This is also the general case. Whenever you have nested structures, you begin referencing with the outermost and end with the innermost.

C Versus C++ Structures

C++ structures are derived from C structures. As such, any C structure is also a valid C++ structure. However, there are two important differences. First, as you will see in a later chapter, C++ structures have some special attributes which allow them to support object-oriented programming. Second, in C, a structure does *not* actually define a new data type. As you know, in C++, when you define a structure, you are defining a new type (which is the name of the structure). This new type may be used to declare variables, function return types, and the like. However, in C, the name of a structure is called its *tag*. The tag, alone, is not a type name. To understand the difference, consider the following C code fragment.

```
struct C_struct {
  int a;
  int b;
};

// declare a C_struct variable
struct C_struct svar;
```

Notice that the structure definition is exactly the same as it is in C++. However, look closely at the declaration of the structure variable **svar**. Its declaration also starts with the keyword **struct**. In C, after you have declared a structure, you must still use the keyword **struct** in conjunction with the structure's tag (in this case, **C_struct**) to specify a complete data type.

If you will be converting older C programs to C++, you won't need to worry about the differences between C and C++ structures because C++ still accepts the C-like declarations. That is, the preceding code fragment will correctly compile as part of the C++ program. It is just that the redundant use of **struct** in the declaration of **svar** is unnecessary in C++.

Bit-fields

C++ allows a variation on the structure called a *bit-field*. A bit-field is a member of a structure that is composed of one or more bits. Using a bit-field, you can access by name one or more bits within a byte or word. To define a bit-field, use the general form

   type name : *size*;

where *type* is either **int** or **unsigned**. If you specify a signed bit-field, then the high-order bit is treated as a sign bit. Notice that a colon separates the name of the bit-field from its size in bits.

Bit-fields are very useful when you want to pack information into the smallest possible space. For example, here is a structure that uses bit-fields to hold inventory information.

```
struct b_type {
  unsigned department: 3; // up to 7 departments
  unsigned instock: 1; // 1 if in stock, 0 if out
  unsigned backordered: 1; // 1 if backordered, 0 if not
  unsigned lead_time: 3; // order lead time in months
} inv[100];
```

In this case, one byte can be used to store information on an inventory item that would normally have taken four bytes without the use of bit-fields. You refer to a bit-field variable just like any other element of a structure. The following statement, for example, assigns the value 3 to the **department** field of item 10.

```
inv[9].department = 3;
```

The following statement determines whether item 5 is out of stock.

```
if(!inv[4].instock) cout << "Out of Stock";
else cout << "In Stock";
```

It is not necessary to completely define all bits within a byte or word. For example, this is perfectly valid:

```
struct b_type {
  int a: 2;
  int b: 3;
};
```

8

The C++ compiler is free to store bit-field variables as it sees fit. However, generally the compiler will automatically store bit-fields in the smallest unit of memory that will hold them. Whether the bit-fields are stored high-order to low-order or the other way around is implementation-dependent.

You can mix bit-fields with regular variables in a structure's definition. For example, this version of the inventory structure also includes room for the name of each item.

```
struct b_type {
  char name[40]; // name of item
  unsigned department; 3: // up to 7 departments
  unsigned instock: 1; // 1 if in stock, 0 if not
  unsigned backordered: 1; // 1 if backordered, 0 if not
  unsigned lead_time: 3; // order lead time in months
} inv[100];
```

It is not necessary to name every bit when using bit-fields. Here, for example, is a structure that uses bit-fields to access the first and last bit in a byte.

```
struct b_type {
  unsigned first: 1;
  int : 6;
  unsigned last: 1;
};
```

The use of unnamed bit-fields makes it easy to reach the bits you are interested in.

Because the smallest addressable unit of memory is a byte, you cannot obtain the address of a bit-field variable. This means that you cannot have a pointer to a bit-field. Also, you cannot have a reference to a bit-field.

Unions

In C++, a union is another aggregate data type that consists of a single memory location that is shared by two or more variables. The variables that share the memory may be of different types. However, only one variable may be used at any one time. A union is defined much like a structure. Its general form is

> union *type-name* {
>   *type member1;*
>   *type member2;*
>   *type member3;*
>   .

```
          .
          .
     type memberN;
} variable-list;
```

As you can see, a union is defined using the keyword **union**. Like a structure, either the *type-name* or the *variable_list* may be missing. Members may be of any valid C++ data type. For example, here is a union that contains three elements: an integer, a character array, and a double.

```
union u_type {
   int i;
   char c[2];
   double d;
} sample;
```

This union will appear in memory as shown in Figure 8-2.

To access an element of a union, use the dot and arrow operators just as you do for structures. For example, this statement assigns 123.098 to **d** of **sample**.

```
sample.d = 123.098;
```

If you are accessing a union through a pointer, you must use the arrow operator. For example, assume that **p** points to **sample**. The following statement assigns **i** the value 101.

```
p->i = 101;
```

It is important to understand that the size of a union is fixed at compile time and is large enough to accommodate the largest element in the union.

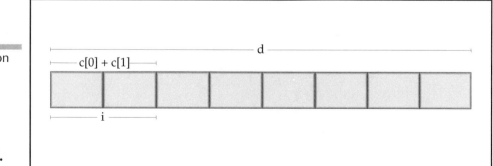

How a union appears in memory (assuming 8-byte doubles)

Figure 8-2.

8

Assuming 8-byte doubles, this means that **sample** will be 8 bytes long. Even if **sample** is currently used to hold an **int** value, it will still be using 8 bytes of memory.

Unions are useful when you need to deal with data in two or more different ways. For example, the **encode( )** function shown below uses a union to encode an integer by swapping its two bytes. (The function assumes that the integers are two bytes long.) The same function can also be used to decode an encoded integer by swapping the already exchanged bytes back to their original positions.

```cpp
#include <iostream.h>

int encode(int i);

main()
{
  int i;

  i = encode(10); // encode it
  cout << "10 encoded is " << i << "\n";

  i = encode(i); // decode it
  cout << "i decoded is " << i << "\n";

  return 0;
}

// Encode an integer, decode an encoded integer.
encode(int i)
{
  struct crypt_type {
    int num;
    char c[2];
  } crypt;
  unsigned char ch;

  crypt.num = i;

  // swap bytes
  ch = crypt.c[0];
  crypt.c[0] = crypt.c[1];
  crypt.c[1] = ch;

  // return encoded integer
  return crypt.num;
}
```

The program displays the following

```
10 encoded is 2560

i decoded is 10
```

Anonymous Unions

There is a special type of union in C++ called an *anonymous union*. An anonymous union does not have a type name and no variables may be declared for this sort of union. Instead, an anonymous union tells the compiler that its members will share the same memory location. However, in all other respects, the members act and are treated like normal variables. That is, the member variables are accessed directly, without the dot operator syntax. For example, examine this program.

```
// Using an anonymous union.
#include <iostream.h>

main()
{
  union {
    unsigned char bytes[8];
    double value;
  };
  int i;

  value = 859345.324;

  // display the bytes within a double
  for(i=0; i<8; i++)
    cout << (int) bytes[i] << " ";

  return 0;
}
```

This program uses an anonymous union to display the individual bytes that comprise a **double**. (This program assumes that **double**s are 8 bytes long.) As you can see, both **value** and **bytes** are accessed as if they were normal variables and not part of a union. Even though they are declared as being part of an anonymous union, their names are at the same scope level as any other local variable declared at the same point. In fact, a member of an anonymous union cannot have the same name as any other variable known to its scope.

8

The reason for the anonymous union is that it gives you a simple way to tell the compiler that you want two or more variables to share the same memory location. Aside from this special attribute, members of an anonymous union behave like other variables.

Enumerations

In C++ you can define an integral type that consists of a list of named integer constants. This is called an *enumeration*. To define an enumeration, use this general form:

> enum *type-name* {*enumeration-list*} *variable-list*;

Here, **enum** is the keyword that declares an enumeration. Either the *type-name* or the *variable-list* is optional. The *type-name* is the type name of the enumeration. The *enumeration-list* is a comma-separated list of names which are the valid values for the enumeration. Here is an example of an enumeration declaration.

```
enum color_type {red, green, yellow} color;
```

The type name of the enumeration is **color_type**, the enumerated constants are **red**, **green**, and **yellow**. These values may be used any place that an integer value may be used. (Put differently, enumerated constants are automatically promoted to **int** in an expression.) **color** is a variable of type **color_type**. **color** can also be used any place that an integer can be used.

Enumeration variables may only be assigned values that are defined in the enumeration. For example, the variable **color** may be assigned only the value **red**, **green**, or **yellow**.

By default, the compiler assigns integer values to the enumerated constants, beginning with 0 at the far left side of the list. Each constant to the right is one greater than the constant that precedes it. Therefore, **red** is 0, **green** is 1, and **yellow** is 2. However, you can override the compiler's default values by explicitly giving a constant a value. For example, in this statement

```
enum color_type {red, green=9, yellow} color;
```

red is still 0, but **green** is 9, and **yellow** is 10.

Once you have defined an enumeration, you can use its type name to declare enumeration variables at other points in the program. For example, assuming the **color_type** enumeration, the following statement is valid and declares **mycolor** as a **color_type** variable.

```
color_type mycolor;
```

The following program creates an enumeration consisting of various computer languages. It assigns **proglang** the value **CPP** and then displays its value (which is 1). Notice how the enumeration type name is used to declare **proglang** as an enumeration variable separately from the actual declaration of **language**.

```cpp
#include <iostream.h>

enum language { C, CPP, Pascal, FORTRAN,
                BASIC, Ada };

main()
{
  language proglang;

  proglang = CPP;

  cout << proglang;

  return 0;
}
```

It takes a little work to display the string equivalent of an enumerated constant. Remember, enumerated constants are not strings; they are named integer constants. The following program uses a **switch** statement to output the name of the computer language which corresponds to its enumerated equivalent.

```cpp
#include <iostream.h>

enum language { C, CPP, Pascal, FORTRAN,
                BASIC, Ada };

main()
{
  language proglang;

  for(proglang=C; proglang<=Ada; proglang++) {
    switch(proglang) {
      case C: cout << "C\n";
        break;
      case CPP: cout << "C++\n";
        break;
      case Pascal: cout << "Pascal\n";
        break;
```

8

```
      case FORTRAN: cout << "FORTRAN\n";
        break;
      case BASIC: cout << "BASIC\n";
        break;
      case Ada: cout << "Ada\n";
        break;
    }
  }

  return 0;
}
```

Notice the use of **proglang** to control the **for** loop and as a selector in the **switch** statement that displays the languages. As stated, since enumerations are integer types, they may be used any place that an integer may be used.

FAST TRACK TIP

C++'s Localization Functions

An interesting use of a structure is found in the subsystem of the C++ standard library that supports localization. This subsystem helps you write programs that can adjust to different geopolitical locales in which your program may be executed. It defines a structure and two functions. The structure is called **lconv**. This structure contains information that relates to the country and/or language environment of the user. It is defined like this:

```
struct lconv {
  char *decimal_point;       /* decimal point character
                                for non-monetary values */
  char *thousands_sep;       /* thousands separator
                                for non-monetary values */
  char *grouping;            /* specifies grouping for
                                non-monetary values */
  char *int_curr_symbol;     /* international currency symbol */
  char *currency_symbol;     /* local currency symbol */
  char *mon_decimal_point;   /* decimal point character
                                for monetary values */
  char *mon_thousands_sep;   /* thousands separator
                                for monetary values */
  char *mon_grouping;        /* specifies grouping for
                                monetary values */
  char *positive_sign;       /* positive value indicator
                                for monetary values */
  char *negative_sign;       /* negative value indicator
                                for monetary values */
  char int_frac_digits;      /* number of digits displayed
```

```
                                          to the right of the decimal
                                          point for monetary values
                                          displayed using international
                                          format */
        char frac_digits;         /* number of digits displayed
                                          to the right of the decimal
                                          point for monetary values
                                          displayed using local format */
        char p_cs_precedes;       /* 1 if currency symbol precedes
                                          positive value,
                                          0 if currency symbol
                                          follows value */
        char p_sep_by_space;      /* 1 if currency symbol is
                                          separated from value by a
                                          space, 0 otherwise */
        char n_cs_precedes;       /* 1 if currency symbol precedes
                                          a negative value, 0 if
                                          currency symbol follows value */
        char n_sep_by_space;      /* 1 if currency symbol is
                                          separated from a negative
                                          value by a space, 0 if
                                          currency symbol follows value */
        char p_sign_posn;         /* indicates position of positive
                                          value symbol */
        char n_sign_posn;         /* indicates position of negative
                                          value symbol */
};
```

The two functions that utilize this structure are called **localeconv( )** and **setlocale( ).** You must include the header file LOCALE.H in order to use these functions or the **lconv** structure.

The **localeconv( )** function returns a pointer to a structure of type **lconv** that contains the current locale settings. The **setlocale( )** function allows you to query or set certain parameters that are sensitive to the geopolitical location where a program is used. For example, in Europe, the comma is used in place of the decimal point.

If you will be writing programs that will be used internationally, then you will want to explore the **lconv** structure and the **localeconv( )** and **setlocale( )** functions.

8

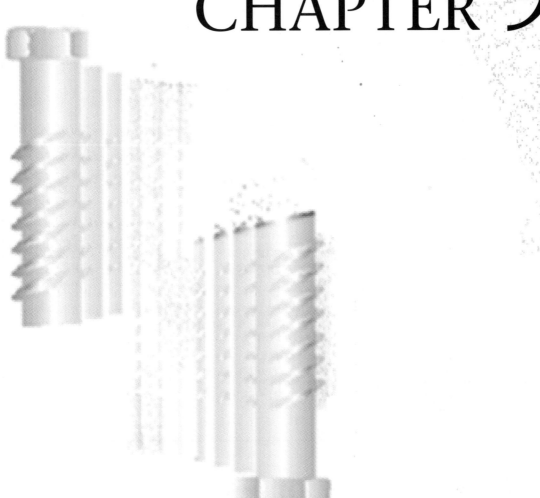

CHAPTER 9

Advanced Data Types
and Operators

The C++ language includes a rich set of data type modifiers that allow you to more finely control various aspects of a variable. This "fine-tuning" includes such things as controlling the variable's lifetime, specifying how a variable is stored, restricting access, and optimizing access speed . Also, C++ includes a number of special operators. These include the bitwise and shift operators, which permit the creation of very efficient routines. This chapter also explains C++'s dynamic allocation operators: **new** and **delete**.

The Storage Class Specifiers

C++ defines four type modifiers that affect how a variable is stored. They are

auto
extern
register
static

These specifiers precede the type name. Let's look at each now.

auto

The **auto** specifier is completely unnecessary. It is provided in C++ to allow compatibility with its predecessor, C. (Humorously, **auto** was included in C only to provide compatibility with its predecessor, B!) Its use is to declare automatic variables. Automatic variables are simply local variables, which are **auto** by default. You will almost never see **auto** used in any C++ program.

extern

Although the programs we have been working with in this book are fairly short, programs in the real world tend to be quite long. As the size of a program grows, it takes longer to compile. For this reason, C++ allows you to break a program into two or more files. You can separately compile these files and then link them together. (The actual method of separate compilation and linking will be explained in the user's manual for your compiler.) However, when working with multifile programs, the following question naturally arises. "How do I share global variables between files?" In C++, a global variable may only be declared once. Because global variables may need to be accessed by two or more files that form the program, a method of informing the compiler about the global data used by the program must be available. The solution to this problem is **extern**. To see how it is used, consider the program in Figure 9-1, which is split between two files.

As you can see, the global variable **count** is used by functions in both files. In File #1, it is declared normally. In File #2, it is declared using the **extern** specifier. The **extern** specifier tells the compiler the type and name of a global variable that is defined in another file, but does not actually create storage for it. When the linker links the two modules together, all references to external variables are resolved. Had File #2 simply declared **count** normally, the linker would have reported an error when it encountered the second definition for **count**.

```
File 1                              File 2

#include <iostream.h>               #include <stdlib.h>

int count;                          extern int count;
void f1();
                                    void f1()
main()                              {
{                                      count = rand();
  int i;                            }

  f1(); // set count's value

  for(i=0; i<count; i++)
    cout << i << " ";

  return 0;
}
```

A multifile
program
Figure 9-1.

While we haven't worried about the distinction between a declaration and a definition of a variable in the previous chapters, it is important here. A *declaration* declares the name and type of a variable. A *definition* causes storage to be allocated for it. In most cases, variable declarations are also definitions. However, by preceding a variable name with the **extern** specifier, you are able to declare a variable without defining it. Therefore, generalizing from the preceding example, when sharing global variables between multiple files, define the variables in one file. In all other files, declare the variables using **extern**.

Before leaving **extern** , one other valid, but uncommon, use needs to be mentioned. Although rarely done, you can use **extern** inside a function to declare global variables that are defined elsewhere in that file. For example, the following is valid.

```
#include <iostream.h>

int count;

main()
{
  extern int count; // this refers to the global count
```

9

```
count = 10;
cout << count;

return 0;
}
```

Here, the variable **count** inside **main( )** is declared as **extern**. This causes the compiler to use the global **count**. The reason you will rarely see this use of **extern** is that it is redundant. Whenever the compiler encounters a variable name not defined by the function as a local variable, it assumes that it is global. Therefore, if a global variable of the same name has been defined, it is assumed to be the one referred to inside the function.

register

One storage class specifier that you will want to use frequently is **register**. The **register** modifier tells the compiler to store a variable in such a way that accesses to it are as fast as possible. Typically, this means storing the variable either in a register of the CPU or in cache memory. As you probably know, access to the registers of the CPU (or to cache memory) is fundamentally faster than is access to the main memory of the computer. Thus, if a variable is stored in a register, access to it will be much faster than if that variable had been stored in RAM, for example. Because the speed by which variables can be accessed has a profound effect on the overall speed of your programs, the careful use of **register** is an important programming technique.

To get an idea about how much faster access to a **register** variable is, try the following program. It makes use of another of C++'s standard library functions called **clock( )**, which returns the number of system clock ticks since the program began execution. It has the prototype

```
clock_t clock( );
```

It uses the TIME.H header. TIME.H also defines the **clock_t** type, which is more or less the same as **long**. To time an event using **clock( )**, call it immediately before the event you wish to time and save the value. Next, call it a second time after the event finishes and subtract the starting value from the ending value. This is the approach used by the program to time how long it takes two loops to execute. One set of loops is controlled by a register variable, the other is controlled by a nonregister variable.

```
#include <iostream.h>
#include <time.h>
```

```
int i; // nonregister variable

main()
{
  register int j;
  int k;
  clock_t start, finish;

  start = clock();
  for(k=0; k<100; k++)
    for(i=0; i<32000; i++) ;
  finish = clock();
  cout << "Nonregister loop: " << finish - start << " ticks\n";

  start = clock();
  for(k=0; k<100; k++)
    for(j=0; j<32000; j++);
  finish = clock();
  cout << "Register loop: " << finish - start << " ticks\n";

  return 0;
}
```

For most compilers, the register-controlled loop will execute about twice as fast as the nonregister controlled loop.

One related point: In the preceding example, the nonregister variable **i** is global because, when feasible, many compilers will automatically convert local variables into register types as an automatic optimization. Thus, making **i** global prevents its possible automatic conversion to **register**.

Technically, **register** is only a request to the compiler, which the compiler is free to ignore. The reason for this is easy to understand: there is a finite amount of registers or fast-access memory and this may differ from environment to environment. Thus, if the compiler runs out of fast access memory, it simply stores the variable normally. Generally, this causes no harm, but (of course) the **register** advantage is lost. For this reason, you must choose carefully which variables you modify with **register**. One good choice is to make a frequently used variable, such as the variable that controls a loop, into a **register** variable. The more times a variable is accessed, the greater the increase in performance when its access time is decreased. Generally, you can assume that at least two variables per function can be truly optimized for access speed.

static

The **static** modifier can be applied to global variables and to local ones. However, it has two slightly different effects, depending upon which type of variable it modifies. Both situations are discussed here.

Local static Variables

The **static** modifier causes a local variable to stay in existence throughout the life of a program. Thus, the contents of a **static** local variable are preserved between function calls. Also, unlike normal local variables, which are initialized each time their block is entered, a **static** local variable is initialized only once, when its block is first entered. For example, take a look at this program.

```
#include <iostream.h>

void f();

main()
{
  int i;

  for(i=0; i<10; i++) f();

  return 0;
}

void f()
{
  static int count = 0;

  count++; // this DOES have lasting effect
  cout << "count is " << count << "\n";
}
```

The program displays the following output.

```
count is 1
count is 2
count is 3
count is 4
count is 5
count is 6
count is 7
count is 8
```

```
count is 9
count is 10
```

As you can see, because **count** is **static**, it retains its value between function calls. The advantage to using a **static** local variable over a global one is that the **static** local variable is still known to and accessible by only the block in which it is declared. In essence, a local **static** variable behaves like a global variable with restricted scope.

Global static Variables

The **static** modifier may also be used on global variables. When it is, it causes the global variable to be known to and accessible by only the functions in the same file in which it is declared. Not only is a function not declared in the same file as a **static** global variable unable to access that global variable, it does not even know its name. This means that there are no name conflicts if a **static** global variable in one file has the same name as another global variable in a different file of the same program.

Access Modifiers

C++ includes two type modifiers that affect the way variables are accessed by both your program and the compiler. These modifiers are **const** and **volatile**. This section examines these type modifiers.

const

If you precede a variable's type with **const**, you prevent that variable from being modified by your program. The variable may be given an initial value, however, through the use of an initialization when it is declared. The compiler is free to locate **const** variables in ROM (read-only memory) in environments that support it. A **const** variable may also have its value changed by hardware-dependent means.

The following program shows how a **const** variable can be given an initial value and used in the program, as long as it is not on the left side of an assignment statement.

```
#include <iostream.h>

main()
{
  const int i = 10;

  cout << i;
```

```
// i = 100; // this line is wrong and will not compile

   return 0;
}
```

Notice the commented-out line. As the comment suggests, if you try to compile this line, the program will not compile because **i** cannot be modified by the program. (You might want to confirm this for yourself.)

The **const** modifier has a second use. It can prevent a function from modifying the object that a parameter points to. That is, when a pointer parameter is preceded by **const**, no statement in the function can modify the variable pointed to by that parameter. The following program shows how a pointer parameter can be declared as **const** to prevent the object it points to from being modified.

```
#include <iostream.h>

void pr_str(const char *p);

main()
{
   char str[80];

   cout << "Enter a string: ";
   cin >> str;
   pr_str(str);

   return 0;
}

void pr_str(const char *p)
{
   while(*p) cout << *p++;
}
```

Here, **p** is a **const** pointer. This means that no statement inside **pr_str( )** can change the string pointed to by **p**. For example, if you change **pr_str( )** as shown here, it will not compile because this version attempts to alter the string pointed to by **p**.

```
// This is wrong.
void pr_str(const char *p)
{
   while(*p) {
      *p = toupper(*p); // this will not compile
      cout << *p++;
```

```
   }
}
```

const can also be applied to reference parameters to prevent functions from modifying the variables that they reference. For example, a function with the following prototype

```
int myfunc(const long &arg);
```

cannot modify the variable referenced by **arg**.

One other important use of **const** is to create named constants. Often, a program will require one or more "magic numbers" that specify such things as array dimensions or file buffer sizes which remain fixed throughout the lifetime of the program. When you need such a value, the best way to create it is using **const**. For example, this creates a constant called **BUFSIZE** that has the value 256.

```
const int BUFSIZE = 256;
```

volatile

When you precede a variable's type with **volatile**, you are telling the compiler that the value of the variable may be changed in ways not explicitly defined in the program. For example, a variable's address might be given to an interrupt service routine, and its value changed each time an interrupt occurs. The reason that **volatile** is important is that most C++ compilers apply complex and sophisticated optimizations to your program to create faster and more efficient executable programs. If the compiler does not know that the contents of a variable may change in ways not explicitly specified by the program, it may not actually examine the contents of the variable each time it is referenced. (It may simply assume that its value is unchanged.) However, specifying a variable as **volatile** causes the compiler to inspect the variable each time it is referenced.

While short examples of **volatile** are hard to find, the following fragment gives you the flavor of its use. Assume that **Some_Interrupt( )** is some type of interrupt service routine which updates the value of **u** each time an interrupt is received.

```
volatile unsigned u;

Some_Interrupt(&u);

for(;;) { // watch value of u
```

```
cout << u;
// ...
```

In this example, if **u** had not been declared **volatile**, the compiler could have optimized the repeated calls to **cout** in such a way that **u** was not reexamined each time. The use of **volatile** forces the compiler to actually obtain the value of **u**.

typedef

Before leaving the topic of data types, there is one more related feature that needs to be discussed. In C++ you can create a new name for an existing type using **typedef**. The general form of **typedef** is

typedef *old-name new-name*;

This new name can be used any place any other type name can. For example, it can be used to declare a variable. In the following program, **smallint** is a new name for a **signed char** and is used to declare **i**.

```
#include <iostream.h>

typedef signed char smallint;

main()
{
  smallint i;

  for(i=0; i<10; i++)
    cout << i;

  return 0;
}
```

Keep three points firmly in mind: First, a **typedef** does not cause the original name to be deactivated. For example, in the program, **signed char** is still a valid type. Second, you can use several **typedef** statements to create many different, new names for the same original type. Third, **typedef** does *not* create a new type of data. It only creates a new name for an existing type.

The new name created by one **typedef** can be used in a subsequent **typedef** to create another name. For example, consider this fragment.

```
typedef int height;
typedef height length;
```

```
typedef length depth;
depth d;
```

Here, **d** is still an integer.

There are basically two reasons to use **typedef**. The first is to create portable programs. For example, if you know that you will be writing a program that will be executed on computers using 16-bit integers as well as on computers using 32-bit integers, and you want to ensure that certain variables are 16 bits long, no matter which machine is executing, you might want to use a **typedef** when compiling the program for the 16-bit machines as follows:

```
typedef int myint;
```

Then, before compiling the code for a 32-bit computer, you can change the **typedef** statement like this:

```
typedef short int myint;
```

This works because on computers using 32-bit integers, a **short int** will be 16 bits long. Assuming that you used **myint** to declare all integer values that you wanted to be 16 bits long, you need change only one statement to change the type of all variables declared using **myint**.

The second reason you might want to use **typedef** is to help provide self-documenting code. For example, if you are writing an inventory program, you might use this **typedef** statement.

```
typedef double subtotal;
```

Now, when anyone reading your program sees a variable declared as **subtotal**, he or she will know that it is used to hold a subtotal.

The Bitwise Operators

C++ contains four special operators that perform their operations on a bit-by-bit basis. These operators are

&	bitwise AND
|	bitwise OR
^	bitwise XOR (eXclusive OR)
~	1's complement

9

These operators work with character and integer types; they cannot be used with floating-point types.

The AND, OR, and XOR operators produce a result based upon a comparison of corresponding bits in each operand. The AND operator turns a bit on if both bits being compared are 1. The OR turns a bit on if either of the bits being comparedis 1. The XOR operation turns a bit on when either of the two bits involved is 1, but not when both are 1 or both are 0. Here is an example of a bitwise AND.

```
    1010 0110
  & 0011 1011
  ---------------
    0010 0010
```

Notice how each resulting bit is set, based on the outcome of the operation being applied to the corresponding bits in each operand.

The 1's complement operator is a unary operator that reverses the state of each bit within an integer or character.

The XOR operation has one interesting property. When the outcome of an XOR operation is XORed with the same value a second time, the initial value is produced. For example, this output.

```
Initial value of i: 100
i after first XOR: 21895
i after second XOR: 100
```

is produced by the following program:

```cpp
#include <iostream.h>

main()
{
  int i;

  i = 100;
  cout << "Initial value of i: " << i << "\n";

  i = i ^ 21987; // first xor
  cout << "i after first XOR: " << i << "\n";

  i = i ^ 21987; // second xor
  cout << "i after second XOR: " << i << "\n";
```

```
     return 0;
}
```

The following program uses a bitwise AND to display, in binary, the ASCII value of the letters of the alphabet.

```
#include <iostream.h>
main()
{
  char ch;
  int i;

  // display binary representation of alphabet
  for(ch='A'; ch<='Z'; ch++) {
    cout << ch << ": ";
    for(i=128; i>0; i=i/2)
      if(i & ch) cout << "1 ";
      else cout << "0 ";
    cout << "\n";
  }

  return 0;
}
```

The program works by adjusting the value of **i** so that only one bit is set each time a comparison is made. Since the high-order bit in a byte represents 128, this value is used as a starting point. Each time through the loop, **i** is halved. This causes the next bit position to be set and all others cleared. Thus, each time through the loop, a bit in **ch** is tested. If it is 1, the comparison produces a true result and a 1 is output. Otherwise, a 0 is displayed. This process continues until all bits have been tested.

By modifying the preceding program as shown here, it can be used to show the effect of the 1's complement operator.

```
#include <iostream.h>

main()
{
  char ch;
  int i;

  ch = 'Z';

  // display binary representation of Z
```

9

```
  for(i=128; i>0; i=i/2)
    if(i & ch) cout << "1 ";
    else cout << "0 ";

  // reverse bit pattern
  ch = ~ch;
  cout << "\n";
  // display binary representation
  for(i=128; i>0; i=i/2)
    if(i & ch) cout << "1 ";
    else cout << "0 ";

  return 0;
}
```

When you run this program, you will see that the state of bits in **ch** are reversed after the operation has occurred.

The following program shows how to use the **&** operator to determine if a signed integer is positive or negative. (The program assumes 16-bit integers.) Since negative numbers are represented with their high-order bits set, the comparison will only be true if **i** is negative. (The value 32768 is the value of an unsigned integer when only its high-order bit is set. This value is 1000 0000 in binary.)

```
#include <iostream.h>

main()
{
  int i;

  cout << "Enter a number: ";
  cin >> i;
  if(i & 32768) cout << "Number is negative.";
  else cout << "Number is positive or zero.";

  return 0;
}
```

The following program makes **i** into a negative number by setting its high-order bit.

```
#include <iostream.h>

main()
{
  int i;
```

```
    i = 1;
    i = i | 32768;
    cout << i;

    return 0;
}
```

The program displays –32,767.

The Shift Operators

C++ includes two operators not commonly found in other computer languages: the left and right bit-shift operators. The left shift operator is **<<**, and the right shift operator is **>>**. These operators may be applied only to character or integer operands. They take these general forms.

> *variable << integer-expression*
> *variable >> integer-expression*

The value of the integer expression determines how many places to the left or right the bits within the variable are shifted. Each left shift causes all bits within the specified variable to be shifted left one position and a zero is brought in on the right. A right shift shifts all bits to the right one position and brings a zero in on the left. However, when right-shifting a signed, negative number, 1s are brought in on the left to preserve the sign bit. For both right and left shifts, when bits are shifted off an end, they are lost.

Note: Although the shift operators use the same symbols as the input and output operators, they have no relationship to them. They perform fundamentally different operations.

A right shift is equivalent to dividing a number by 2, and a left shift is the same as multiplying the number by 2. However, because of the internal operation of virtually all CPUs, shift operations are faster than their equivalent arithmetic operations.

This program demonstrates the right and left shift operators.

```
#include <iostream.h>

void show_binary(unsigned u);

main()
```

```
{
  unsigned u;

  u = 45678;
  show_binary(u);

  u = u << 1;
  show_binary(u);

  u = u >> 1;
  show_binary(u);

  return 0;
}

void show_binary(unsigned u)
{
  unsigned long val;

  for(val=32768; val; val=val/2)
    if(u & val) cout << "1 ";
    else cout << "0 ";

  cout << "\n";
}
```

The output from this program is

```
1 0 1 1 0 0 1 0 0 1 1 0 1 1 1 0
0 1 1 0 0 1 0 0 1 1 0 1 1 1 0 0
0 0 1 1 0 0 1 0 0 1 1 0 1 1 1 0
```

Notice that after the left shift, a bit of information has been lost. When the right shift occurs, a zero is brought in. As stated earlier, bits that are shifted off one end are lost.

Since a right shift is the same as a division by two, but faster, the **show_binary( )** function can be made more efficient as shown here.

```
void show_binary(unsigned u)
{
  unsigned long val;

  for(val=32768; val; val = val>>1)
    if(u & val) cout << "1 ";
    else cout << "0 ";
```

```
    cout << "\n";
}
```

In this case,

```
val = val >> 1
```

is substituted for

```
val = val /2
```

Rotating an Integer

Although C++ contains operators that perform a left shift and right shift, it does not have ones that perform a left or right rotate. As you probably know, a *rotate* is similar to a shift except that the bit shifted off one end is inserted onto the other. For example, given the following binary value

```
1 0 1 1   0 0 1 0
```

a left rotate will produce the following binary value

```
0 1 1 0   0 1 0 1
```

As you can see, the 1 shifted off the left side of the original value is brought into the right side.

Although C++ does not have rotate operators, it is easy to create rotation functions. For example, the following program creates a left rotate function that can be used on integer values. Notice how it employs a **union** to "catch" any bits that are shifted off.

```
// A left rotate function.
#include <iostream.h>

union rotate {
  unsigned char ch[3];
  unsigned long ul;
  unsigned u;
};

void leftrot(rotate &arg);
```

```
main()
{
  rotate num;
  int i;

  num.u = 1;

  for(i=0; i<32; i++) {
    leftrot(num);
    cout << num.u << "\n";
  }

  return 0;
}

void leftrot(rotate &arg)
{
  arg.ch[2] = 0; // clear the high-order byte

  arg.ul = arg.ul << 1;

  // if bit rotated out, add back onto right
  if(arg.ch[2]) arg.ch[0] = arg.ch[0] | 1;
}
```

The **leftrot( )** function works like this. The integer you want to rotate left is put into the **u** member of the **rotate** union. The **leftrot( )** function then left-shifts the long integer **ul.** It then checks to see if a bit has been shifted off into the third character of **ch.** If it has, it is inserted onto the right side. On your own, you might want to try creating your own version of a right shift using a similar mechanism.

The ? Operator

C++ contains one ternary operator: the **?.** A ternary operator requires three operands. The **?** operator is commonly used to replace statements such as

> if(*condition*) *var* = *exp1*;
> else *var* = *exp2*;

The general form of the **?** operator is

> *var* = *condition* ? *exp1*: *exp2*;

Here, *condition* is an expression that evaluates to true or false. If it is true, *var* is assigned the value of *exp1*. If it is false, *var* is assigned the value of *exp2*. The reason for the **?** operator is that a compiler can produce more efficient code using it instead of the equivalent **if/else** statement.

The following program illustrates the **?** operator. It inputs a number and then converts the number into 1 if the number is positive and –1 if it is negative.

```
#include <iostream.h>

main()
{
  int i;

  cout << "Enter a number: ";
  cin >> i;
  i = i>0 ? 1: -1;
  cout << i;

  return 0;
}
```

The next program is a computerized coin toss. It repeatedly generates random numbers until you to press a key. It then prints either **heads** or **tails,** depending upon the value of the random number when you press the key. This program uses the nonstandard function **kbhit( )** to detect when the user presses a key on the keyboard. (**kbhit( )** is described in the following Fast Track Tip.)

```
#include <iostream.h>
#include <stdlib.h>
#include <conio.h>

main()
{
  int i;

  cout << "Press a key.\n";
  while(!kbhit()) rand(); // wait for keypress

  i = rand()%2 ? 1: 0;
  if(i) cout << "heads";
  else cout << "tails";

  return 0;
}
```

9

The coin-toss program can be written in a more efficient way. There is no technical reason that the **?** operator need assign its value to any variable. Therefore, the coin toss program can be written as

```cpp
#include <iostream.h>
#include <stdlib.h>
#include <conio.h>

main()
{

  cout << "Press a key.\n";

  while(!kbhit()) rand(); // wait for keypress
  rand()%2 ? cout << "heads" : cout << "tails";

  return 0;
}
```

Remember, since a call to a function is a valid C++ expression, it is perfectly valid to call **cout** in the **?** statement.

FAST TRACK TIP

The kbhit( ) Function

While not defined by either the ANSI C or the draft ANSI C++ standard, the **kbhit( )** function is one of the more useful, nonstandard functions. It determines whether or not the user has pressed a key on the keyboard. It has this prototype.

```cpp
int kbhit( );
```

It returns nonzero if the user has hit a key or zero otherwise. The function does not wait for a keypress. It only checks to see if a key has been pressed. Also, if a key has been pressed, it does not remove that key from the input buffer. The function requires the nonstandard header file CONIO.H.

The reason that **kbhit( )** is valuable is that it allows your program to check for user input without a disruption in the program's execution. For example, **kbhit( )** is often used inside a loop, such as the one shown here.

```cpp
do {
  if(kbhit()) break;
```

```
          // otherwise, continue processing ...
      }
```

If the user does not press a key, processing continues uninterrupted. However, if the user presses a key, then the loop is broken.

kbhit( ) is just one of several nonstandard I/O functions supported by most C++ compilers. You will want to check your compiler's library manual for others.

Assignment Options

The assignment operator is more powerful in C++ than in most other computer languages. In this section, you will see how.

You can assign several variables the same value using the general form

   var1 = var2 = var3 = ...= varN = value;

For example, this statement

```
i = j = k = 100;
```

assigns **i**, **j**, and **k** the value 100. In professionally written C++ code, it is common to see such multiple-variable assignments.

Another variation on the assignment statement is sometimes called C++ shorthand. In C++, you can transform a statement like

```
a = a + 3;
```

into a statement like

```
a += 3;
```

In general, any time you have a statement of the form

   var = var op expression;

you can write it in shorthand form as

   var op= expression;

9

Here, *op* is one of the following operators:

```
+ - * / % << >> & | ^
```

Here is another example. This statement

```
x = x / 10;
```

can be rewritten as

```
x /= 10;
```

Remember that there must be no space between the operator and the equal sign. You will want to use the shorthand form not because it saves you a little typing effort, but because the C++ compiler may be able to create more efficient executable code.

The Comma Operator

The next operator we will examine is the comma. It has a very unique function: it tells the compiler to "do this and this and this." That is, the comma is used to string together several operations. The most common use of the comma is in the **for** loop. In the following loop, the comma is used in the initialization portion to initialize two loop-control variables, and in the increment portion to increment **i** and decrement **j**.

```
for(i=0; j=0; i+j<count; i++, j--) . . .
```

The value of a comma-separated list of expressions is the rightmost expression. For example, the following statement assigns 100 to **value**. The other values are discarded.

```
value = (count, 99, 33, 100);
```

The parentheses are necessary because the comma operator is lower in precedence than the assignment operator.

Using sizeof

Sometimes it is helpful to know the size, in bytes, of a type of data. Since the sizes of C++'s built-in types can differ among computing environments, knowing the size of a variable in all situations can sometimes be difficult. To solve this problem, C++ includes the **sizeof** compile-time operator, which has these general forms:

sizeof (*type*)
sizeof *var_name*

The first version returns the size of the specified data type and the second returns the size of the specified variable. As you can see, if you want to know the size of a data type, such as **int**, you must enclose the type name in parentheses. If you want to know the name of a variable, no parentheses are needed, although they may still be used, if you desire.

To see how **sizeof** works, try this short program. (For most environments, it displays the values 1, 2, 4, and 8.)

```
// Demonstrate sizeof.
#include <iostream.h>

main()
{
  char ch;
  int i;

  cout << sizeof ch << ' '; // size of char
  cout << sizeof i << ' ';  // size of int
  cout << sizeof (float) << ' '; // size of float
  cout << sizeof (double) << ' '; // size of double

  return 0;
}
```

As mentioned, **sizeof** is a compile-time operator. All information necessary to compute the size of a variable or data type is known during compilation.

You may apply **sizeof** to any data type. For example, when it is applied to an array, it returns the number of bytes used by the array. When applied to a structure, it returns the physical size of the structure, which may be larger than the size of its individual members added together. The reason for this is that the compiler is free to pad a structure so that alignment on word or paragraph (16-byte) boundaries is achieved. When applied to a union, it returns the size of the largest element that the union may hold.

sizeof primarily helps you to generate portable code that depends upon the size of the C++ data types. Remember, since the size of C++'s types is defined by the implementation, it is bad style to make assumptions about size in code that you write.

Dynamic Allocation Using new and delete

There are two primary ways in which a C++ program can store information in the main memory of the computer. The first is through the use of variables. The storage provided for variables is fixed at compile-time and cannot be altered during the execution of a program. The second way information can be stored is through the use of C++'s dynamic allocation system. In this method, storage for data is allocated as needed from the free memory area that lies between your program (and its permanent storage area) and the stack. This region is called the *heap*. (Figure 9-2 shows conceptually how a C++ program appears in memory.) Dynamically allocated storage is determined at run time. Using dynamic allocation, it is possible for your program to create variables that it needs during its execution. Thus, it can create as many or as few variables as required, depending upon the situation.

Memory to satisfy a dynamic allocation request is taken from the heap. As you might guess, it is possible, under fairly extreme cases, for free memory to become exhausted. Therefore, while dynamic allocation offers greater flexibility, it, too, is finite.

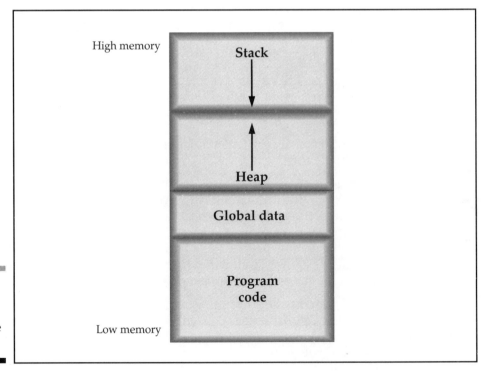

A conceptual view of a C++ program's memory usage
Figure 9-2.

Dynamic allocation is typically used to support such data structures as linked lists, binary trees, and sparse arrays. (These topics are beyond the scope of this book.) However, you are free to use dynamic allocation wherever you determine it to be of value. Because real-world applications of dynamic allocation tend to be large and complex, only the mechanics of dynamic allocation using C++ are discussed here. However, good uses for dynamic allocation can be found in any book on data structures.

C++ contains two operators which perform the function of allocating and freeing memory. The operators are **new** and **delete**. Their general forms are shown here:

> *pointer_var* = new *var_type*;
> delete *pointer_var*;

Here, *pointer_var* is a pointer of type *var_type*. The **new** operator allocates sufficient memory to hold a value of type *var_type* and returns a pointer to it. Any valid data type can be allocated using **new**. The **delete** operator frees the memory pointed to by *pointer_var*. Once freed, this memory can be reallocated to different purposes by a subsequent **new** allocation request.

Since the heap is finite, it could become exhausted. If there is not enough free memory available in the heap to fill a memory request, then the request fails and **new** returns a null pointer. Therefore, you must always check the pointer produced by **new** before using it.

Because of the way dynamic allocation is managed, you must only use **delete** with a pointer memory that was allocated using **new**. Using **delete** with any other type of address will cause serious problems.

Here is a simple example of **new** and **delete**.

```
#include <iostream.h>

main()
{
  int *p;

  p = new int; // allocate memory for int
  if(!p) {
    cout << "Allocation failure\n";
    return 1;
  }

  *p = 100; // assign that memory the value 100
  cout << *p; // prove that it works by displaying value
```

9

```
  delete p; // free the memory

  return 0;
}
```

This program assigns to **p** an address in the heap that is large enough to hold an integer. It then assigns that memory the value 100 and displays the contents of that memory on the screen. Finally, it frees the dynamically allocated memory.

Initializing Dynamically Allocated Memory

You can initialize dynamically allocated memory using the **new** operator. To do this, specify the initial value inside parentheses after the type name. For example, this program uses initialization to give the memory pointed to by **p** the value 1997.

```
#include <iostream.h>

main()
{
  int *p;

  p = new int (1997);  // initialize with 1997
  if(!p) {
    cout << "Allocation failure\n";
    return 1;
  }

  cout << *p;

  delete p;

  return 0;
}
```

Allocating Arrays

You can allocate arrays using **new**. The general form for a singly dimensioned array is shown here.

   pointer_var = new *var_type* [*size*];

Here, *size* specifies the number of elements in the array.

To free a dynamically allocated array, use this form of **delete**.

delete [ ] *pointer_var;*

Here, *pointer_var* is the address obtained when the array was allocated. The use of the **[ ]** tells C++ that a dynamically allocated array is being deleted and it automatically frees all the memory allocated to the array.

Note: Older C++ compilers may require that you specify the size of the array being deleted. Older versions of C++ required this form of **delete** when freeing an array:

delete *[size] pointer_var;*

where *size* is the number of elements in the array. The modern specification for C++ no longer requires that the size of the array be specified.

The next program allocates space for a 10-element array of **float**s, assigns the array the values 100 to 109, and displays the contents of the array on the screen.

```
#include <iostream.h>

main()
{
  float *p;
  int i;

  p = new float [10]; // get a 10-element array
  if(!p) {
    cout << "Allocation failure\n";
    return 1;
  }

  // assign the values 100 through 109
  for(i=0; i<10; i++) p[i] = 100.00 + i;

 // display the contents of the array
  for(i=0; i<10; i++)  cout << p[i] << " ";

  delete [ ] p; // delete the entire array

  return 0;
}
```

There is one important point to remember about allocating an array: you cannot initialize it.

9

Operator Precedence Summary

Table 9-1 shows the precedence of all the C++ operators. It includes a few operators that have not yet been discussed. They will be explained later in this book.

Highest	( ) [ ] -> :: .
	! ~ –– – + (type cast) * &
	sizeof new delete typeid
	.* –>*
	* / %
	+ –
	<< >>
	< <= > >=
	== !=
	&
	^
	|
	&&
	||
	?
	= += = *= /= etc.
Lowest	,

The Precedence of the C++ Operators

Table 9-1.

C-Based Dynamic Allocation

The C language does not contain the **new** and **delete** operators. Instead, C uses library functions rather than operators to allocate and free memory. For compatibility, C++ still provides support for C's dynamic allocation system. Since it is still quite common to find the C-like dynamic allocation system used in both C and C++ programs, the following discussion will explain its basics.

At the core of C's allocation system are the functions **malloc( )** and **free( )**. The **malloc( )** function allocates memory and the **free( )** function releases it. That is, each time a **malloc( )** memory request is made, a portion of the remaining free memory is allocated. Each time a **free( )** memory release call is made, memory is returned to the system. Any program that uses these functions should include the header file STDLIB.H.

The **malloc( )** function has this prototype.

    void *malloc(size_t *num_bytes*);

Here, *num_bytes* is the number of bytes of memory you wish to allocate. (**size_t** is a defined type that is (more or less) an **unsigned** integer.) The **malloc( )** function returns a pointer of type **void**. You must use a type cast to convert this pointer into the type of pointer needed by your program. After a successful call, **malloc( )** will return a pointer to the first byte of the region of memory allocated from the heap. If there is not enough available memory to satisfy the **malloc( )** request, an allocation failure occurs and **malloc( )** returns a null.

The **free( )** function is the opposite of **malloc( )** in that it returns previously allocated memory to the system. Once the memory has been released, it may be reused by a subsequent call to **malloc( )**. The function **free( )** has this prototype.

    void free(void *ptr*);

Here, *ptr* is a pointer to memory previously allocated using **malloc( )**. You must never call **free( )** with an invalid argument because if you do, the free list will be destroyed.

While **malloc( )** and **free( )** are fully capable dynamic allocation functions, there are several reasons why C++ defines its own approach to dynamic allocation. First, **new** automatically computes the size of the type of object being allocated. Using **malloc( )**, your program must manually make this determination (usually using **sizeof**). Second, **new** automatically returns the correct pointer type—you don't need to use a type cast. Third, it is possible to initialize the object being allocated using **new**. This is not possible using **malloc( )**. Finally, as you will see later in this book, it is possible to create your own, customized versions of **new** (and **delete**).

One last point: Because of possible incompatibilities, you should not mix **malloc( )** and **free( )** with **new** and **delete** within the same program.

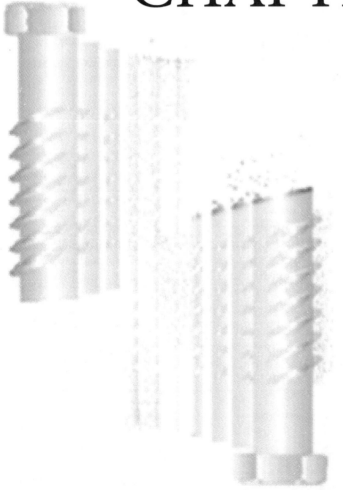

CHAPTER 10

Introducing the Class

This chapter introduces the class. The class forms the basis for object-oriented programming and is C++'s fundamental unit of encapsulation. A class is used to create an *object*. As you can guess, the class is at the foundation of C++'s more advanced features.

Note: From this point forward, you will be using all of the skills that you have acquired from the preceding nine chapters. Now might be a good time to skim through the first part of this book again and review what you already know. Although nothing in this, or any subsequent chapter, is more difficult than what you have already learned, the object-oriented features of C++ require a firm understanding of the C++ fundamentals.

A First Look at the Class

Classes are created using the keyword **class**. The syntax of a **class** declaration is similar to that of a structure. Its general form is shown here:

```
class class-name {
    private functions and variables
public:
    public functions and variables
} object-list;
```

In a **class** declaration, the *object-list* is optional. As with a structure, you can declare class objects later, as needed. While the *class-name* is also technically optional, from a practical point of view it is virtually always needed. The reason for this is that the *class-name* becomes a new type name that is used to declare objects of the class. Notice that a **class** declaration may include both variables and functions.

Functions and variables declared inside a **class** declaration are said to be *members* of that class. By default, all functions and variables declared inside a class are private to that class. This means that they are accessible only by other members of that class. To declare public class members, the **public** keyword is used, followed by a colon. All functions and variables declared after the **public** specifier are accessible both by other members of the class and by any other part of the program.

Here is a simple class declaration:

```
class myclass {
  // private to myclass
  int a;
public:
  void set_a(int num);
  int get_a();
};
```

This class has one private variable, called **a**, and two public functions, **set_a( )** and **get_a( )**. Notice that functions are declared within a class using their prototype forms. Functions that are declared to be part of a class are called *member functions*.

Since **a** is private, it is not accessible by any code outside **myclass**. However, since **set_a( )** and **get_a( )** are members of **myclass**, they may access **a**. Further, **get_a( )** and **set_a( )** are declared as public members of **myclass** and can be called by any other part of the program that contains **myclass**.

Although the functions **get_a( )** and **set_a( )** are declared by **myclass**, they are not yet defined. To define a member function, you must link the type name of its class with the name of the function. You do this by preceding the function name with the class name followed by two colons. The two colons are called the *scope resolution operator*. For example, here is the way the member functions **set_a( )** and **get_a( )** are defined:

```
void myclass::set_a(int num)
{
  a = num;
}

int myclass::get_a()
{
  return a;
}
```

Notice that both **set_a( )** and **get_a( )** have access to **a**, which is private to **myclass**. As stated, because **set_a( )** and **get_a( )** are members of **myclass**, they may directly access its private data.

When you define a member function, use this general form:

> *type class-name::func-name(parameter-list)*
> *{*
> * // body of function*
> *}*

The declaration of **myclass** does not define any objects of type **myclass**—it only defines the type of object that will be created when one is actually declared. To create an object, use the class name as a type specifier. For example, this line declares two objects of type **myclass**:

```
myclass ob1, ob2; // these are objects of type myclass
```

Remember: A class declaration is a logical abstraction that defines a new data type. An object declaration creates a physical entity of that type. (That is, an object occupies memory space, but a type definition does not.)

Once an object of a class has been created, your program may reference its public members by using the dot (period) operator in much the same way that structure members are accessed. Assuming the preceding object declaration, this statement calls **set_a( )** for objects **ob1** and **ob2**:

```
ob1.set_a(10); // sets ob1's version of a to 10
ob2.set_a(99); // sets ob2's version of a to 99
```

As the comments indicate, these statements set **ob1**'s copy of **a** to 10 and **ob2**'s to 99. Each object contains its own copy of all data declared in the class. This means that **ob1**'s **a** is distinct and different from the one linked to **ob2**.

Remember: Each object of a class has its own copy of all variables declared within the class.

This program illustrates **myclass.** It sets the value of **a** for **ob1** and **ob2** and displays **a**'s value for each object:

```
#include <iostream.h>

class myclass {
  // private to myclass
  int a;
public:
  void set_a(int num);
  int get_a();
};

void myclass::set_a(int num)
{
  a = num;
}

int myclass::get_a()
{
  return a;
}
```

```
main()
{
  myclass ob1, ob2;

  ob1.set_a(10); // set ob1's a
  ob2.set_a(99); // set ob2's a

  cout << ob1.get_a() << "\n";
  cout << ob2.get_a() << "\n";

  return 0;
}
```

As you should expect, this program displays the values 10 and 99 on the screen.

In **myclass**, **a** is private. This means that only member functions of **myclass** may access it directly. (This is one reason why the public function **get_a( )** is required.) If you try to access a private member of a class from some part of your program that is not a member of that class, a compile-time error will result. For example, assuming **myclass** is defined as shown in the preceding example, this **main( )** function will cause an error:

```
// This fragment contains an error.
main()
{
  myclass ob1, ob2;

  ob1.a = 10; // ERROR! cannot access private member
  ob2.a = 99; // by non-member functions.

  cout << ob1.get_a() << "\n";
  cout << ob2.get_a() << "\n";

  return 0;
}
```

Just as there may be public member functions, there may be public member variables as well. For example, if **a** were declared in the public section of **myclass**, then **a** could be accessed by any part of the program, as shown here:

```
#include <iostream.h>

class myclass {
public:
  // now a is public
```

```
  int a;
  // and there is no need for set_a() or get_a()
};

main()
{
  myclass ob1, ob2;

  // here, a is accessed directly
  ob1.a = 10;
  ob2.a = 99;

  cout << ob1.a << "\n";
  cout << ob2.a << "\n";

  return 0;
}
```

In this example, since **a** is declared as a public member of **myclass**, it is directly accessible from **main( )**. Notice how the dot operator is used to access **a**. In general, whether you are calling a member function or accessing a member variable, the object's name followed by the dot operator followed by the member's name is required to fully specify which object's member you are referring to.

A Stack Class

To taste the power of objects, let's look at a more practical example. This program creates a class called **stack** that implements a stack that can be used to store characters:

```
#include <iostream.h>

const int SIZE=10;

// Declare a stack class for characters
class stack {
  char stck[SIZE]; // holds the stack
  int tos; // index of top-of-stack
public:
  void init(); // initialize stack
  void push(char ch); // push character on stack
  char pop(); // pop character from stack
};

// Initialize the stack
```

10

```cpp
void stack::init()
{
  tos = 0;
}

// Push a character.
void stack::push(char ch)
{
  if(tos==SIZE) {
    cout << "Stack is full.\n";
    return;
  }
  stck[tos] = ch;
  tos++;
}

// Pop a character.
char stack::pop()
{
  if(tos==0) {
    cout << "Stack is empty.\n";
    return 0; // return null on empty stack
  }
  tos--;
  return stck[tos];
}

main()
{
  stack s1, s2;  // create two stacks
  int i;

  // initialize the stacks
  s1.init();
  s2.init();

  s1.push('a');
  s2.push('x');
  s1.push('b');
  s2.push('y');
  s1.push('c');
  s2.push('z');

  for(i=0; i<3; i++) cout << "Pop s1: " << s1.pop() << "\n";
  for(i=0; i<3; i++) cout << "Pop s2: " << s2.pop() << "\n";
```

```
   return 0;
}
```

This program displays the following output:

```
Pop s1: c
Pop s1: b
Pop s1: a
Pop s2: z
Pop s2: y
Pop s2: x
```

Let's take a close look at this program now. The class **stack** contains two private variables: **stck** and **tos**. The array **stck** actually holds the characters pushed onto the stack, and **tos** contains the index to the top of the stack. The public stack functions are **init( )**, **push( )**, and **pop( )**, which initialize the stack, push a value, and pop a value, respectively.

Inside **main( )**, two stacks, **s1** and **s2,** are created, and three characters are pushed onto each stack. It is important to understand that each stack object is separate from the other. That is, the characters pushed onto **s1** *in no way* affect the characters pushed onto **s2**. Each object contains its own copy of **stck** and **tos**. This concept is fundamental to understanding objects. Although all objects of a class share their member functions, each object creates and maintains *its own data.*

Understanding Member Access

In the preceding examples, you have seen class members accessed by other class members and by other parts of the program. Before moving on, let's review the rules that govern class member access.

First, a member function may directly access member variables or call other member functions *without* qualifying them with an object name. For example:

```
class sample {
  int x;
public:
  int y;
  void setx(int i);
  // ...
};

void sample::setx(int i)
{
```

```
    x = i;
}

main()
{
  sample ob;

  ob.setx(10);
  ob.y = 20;
  // ...
}
```

Here, the member function **setx( )** directly refers to **x.** That is, inside **setx( )**, **x** is not qualified with an object name. The reason that **x** may be accessed directly is because the object upon which **setx( )** is operating is already known. Remember, outside **sample**, **setx( )** may only be called in conjunction with an object. For example, in **main( )**, **setx( )** is invoked for **ob.** Thus, when **setx( )** executes the line **x = i**; it is **ob**'s **x** that is being operated upon.

Second, although member functions may directly operate upon member variables or directly call other member functions, code outside the class may not. Instead, code outside the class must always link an object name with a member name (as preceding examples have shown). For example, even though **setx( )** and **y** are public members of **sample**, they may only be accessed via an object by code outside the class. To understand why, consider this line from the preceding fragment:

```
ob.y = 20;
```

This assigns the value of 20 to **ob**'s copy of **x.** Remember, each object has its own copy of the member variables. Therefore, there is no concept (in this context) of assigning **y** a value independent of any object. **y** only exists relative to an object.

At this point, member access may still seem a little fuzzy. However, as you work through the next few chapters, it will become clear.

Constructors and Destructors

If you have been writing programs for very long, you know that it is very common for parts of your program to require initialization. The need for initialization is even more common when working with objects. In fact, when applied to real problems, virtually every object you create will require some sort of initialization. To address this situation, C++ allows a *constructor function* to be included in a class declaration. A class's constructor is called each time an object of that class is created. Thus, any initializations that need to be performed on an object can be done automatically by the constructor function.

A constructor function has the same name as the class of which it is a part and has no return type. For example, here is a short class that contains a constructor function:

```cpp
#include <iostream.h>

class myclass {
   int a;
public:
   myclass(); // constructor
   void show();
};

myclass::myclass()
{
   cout << "In constructor\n";
   a = 10;
}

void myclass::show()
{
   cout << a;
}

main()
{
   myclass ob;

   ob.show();

   return 0;
}
```

In this simple example, the value of **a** is initialized by the constructor **myclass( )**. The constructor is called when the object **ob** is created. An object is created when that object's declaration statement is executed. It is important to understand that in C++, a variable declaration statement is an "action statement." When programming in other languages, it is easy to think of declaration statements as simply establishing variables. However, in C++, because an object may have a constructor, a variable declaration statement may, in fact, cause considerable actions to occur.

Notice how **myclass( )** is defined. As stated, it has no return type. In fact, according to the C++ formal syntax rules, it is illegal for a constructor to have a return type.

For global objects, an object's constructor is called once, when the program first begins execution. For local objects, the constructor is called each time the declaration statement is executed.

To fully appreciate the benefits of constructors, recall that the **stack** class created earlier required an initialization function to set the stack index variable to zero. This is precisely the sort of operation that a constructor function was designed to perform. Here is an improved version of the **stack** class that uses a constructor to automatically initialize a stack object when it is created:

```
#include <iostream.h>

#define SIZE 10

// Declare a stack class for characters
class stack {
  char stck[SIZE]; // holds the stack
  int tos; // index of top-of-stack
public:
  stack(); // constructor
  void push(char ch); // push character on stack
  char pop(); // pop character from stack
};

// Initialize the stack
stack::stack()
{
  cout << "Constructing a stack.\n";
  tos = 0;
}

// Push a character.
void stack::push(char ch)
{
  if(tos==SIZE) {
    cout << "Stack is full.\n";
    return;
  }
  stck[tos] = ch;
  tos++;
}
```

```
// Pop a character.
char stack::pop()
{
  if(tos==0) {
    cout << "Stack is empty.\n";
    return 0; // return null on empty stack
  }
  tos--;
  return stck[tos];
}

main()
{
  // create two stacks that are automatically initialized
  stack s1, s2;
  int i;

  s1.push('a');
  s2.push('x');
  s1.push('b');
  s2.push('y');
  s1.push('c');
  s2.push('z');

  for(i=0; i<3; i++) cout << "Pop s1: " << s1.pop() << "\n";
  for(i=0; i<3; i++) cout << "Pop s2: " << s2.pop() << "\n";

  return 0;
}
```

As you can see, now the initialization task is performed automatically by the constructor function rather than by a separate function that must be explicitly called by the program. This is an important point. When an initialization is performed automatically when an object is created, it eliminates any prospect that, by error, the initialization will not be performed. This is another way that objects help reduce program complexity. You, as the programmer, don't need to worry about initialization—it is performed automatically when the object is brought into existence.

The complement of a constructor is the *destructor*. This function is called when an object is destroyed. When working with objects, it is very common to have to perform some actions when an object is destroyed. For example, an object that allocates memory when it is created will want to free that

10

memory when it is destroyed. The name of a destructor is the name of the class of which it is part preceded by a ~. For example, this class contains a destructor function:

```cpp
#include <iostream.h>

class myclass {
   int a;
public:
   myclass(); // constructor
   ~myclass(); // destructor
   void show();
};

myclass::~myclass()
{
   cout << "In constructor\n";
   a = 10;
}

myclass::~myclass()
{
   cout << "Destructing...\n";
}

void myclass::show()
{
   cout << a << "\n";
}

main()
{
   myclass ob;

   ob.show();

   return 0;
}
```

The output produced by this program is shown here.

```
In constructor
10
Destructing...
```

A class's destructor is called when an object is destroyed. Local objects are destroyed when they go out of scope. Global objects are destroyed when the program ends.

Technically, a constructor or a destructor may perform any type of operation. The code that occurs within these functions does not *have* to initialize or reset anything related to the class for which they are defined. For example, a constructor for the preceding examples could have computed pi to 100 places. However, having a constructor or destructor perform actions not directly related to the initialization or orderly destruction of an object makes for very poor programming style and should be avoided.

There is one restriction that applies to both constructors and destructors: It is not possible to obtain the address of either.

Parameterized Constructors

It is possible to pass arguments to a constructor function. To allow this, simply add the appropriate parameters to the constructor function's declaration and definition. Then, when you declare an object, specify the parameters as arguments. To see how this is accomplished, let's begin with the short example shown here:

```cpp
#include <iostream.h>

class myclass {
  int a;
public:
  myclass(int x); // constructor
  void show();
};

myclass::myclass(int x)
{
  cout << "In constructor\n";
  cout << "x is " << x << "\n";
  a = x;
}

void myclass::show()
{
  cout << a << "\n";
}

main()
{
```

```
    myclass ob(4);

    ob.show();

    return 0;
}
```

Here, the constructor for **myclass** takes one parameter. The value passed to **myclass( )** is used to initialize **a**. Pay special attention to how **ob** is declared in **main( )**. The value 4, specified in the parentheses following **ob**, is the argument that is passed to **myclass( )**'s parameter **x**, which is used to initialize **a**.

The syntax for passing an argument to a parameterized constructor has a second, longer form, which is shown here.

```
myclass ob = myclass(4);
```

However, most C++ programmers use the short form shown in the program. Actually, there is a slight technical difference between the two forms which relates to copy constructors. (Copy constructors are discussed later in this book.) But you don't need to worry about this distinction now.

Unlike constructor functions, destructor functions may not have parameters. The reason for this is simple enough to understand: there exists no mechanism by which to pass arguments to an object that is being destroyed.

It is possible—in fact, quite common—to pass a constructor more than one argument. Here, **myclass( )** is passed two arguments:

```
#include <iostream.h>

class myclass {
  int a, b;
public:
  myclass(int x, int y); // constructor
  void show();
};

myclass::myclass(int x, int y)
{
  cout << "In constructor\n";
  cout << "x is " << x << ", y is " << y << "\n";
  a = x;
  b = y;
}
```

```
void myclass::show()
{
  cout << a << ' ' << b << "\n";
}

main()
{
  myclass ob(4, 7);

  ob.show();

  return 0;
}
```

Here, 4 is passed to **x** and 7 is passed to **y**. This same general approach is used to pass any number of arguments you like (up to the limit set by the compiler, of course).

Initializing Constructors with One Parameter

If a constructor function only has one parameter, then there is a third way to pass an initial value to that constructor. For example, consider the following short program.

```
#include <iostream.h>

class myclass {
  int a;
public:
  myclass(int j);
  int geta();
};

myclass::myclass(int j)
{
  a = j;
}

int myclass::geta()
{
```

```
    return a;
}

main()
{
  myclass ob = 2001; // passes 2001 to j

  cout << ob.geta(); // outputs 2001
```

Introducing Inheritance

Although inheritance is discussed more fully in Chapter 4, a brief overview is appropriate here. As it applies to C++, inheritance is the mechanism by which one class can inherit the properties of another. Inheritance allows a hierarchy of classes to be built, moving from the most general to the most specific.

To begin, it is necessary to define two terms commonly used when discussing inheritance. When one class is inherited by another, the class that is inherited is called the *base class*. The inheriting class is called the *derived class*. In general, the process of inheritance begins with the definition of a base class. The base class defines all qualities that will be common to any derived class. In essence, the base class represents the most general description of a set of traits. A derived class inherits those general traits and adds those properties that are specific to that class.

To understand how one class can inherit another, let's first begin with an example that, although simple, illustrates many key features of inheritance. To start, here is the declaration for the base class:

```
// Define base class.
class B {
  int i;
public:
  void set_i(int n);
  int get_i();
};
```

Using this base class, here is a derived class that inherits it:

```
// Define derived class.
class D : public B {
  int j;
public:
  void set_j(int n);
  int mul();
};
```

Look closely at this declaration. Notice that after the class name **D**, there is a colon followed by the keyword **public** and the class name **B**. This tells the compiler that class **D** will inherit class **B**. The keyword **public** tells the compiler that **B** will be inherited such that all public elements of the base class will also be public elements of the derived class. However, all private elements of the base class remain private to it and are not directly accessible by the derived class. Here is an entire program that uses the **B** and **D** classes:

```
// A simple example of inheritance.
#include <iostream.h>

// Define base class.
class B {
  int i;
public:
  void set_i(int n);
  int get_i();
};

// Define derived class.
class D : public B {
  int j;
public:
  void set_j(int n);
  int mul();
};

// Set value i in B.
void B::set_i(int n)
{
  i = n;
}

// Return value of i in B.
int B::get_i()
{
  return i;
```

```
}

// Set value of j in D.
void D::set_j(int n)
{
  j = n;
}

// Return value of B's i times D's j.
int D::mul()
{
  // derived class can call base class public member functions
  return j * get_i();
}

main()
{
  D ob;

  ob.set_i(10); // load i in B
  ob.set_j(4);  // load j in D

  cout << ob.mul();  // displays 40

  return 0;
}
```

Look at the definition of **mul( )**. Notice that it calls **get_i( )**, which is a member of the base class **B**, not of **D**, without linking it to any specific object. This is possible because the public members of **B** become public members of **D**. However, **mul( )** must call **get_i( )** instead of accessing **i** directly because the private members of a base class (in this case, **i**) remain private to it and not accessible by any derived class. The reason that private members of a class are not accessible to derived classes is to maintain encapsulation. If the private members of a class could be made public simply by inheriting the class, encapsulation could be easily circumvented.

The general form used to inherit a base class is shown here:

> class *derived-class-name : access-specifier base-class-name* {
>   *// ...*
> };

Here, *access-specifier* is one of the following three keywords: **public**, **private**, or **protected.** For now, just use **public** when inheriting a class. A complete description of the access specifiers will be given later in this book.

Pointers to Class Objects

So far, you have been accessing members of an object by using the dot operator. This is the correct method when you are working with an object. However, it is also possible to access a member of an object via a pointer to that object. When this is the case, the arrow operator (–>) rather than the dot operator is employed. (This is exactly the same way the arrow operator is used when given a pointer to a structure.)

You declare an object pointer just like you declare a pointer to any other type of variable. Specify its class name, and then precede the variable name with an asterisk. To obtain the address of an object, precede the object with the **&** operator, just as you do when taking the address of any other type of variable.

Just like pointers to other types, when you increment an object pointer, it will point to the next object of its type.

Here is a simple example that uses an object pointer:

```cpp
#include <iostream.h>

class myclass {
  int a;
public:
  myclass(int x); // constructor
  int get();
};

myclass::myclass(int x)
{
  a = x;
}

int myclass::get()
{
  return a;
}

main()
{
  myclass ob(120);  // create object
  myclass *p;  // create pointer to object

  p = &ob; // put address of ob into p

  cout << "Value using object: " << ob.get();
  cout << "\n";
```

```
   cout << "Value using pointer: " << p->get();

   return 0;
}
```

Notice how the declaration

```
myclass *p;
```

creates a pointer to an object of **myclass**. It is important to understand that creation of an object pointer does *not* create an object—it creates just a pointer to one.

References to Objects

Class objects may be referenced in the same way as any other data type. There are no special restrictions or instructions that apply. When accessing a class member through a reference, use the dot (not the arrow) operator. Once again, it is important to remember that references are not pointers. As you will see in later chapters, the use of object references does help solve some special problems that can develop when using classes.

Classes, Structures, and Unions are Related

Structures and unions are related to the class. In this section, you will see how.

Structures and Classes

As you have seen, the **class** is syntactically similar to the **struct**. You might be surprised to learn, however, that the class and the structure have virtually identical capabilities. In C++, the definition of a structure can also include member functions, including constructor and destructor functions, in just the same way that a class can. In fact, the only difference between a structure and a class is that, by default, the members of a class are private but the members of a structure are public. The expanded syntax of a structure is shown here:

```
   struct type-name {
     // public function and data members
   private:
     // private function and data members
   } object-list;
```

According to the formal C++ syntax, both **struct** and **class** create new class *types*. Notice that a new keyword is introduced. It is **private,** and it tells the compiler that the members that follow are private to that class.

On the surface, there is a seeming redundancy in the fact that structures and classes have virtually identical capabilities. Many newcomers to C++ wonder why this apparent duplication exists. In fact, it is not uncommon to hear the suggestion that the **class** keyword is unnecessary. The answer to this line of reasoning has both a "strong" and "weak" form. The "strong" (or compelling) reason concerns maintaining compatibility with C. As C++ is currently defined, a standard C structure is also perfectly acceptable in a C++ program. Since in C all structure members are public by default, this convention is also maintained in C++. Further, because **class** is a syntactically separate entity from **struct**, the definition of a class is free to evolve in a way that will not be compatible with a C-like structure definition. Since the two are separated, the future direction of C++ is not restricted by compatibility concerns. The "weak" reason for having two similar constructs is that there is no disadvantage to expanding the definition of a structure in C++ to include member functions.

Although structures have the same capabilities as classes, most programmers restrict their use of structures to their C-like form and do not use them to include function members. Most programmers use the **class** keyword when defining objects that contain both data and code. However, this is a stylistic matter and is subject to your own preference. (After this section, this book reserves the use of **struct** for objects that do not have function members.)

Here is a short program that uses a **struct** to create a class:

```
#include <iostream.h>
#include <string.h>

// use struct to define a class type
struct st_type {
  st_type(double b, char *n);
  void show();
private:
  double balance;
  char name[40];
} ;

st_type::st_type(double b, char *n)
{
  balance = b;
  strcpy(name, n);
}
```

```
void st_type::show()
{
  cout << "Name: " << name;
  cout << ": $" << balance;
  if(balance<0.0) cout << "***";
  cout << "\n";
}

main()
{
  st_type acc1(100.12, "Johnson");
  st_type acc2(-12.34, "Hedricks");

  acc1.show();
  acc2.show();
  return 0;
}
```

Notice that, as stated, the members of a structure are public by default. The **private** keyword must be used to declare private members.

Unions and Classes

If you found the connection between classes and structures interesting, so will you find this next revelation about C++: unions and classes are also related! In C++, **union** also defines a class type which may contain both functions and data as members. A union is like a structure in that, by default, all members are public until the **private** specifier is used. It is just that in a union, all data members share the same memory location. Unions may also contain constructor and destructor functions.

Although structures and classes seem on the surface to be redundant, this is not the case with unions. In an object-oriented language, it is important to preserve encapsulation. Thus, the union's ability to link code and data allows you to create class types in which all data uses a shared location. This is something that you cannot do using a class.

Here is an example that uses a union to display the binary bit pattern, byte by byte, contained within a **double** value.

```
#include <iostream.h>

union bits {
  bits(double n);
  void show_bits();
  double d;
  unsigned char c[sizeof(double)];
```

```
};

bits::bits(double n)
{
  d = n;
}

void bits::show_bits()
{
  int i, j;

  for(j = sizeof(double)-1; j>=0; j--) {
    cout << "Bit pattern in byte " << j << ": ";
    for(i = 128; i; i >>= 1)
      if(i & c[j]) cout << "1";
      else cout << "0";
    cout << "\n";
  }
}

main()
{
  bits ob(1991.829);

  ob.show_bits();

  return 0;
}
```

The output of this program is

```
Bit pattern in byte 7: 01000000
Bit pattern in byte 6: 10011111
Bit pattern in byte 5: 00011111
Bit pattern in byte 4: 01010000
Bit pattern in byte 3: 11100101
Bit pattern in byte 2: 01100000
Bit pattern in byte 1: 01000001
Bit pattern in byte 0: 10001001
```

There are several restrictions that apply to unions as they relate to C++. They cannot inherit any other class and they cannot be used as a base class for any other type. Unions must not have any **static** members (which are described later). They also must not contain any object that has a constructor or destructor. (The union *can* have a constructor and destructor, though.)

FAST TRACK TIP

C-based Structures and Unions

10

In C, structures and unions may not have function members. Also, they may not contain constructors or destructors. However, C-based structures and unions are fully compatible with C++. Thus, if you will be converting C code to C++, then you do not need to alter structure or union declarations. They will compile correctly, as is. However, if you are porting code from C++ to C, then you will need to remove any function members contained in structures or unions.

When porting from C to C++, you will want to watch for opportunities to convert structures into classes. Many times, there are equivalents of member functions used by a C program even though they cannot actually be members of a structure. For example, in a C program you sometimes see code such as this:

```
struct X {
  int a, b;
  /* ... */
} ;
/* ... */
void init(struct X Xvar, int k, int j)
{
  Xvar.a = k;
  Xvar.b = j;
  /* ... */
}
```

You can easily convert such code into a class that contains a constructor function.

Using Inline Functions

Before continuing our examination of the class, a short but related digression is needed. In C++, it is possible to define functions that are not actually called but, rather, are expanded in line, at the point of each call. The advantage of *inline* functions is that they have no overhead associated with the function call and return mechanism. This means that inline functions can be executed much faster than normal functions. (Remember, the machine instructions that generate the function call and return take time each time a function is called. If there are parameters, even more time overhead is generated.) The disadvantage of inline functions is that if they are too large and called too often, your program grows larger. For this reason, inline functions are usuallly reserved for short functions.

To declare an inline function, simply precede the function's definition with the **inline** specifier. For example, this short program shows how to declare an inline function:

```
// Example of an inline function
#include <iostream.h>

inline int even(int x)
{
  return !(x%2);
}

main()
{
  if(even(10)) cout << "10 is even.\n";
  if(even(11)) cout << "11 is even.\n";

  return 0;
}
```

In this example, the function **even( )**, which returns true if its argument is even, is declared as being inline. This means that the line

```
if(even(10))  cout << "10 is even\n";
```

is functionally equivalent to

```
if(!(10%2)) cout << "10 is even\n";
```

This example also points out another important feature of using **inline**: an inline function must be defined *before* it is first called. If it isn't, the compiler has no way to know that it is supposed to be expanded in line. This is why **even( )** was defined before **main( ).**

It is important to understand that the **inline** specifier is a *request,* not a command, to the compiler. If, for various reasons, the compiler is unable to fulfill the request, the function is compiled as a normal function and the **inline** request is ignored**.**

Depending upon your compiler, several restrictions to inline functions may apply. For example, some compilers will not inline a function that is recursive or that contains a **static** variable, a loop statement, a **switch** or a **goto**. You should check your compiler's user manual for specific restrictions to inline functions that may affect you. Remember: If any inline restriction is violated, the compiler is free to generate a normal function.

Any type of function may be inlined, including functions that are members of classes. For example, here the member function **divisible( )** is inlined for fast execution. (The function returns true if its first argument can be evenly divided by its second.)

```
// Demonstrate inlining a member function.
#include <iostream.h>

class samp {
  int i, j;
public:
  samp(int a, int b);
  int divisible(); // inlined in its definition
};

samp::samp(int a, int b)
{
  i = a;
  j = b;
}

/* Return 1 if i is evenly divisible by j.
   This member function is expanded in line.
*/
inline int samp::divisible()
{
  return !(i%j);
}

main()
{
  samp ob1(10, 2), ob2(10, 3);

  // this is true
  if(ob1.divisible()) cout << "10 is divisible by 2\n";

  // this is false
  if(ob2.divisible()) cout << "10 is divisible by 3\n";

  return 0;
}
```

It is perfectly permissible to inline an overloaded function. For example, this program overloads **min( )** three ways. Each way is also declared as **inline.**

```
#include <iostream.h>
```

```
// Overload min() three ways.

// integers
inline int min(int a, int b)
{
  return a<b ? a : b;
}

// longs
inline long min(long a, long b)
{
  return a<b ? a : b;
}

// doubles
inline double min(double a, double b)
{
  return a<b ? a : b;
}
main()
{
  cout << min(-10, 10) << "\n";
  cout << min(-10.01, 100.002) << "\n";
  cout << min(-10L, 12L) << "\n";

  return 0;
}
```

Automatic Inlining

If a member function's definition is short enough, its definition may be included inside the class declaration. Doing so causes the function to automatically become an inline function, if possible. When a function is defined within a class declaration, the **inline** keyword is no longer necessary. (However, it is not an error to use it in this situation.) For example, the **divisible( )** function from the preceding section can be automatically inlined as shown here:

```
#include <iostream.h>

class samp {
  int i, j;
public:
  samp(int a, int b);

  // divisible is defined here and automatically inlined.
  int divisible() { return !(i%j); }
```

```
};

samp::samp(int a, int b)
{
  i = a;
  j = b;
}

main()
{
  samp ob1(10, 2), ob2(10, 3);

  // this is true
  if(ob1.divisible()) cout << "10 is divisible by 2\n";

  // this is false
  if(ob2.divisible()) cout << "10 is divisible by 3\n";

  return 0;
}
```

As you can see, the code associated with **divisible( )** occurs inside the declaration for the class **samp.** Further notice that no other definition of **divisible( )** is needed—or permitted. Defining **divisible( )** inside **samp** causes it automatically to be made into an inline function.

Notice how **divisible( )** is defined within **samp**, particularly its body. It occurs all on one line. This format is very common in C++ programs when a function is declared within a class declaration. It allows the declaration to be more compact. However, the **samp** class could have been written like this:

```
class samp {
  int i, j;
public:
  samp(int a, int b);

  /* divisible is defined here and automatically
     inlined. */
  int divisible()
  {
    return !(i%j);
  }
};
```

In this version, the layout of **divisible( )** uses the more or less standard indentation style. From the compiler's point of view, there is no difference between the compact style and the standard style. However, the compact style is commonly found in C++ programs when short functions are defined inside a class definition.

The same restrictions that apply to "normal" inline functions apply to automatic inline functions within a class declaration. When a function defined inside a class declaration cannot be made into an inline function (because a restriction has been violated) it will be made into a regular function.

Perhaps the most common use of inline functions defined within a class is to define constructor and destructor functions. For example, the **samp** class can more efficiently be defined like this:

```
#include <iostream.h>

class samp {
  int i, j;
public:
  // inline constructor
  samp(int a, int b) { i = a; j = b; }
  int divisible() { return !(i%j); }
};
```

The definition of **samp( )** within the class **samp** is sufficient, and no other definition of **samp( )** is needed or allowed.

Sometimes a short function will be included in a class declaration even though the automatic inlining feature is of little or no value. Consider this class declaration:

```
class myclass {
  int i;
public:
  myclass(int n) { i = n; }
  void show() { cout << i; }
};
```

Here, the function **show( )** is made into an inline function automatically. However, as you should know, I/O operations are (generally) so slow relative to CPU/memory operations that any effect of eliminating the function call overhead is virtually lost. Despite this, in C++ programs, it is still common to see small functions of this type declared within a class simply for the sake of convenience and because no harm is caused.

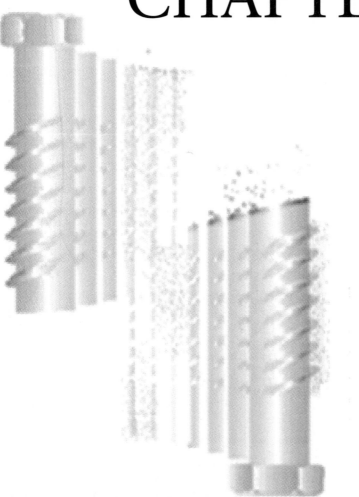

CHAPTER 11

A Closer Look at Classes

In this chapter you will continue to explore the class. You will learn about assigning objects, passing objects to functions, returning objects from functions, overloading constructors, and the friend function. You will also learn about copy constructors and the **this** pointer.

Assigning Class Objects

One class object may be assigned to another provided that both objects are of the same type. By default, when one object is assigned to another, a bitwise copy of all the data members is performed. For example, when an object called **A** is assigned to another object called **B**, the contents of all of **A**'s data are copied into the equivalent members of **B**. For example, consider this short program:

```
// An example of object assignment.
#include <iostream.h>

class myclass {
  int a, b;
public:
  void set(int i, int j) { a = i; b = j; }
  void show() { cout << a << ' ' << b << "\n"; }
};

main()
{
  myclass o1, o2;

  o1.set(10, 4);

  // assign o1 to o2
  o2 = o1;

  o1.show();
  o2.show();

  return 0;
}
```

In this example, object **o1** has its member variables **a** and **b** set to the values 10 and 4, respectively. Next, **o1** is assigned to **o2**. This causes the current value of **o1.a** to be assigned to **o2.a** and **o1.b** to be assigned to **o2.b**. Thus, when run, this program displays

```
10 4
10 4
```

Keep in mind that an assignment between two objects simply makes the data in those objects identical. The two objects are still completely separate. For example, after the assignment, calling **o1.set( )** has no effect on **o2**.

Only objects of the same type may be used in an assignment statement. If the objects are not of the same type, a compile-time error is reported. Further, it is not sufficient that the types just be physically similar—their type names must be the same.

A Potential Problem with Object Assignment

You must exercise some care when assigning one object to another. To understand why, consider the following example. It defines a simple string class called **strtype**. **strtype** stores a pointer to a dynamically allocated string. Objects of type **strtype** must be initialized using a null-terminated string. Its constructor automatically allocates sufficient memory to hold the string. However, this program contains a serious error. See if you can find it.

11

```
// This program contains an error.

#include <iostream.h>
#include <malloc.h>
#include <string.h>
#include <stdlib.h>

class strtype {
  char *p; // pointer to string
  int len; // length of string
public:
  strtype(char *ptr);
  ~strtype();
  void show();
};

strtype::strtype(char *ptr)
{
  len = strlen(ptr);
  p = new char [len+1];
  if(!p) {
    cout << "Allocation error.\n";
    exit(1);
  }
  strcpy(p, ptr);
}

strtype::~strtype()
{
  cout << "Freeing p\n";
  delete [] p;
}
```

```
void strtype::show()
{
  cout << p << " - length: " << len;
  cout << "\n";
}

main()
{
  strtype s1("This is a test"), s2("I like C++");

  s1.show();
  s2.show();

  // assign s1 to s2 - - this generates an error
  s2 = s1;

  s1.show();
  s2.show();

  return 0;
}
```

The trouble with this program is quite insidious. When **s1** and **s2** are created, both allocate memory to hold their respective strings. A pointer to each object's dynamically allocated memory is stored in **p**. When a **strtype** object is destroyed, this memory is released. However, when **s1** is assigned to **s2**, **s2**'s **p** now points to the same memory as **s1**'s **p**. Thus, when these objects are destroyed, the memory pointed to by **s1**'s **p** is freed *twice* and the memory originally pointed to by **s2**'s **p** is not freed *at all*. While benign in this context, this sort of problem occurring in a real program will cause the dynamic allocation system to fail and possibly even cause a program crash.

As you can see from the preceding example, when assigning one object to another, you must make sure you are not overwriting information that may be needed later. Later in this book you will learn how to define the assignment operation relative to classes that you create, thus avoiding this type of problem.

Passing Class Objects to Functions

Class objects may be passed to functions as arguments in just the same way that other types of data are passed. Simply declare the function's parameter as a class type and then use an object of that class as an argument when calling the function. As with other types of data, by default all objects are passed by value to a function.

Here is a short example that passes an object to a function:

```cpp
#include <iostream.h>

class samp {
  int i;
public:
  samp(int n) { i = n; }
  int get_i() { return i; }
};

// Return square of o.i.
int sqr_it(samp o)
{
  return o.get_i() * o.get_i();
}

main()
{
  samp a(10), b(2);

  cout << sqr_it(a) << "\n";
  cout << sqr_it(b) << "\n";

  return 0;
}
```

11

This program creates a class called **samp** that contains one integer variable called **i**. The function **sqr_it( )** takes an argument of type **samp** and returns the square of that object's **i** value. The output from this program is **100** followed by **4**.

Constructors, Destructors, and Argument Passing

When an object is passed to a function using C++'s normal call-by-value parameter passing mechanism, a copy of that object is made. This means that a new object comes into existence. Also, when the function that the object was passed to terminates, the copy of the argument (that is, the function's parameter) is destroyed. This raises two questions. First, is the object's constructor called when the copy is made? Second, is the object's destructor called when the copy is destroyed? The answer may, at first, seem surprising.

When a copy of an object is made to be used in a function call, the constructor function is *not* called. The reason for this is simple to understand if you think about it. Since a constructor function is generally used to initialize some aspect of an object, it must not be called when making a copy of an already existing object passed to a function. Doing so would alter the contents of the object. When passing an object to a function, you want the current state of the object, not its initial state. However, when the function terminates and the copy is destroyed, the destructor function *is* called. This is because the object might perform some operation that must be undone when it goes out of scope. For example, the copy may allocate memory that must be released.

To summarize, when a copy of an object is created because it is used as an argument to a function, the constructor function is not called. However, when the copy is destroyed (usually by going out of scope when the function returns), the destructor function is called.

The following program illustrates the preceding discussion:

```cpp
#include <iostream.h>

class samp {
    int i;
public:
    samp(int n) {
        i = n;
        cout << "Constructing\n";
    }
    ~samp() { cout << "Destructing\n"; }
    int get_i() { return i; }
};

// Return square of o.i.
int sqr_it(samp o)
{
    return o.get_i() * o.get_i();
}

main()
{
    samp a(10);

    cout << sqr_it(a) << "\n";

    return 0;
}
```

This function displays the following:

```
Constructing
Destructing
100
Destructing
```

As you can see, only one call to the constructor function is made. This occurs when **a** is created. However, two calls to the destructor are made. One is for the copy created when **a** is passed to **sqr_it( )**. The other is for **a**, itself.

11

A Potential Problem When Passing Objects

Care must be exercised when passing certain types of class objects to functions. Here is why. When a function terminates, its parameters go out of scope. This means that the destructors for its parameters are called. However, by default, a parameter is merely a copy of the argument used to call the function. Therefore, if the copy's destructor destroys something still needed by the original, serious problems will follow. For example, if the object used as the argument allocates dynamic memory and frees that memory when destroyed, then its copy will free the same memory when its destructor is called. This will leave the original object damaged and effectively useless. It is important to guard against this type of error and to make sure that the destructor function of the copy does not cause side effects that affect the original argument.

As you might guess, one way around the problem of a parameter's destructor function destroying data needed by the calling argument is to pass the address of the object (and not the object itself) using either a pointer or a reference. When an address is passed, no new object is created, and therefore, no destructor is called when the function returns. However, an even better solution exists, which utilizes a *copy constructor*. A copy constructor lets you define precisely how copies of objects get made. It is described later in this chapter.

Returning Objects

Just as you may pass objects to functions, functions may return objects. To do so, first declare the function as returning a class type. Second, return an object of that type using the normal **return** statement. Here is an example of a function that returns an object:

```
// Returning an object
#include <iostream.h>
#include <string.h>

class samp {
```

```
    char s[80];
public:
  void show() { cout << s << "\n"; }
  void set(char *str) { strcpy(s, str); }
};

// Return an object of type samp
samp input()
{
  char s[80];
  samp str;

  cout << "Enter a string: ";
  cin >> s;

  str.set(s);

  return str;
}

main()
{
  samp ob;

  // assign returned object to ob
  ob = input();
  ob.show();

  return 0;
}
```

In this example, **input( )** creates a local object called **str** and then reads a string from the keyboard. This string is copied into **str.s** and then **str** is returned by the function. This object is then assigned to **ob** inside **main( )** when it is returned by the call to **input( )**.

There is one important point to understand about returning objects from functions. It is this: when an object is returned by a function, a temporary object is automatically created that holds the return value. It is this object that is actually returned by the function. After the value has been returned, this object is destroyed. The destruction of this temporary object may cause unexpected side effects in some situations. For example, if the object returned by the function has a destructor that frees dynamically allocated memory, that memory will be freed even though the object that is assigned the return value is still using it. For example, consider this incorrect version of the preceding program:

11

```cpp
// An error generated by returning an object.
#include <iostream.h>
#include <string.h>
#include <stdlib.h>

class samp {
  char *s;
public:
  samp() { s = '\0'; }
  ~samp() { if(s) delete [] s; cout << "Freeing s\n"; }
  void show() { cout << s << "\n"; }
  void set(char *str);
};

// Load a string.
void samp::set(char *str)
{
  s = new char [strlen(str)+1];
  if(!s) {
    cout << "Allocation error.\n";
    exit(1);
  }

  strcpy(s, str);
}

// Return an object of type samp.
samp input()
{
  char s[80];
  samp str;
  cout << "Enter a string: ";
  cin >> s;

  str.set(s);
  return str;
}

main()
{
  samp ob;

  // assign returned object to ob
  ob = input();   // This causes an error!!!!
  ob.show();

  return 0;
}
```

The output from this program is shown here:

```
Enter a string: Hello
Freeing s
Freeing s
Hello
Freeing s
Null pointer assignment
```

Notice that **samp**'s destructor function is called three times. First, it is called when the local object **str** goes out of scope when **input( )** returns. The second time ~**samp( )** is called is when the temporary object returned by **input( )** is destroyed. Remember, when an object is returned from a function, an invisible (to you) temporary object is automatically generated which holds the return value. In this case, this object is simply a copy of **str,** which is the return value of the function. Therefore, after the function has returned, the temporary object's destructor is executed. Finally, the destructor for object **ob**, inside **main( ),** is called when the program terminates. The trouble is that in this situation, the first time the destructor executes, the memory allocated to hold the string input by **input( )** is freed. Thus, not only do the other two calls to **samp**'s destructor try to free an already released piece of dynamic memory, but they destroy the dynamic allocation system in the process, as evidenced by the run-time message "Null pointer assignment." (Depending upon your compiler, the memory model used for compilation, and the like, you may or may not see this message if you try this program.)

The key point to be understood from this example is that when an object is returned from a function, the temporary object used to effect the return will have its destructor function called. Thus, you should avoid returning objects in which this situation is harmful. (As you will soon see, it is possible to use a copy constructor to manage this situation.)

FAST TRACK TIP

The Standard Class Libraries

As you have seen in this and the preceding chapter, the class is the foundation upon which new and complex data types are constructed. Once a new class has been defined, it is possible to place that class in a *class library* so that it may be reused. Because there are several general-purpose class types that have wide applicability, the ANSI C++ standardization committee is currently in the process of defining a standard set of class libraries. At the time of this writing, these libraries are still "a work in progress" and are not fully implemented by any currently available C++

compiler. For these reasons, it was not feasible to discuss most of the class libraries in this book. (The major exception to this is the I/O library, which all C++ compilers currently implement, and which is fully discussed in Chapter 13.) However, since future compilers will implement these class libraries, it is important for you to know what will become available. The libraries currently being defined by the proposed ANSI C++ standard are listed here.

◆ Language support

◆ Diagnostics

◆ General utilities

◆ Strings

◆ Localization

◆ Containers

◆ Iterators

◆ Algorithms

◆ Numerics

◆ Input/Output

Although the ANSI C++ standard is still in the development stage, you will want to check your compiler manuals to see which of these class libraries are currently supported.

Remember, the class libraries are in addition to the standard function library, which is included in all C++ compilers.

Overloading Constructor Functions

It is possible—indeed, common—to overload a class's constructor function. (It is not possible to overload a destructor, however.) There are several reasons why you will want to overload a constructor function, but the central theme is flexibility. For any given class, there must be a constructor function that can accommodate each way that an object of that class is declared. If no matching constructor is found for a declaration, a compile-time error occurs. This is why overloaded constructor functions are so common in C++ programs.

Perhaps the most frequent use of overloaded constructor functions is to provide the option of either giving an object an initialization or not giving it one. For example, in the following program, **o1** is given an initial value, but **o2** is not. If you remove the constructor that has the empty argument list, the program will not compile because there is no constructor that matches a noninitialized object of type **samp**. Vice versa, if you remove the parameterized constructor, the program will not compile because there is no match for an initialized object. Both are needed for this program to compile correctly.

```cpp
#include <iostream.h>

class myclass {
  int x;
public:
  // overload constructor two ways
  myclass() { x = 0; } // no initializer
  myclass(int n) { x = n; } // initializer
  int getx() { return x; }
};

main()
{
  myclass o1(10); // declare with initial value
  myclass o2; // declare without initializer

  cout << "o1: " << o1.getx() << '\n';
  cout << "o2: " << o2.getx() << '\n';

  return 0;
}
```

Another reason for overloading constructor functions is to allow the programmer to select the most convenient method of initializing an object. To see how, first examine the next example, which creates a class that holds a calendar date. It overloads the **date( )** constructor two ways. One way, it accepts the date as a character string. The other way, the date is passed as three integers.

```cpp
#include <iostream.h>
#include <stdlib.h>

class date {
  int day, month, year;
public:
  date(char *str);

  // Construct date using three integers.
  date (int m, int d, int y) {
```

```
      day = d;
      month = m;
      year = y;
    }
    void show() {
      cout << month << '/' << day << '/';
      cout << year << '\n';
    }
};
```

11

```
// Construct date using a string.
date::date(char *str)
{
  char temp[80];
  int i;

  // get month
  for(i=0; *str!='/' && *str!='\0'; i++)
    temp[i] = *str++;
  temp[i] = '\0'; // null terminate
  month = atoi(temp);

  // get day
  str++; // advance past slash
  for(i=0; *str!='/' && *str!='\0'; i++)
    temp[i] = *str++;
  temp[i] = 0; // null terminate
  day = atoi(temp);

  // get year
  str++; // advance past slash
  for(i=0; *str != '\0'; i++) temp[i] = *str++;
  temp[i] = '\0'; // null terminate
  year = atoi(temp);
}

main()
{
  // construct date object using string
  date sdate("7/10/97");

  // construct date object using integers
  date idate(7, 10, 97);

  sdate.show();
  idate.show();

  return 0;
}
```

The advantage of overloading the **date( )** constructor as shown in the program is that you are free to use whichever version most conveniently fits the situation. For example, if a **date** object is being created from user input, then the string version is the easiest to use. However, if the **date** object is being constructed through some sort of internal computation, then the three-integer parameter version probably makes more sense.

Although it is possible to overload a constructor as many times as you want, doing so excessively has a destructuring effect on the class. From a stylistic point of view, it is best to overload a constructor to accommodate only those situations that are likely to occur frequently. For example, overloading **date( )** a third time so the date can be entered as three octal integers makes little sense. However, overloading it to accept an object of type **time_t** (a type that stores the system date and time) could be very valuable.

There is one other situation in which you will need to overload a class's constructor function: when a dynamic array of that class will be allocated. As you should recall from the preceding chapter, a dynamic array cannot be initialized. Thus, if the class contains a constructor that takes an initializer, you must include an overloaded version that takes no initializer.

Creating and Using a Copy Constructor

One of the more important forms of an overloaded constructor is the *copy constructor*. As examples from the preceding sections have shown, problems can occur when an object is passed to or returned from a function. As you will learn in this section, one way to avoid these (and other) problems is to define a copy constructor, which is a special type of overloaded constructor function.

To begin, let's restate the problems that a copy constructor is designed to solve. When an object is passed to a function, a bitwise (that is, exact) copy of that object is made and given to the function parameter that receives the object. However, there are cases in which this identical copy is not desirable. For example, if the object contains a pointer to allocated memory, then the copy will point to the *same* memory as does the original object. Therefore, if the copy makes a change to the contents of this memory, it will be changed for the original object, too! Also, when the function terminates, the copy will be destroyed, causing its destructor to be called. This may also lead to undesired side effects that affect the original object.

A similar situation occurs when an object is returned by a function. Commonly, the compiler will generate a temporary object that holds a copy of the value returned by the function. (This is done automatically and is beyond your control.) This temporary object goes out of scope once the value is returned to the calling routine, causing the temporary's destructor to be called. However, if the destructor destroys something needed by the calling routine (such as freeing dynamically allocated memory), then trouble will follow.

At the core of these problems is the fact that a bitwise copy of the object is being made. To prevent these problems, you, the programmer, need to define precisely what occurs when a copy of an object is made so that you can avoid undesired side effects. The way you accomplish this is by creating a copy constructor. By defining a copy constructor, you can fully specify exactly what occurs when a copy of an object is made.

11

Before describing the copy constructor, it is important for you to understand that C++ defines two distinct types of situations in which the value of one object is given to another. The first situation is assignment. The second situation is initialization, which can occur three ways:

◆   When an object is used to initialize another in a declaration statement

◆   When an object is passed as a parameter to a function, and

◆   When a temporary object is created for use as a return value by a function

The copy constructor only applies to initializations. It does not apply to assignments.

By default, when an initialization occurs, the compiler will automatically provide a bitwise copy. (That is, C++ automatically provides a default copy constructor that simply duplicates the object.) However, it is possible to specify precisely how one object will initialize another by defining a copy constructor. Once defined, the copy constructor is called whenever an object is used to initialize another. Remember that copy constructors do not affect assignment operations.

The general form of a copy constructor is shown here:

```
classname (const classname &obj) {
  // body of constructor
  }
```

Here, *obj* is a reference to an object that is being used to initialize another object. It is permissible for a copy constructor to have additional parameters as long as they have default arguments defined for them. However, in all cases the first parameter must be a reference to the object doing the initializing. It is also permissible for *obj* not to be **const,** but it usually is. (Technically, if *obj* is not specified as **const** you cannot use a **const** object to initialize another object.)

Once a copy constructor has been defined for a class, any time an initialization occurs, the copy constructor will be called. For example, assuming a class called **myclass** and that **y** is an object of type **myclass**, then these statements would invoke the **myclass** copy constructor.

```
myclass x = y; // y explicitly initializing x
func1(y);      // y passed as a parameter
y = func2();   // y receiving a returned object
```

In the first two cases, a reference to **y** would be passed to the copy constructor. In the third, a reference to the object returned by **func2( )** is passed to the copy constructor.

Here is an example that illustrates why an explicit copy constructor function is needed. This program creates a very limited "safe" integer array type which prevents array boundaries from being overrun. Storage for each array is allocated using **new** and a pointer to the memory is maintained within each array object.

```
/* This program creates a "safe" array class. Since space
   for the array is dynamically allocated, a copy constructor
   is provided to allocate memory when one array object is
   used to initialize another.
*/
#include <iostream.h>
#include <stdlib.h>

class array {
  int *p;
  int size;
public:
  array(int sz) { // constructor
    p = new int[sz];
    if(!p) exit(1);
    size = sz;
    cout << "Using 'normal' constructor.\n";
  }
  ~array() {delete [] p;}

  // copy constructor
  array(const array &a);

  void put(int i, int j) {
    if(i>=0 && i<size) p[i] = j;
  }
  int get(int i) {
    return p[i];
```

11

```
  }
};

/* Copy constructor.

   In this case, memory is allocated specifically for
   the copy and the address of this memory is assigned
   to p. In this way, p is not pointing to the same
   dynamically allocated memory as the original object.
*/
array::array(const array &a) {
  int i;

  p = new int[a.size];  // allocate memory for copy
  if(!p) exit(1);
  for(i=0; i<a.size; i++) p[i] = a.p[i]; // copy contents
  cout << "Using copy constructor.\n";
}

main()
{
  array num(10);  // this calls "normal" constructor
  int i;

  // put some values into the array
  for(i=0; i<10; i++) num.put(i, i);

  // display num
  for(i=9; i>=0; i--) cout << num.get(i);
  cout << "\n";

  // create another array and initialize with num
  array x = num;  // this invokes copy constructor

  // display x
  for(i=0; i<10; i++) cout << x.get(i);

  return 0;
}
```

When **num** is used to initialize **x**, the copy constructor is called, memory for the new array is allocated and stored in **x.p**, and the contents of **num** are copied to **x**'s array. In this way, **x** and **num** have arrays that have the same values, but each array is separate and distinct. (That is, **num.p** and **x.p** do not point to the same piece of memory.) If the copy constructor had not been created, then the statement **array x = num** would have resulted in **x** and **num** sharing the same memory for their arrays! (That is, **num.p** and **x.p** would have, indeed, pointed to the same location.)

Remember that the copy constructor is called only for initializations. For example, this sequence does not call the copy constructor defined in the preceding program.

```
array a(10);
array b(10);

b = a; // does not call copy constructor
```

In this case, **b = a** performs the assignment operation.

To see how the copy constructor helps prevent some of the problems associated with passing certain types of objects to functions, consider this (incorrect) program.

```
// This program has an error.
#include <iostream.h>
#include <string.h>
#include <stdlib.h>

class strtype {
  char *p;
public:
  strtype(char *s);
  ~strtype() { delete [] p; }
  char *get() { return p; }
};

strtype::strtype(char *s)
{
  int l;

  l = strlen(s) + 1;

  p = new char [l];
  if(!p) {
    cout << "Allocation error.\n";
    exit(1);
  }

  strcpy(p, s);
}
```

```
void show(strtype x)
{
  char *s;

  s = x.get();
  cout << s << "\n";
}

main()
{
  strtype a("Hello"), b("There");

  show(a);
  show(b);

  return 0;
}
```

11

In this program, when a **strtype** object is passed to **show( )** a bitwise copy is made (since no copy constructor has been defined) and put into parameter **x**. Thus, when the function returns, **x** goes out of scope and is destroyed. This, of course, causes **x**'s destructor to be called, which frees **x.p**. However, the memory being freed is the same memory that is still being used by the object used to call the function. This results in an error.

The solution to the preceding problem is to define a copy constructor for the **strtype** class that allocates memory for the copy when the copy is created. This approach is used by the following, corrected, program.

```
/* This program uses a copy constructor to allow
   strtype objects to be passed to functions. */
#include <iostream.h>
#include <string.h>
#include <stdlib.h>

class strtype {
  char *p;
public:
  strtype(char *s); // constructor
  strtype(const strtype &o); // copy constructor
  ~strtype() { delete [] p; } // destructor
  char *get() { return p; }
};

// "Normal" constructor
```

```
strtype::strtype(char *s)
{
  int l;

  l = strlen(s)+1;

  p = new char [l];
  if(!p) {
    cout << "Allocation error.\n";
    exit(1);
  }

  strcpy(p, s);
}

// Copy constructor
strtype::strtype(const strtype &o)
{
  int l;

  l = strlen(o.p) + 1;

  p = new char [l]; // allocate memory for new copy
  if(!p) {
    cout << "Allocation error\n";
    exit(1);
  }

  strcpy(p, o.p); // copy string into copy
}

void show(strtype x)
{
  char *s;

  s = x.get();
  cout << s << "\n";
}

main()
{
  strtype a("Hello"), b("There");

  show(a);
  show(b);

  return 0;
}
```

Now, when **show( )** terminates and **x** goes out of scope, the memory pointed to by **x.p** (which will be freed) is not the same as the memory still in use by the object passed to the function.

At this point, copy constructors may still seem a bit esoteric. However, you should learn to use them because nearly all real-world classes require them.

Introducing Friend Functions

There will be times when you want a function to have access to the private members of a class without the function actually being a member of the class. Towards this end, C++ supports *friend functions*. A friend is not a member of a class but still has access to its private elements. Two reasons that friend functions are useful have to do with operator overloading and the creation of certain types of I/O functions. You will have to wait until later to see these uses of a friend in action. However, a third reason for friend functions is that there will be times when you want one function to have access to the private members of *two or more* different classes. This use is examined here, after the basics have been discussed.

A friend function is defined as a regular, nonmember function. However, inside the class declaration for which it will be a friend, its prototype is also included, prefaced by the keyword **friend**. To understand how this works, examine this short program. In it, the friend function **isfactor( )** returns true if **d** is a factor of **n**.

```
// A example of a friend function.
#include <iostream.h>

class myclass {
  int n, d;
public:
  myclass(int i, int j) { n = i; d = j; }
  // declare a friend of myclass
  friend int isfactor(myclass ob);
};

/* Here is friend function definition. It returns true
   if d is a factor of n. Notice that the keyword
   friend is not used in the definition of isfactor().
*/
int isfactor(myclass ob)
{
  if(!(ob.n % ob.d)) return 1;
  else return 0;
}
```

```
main()
{
  myclass ob1(10, 2), ob2(13, 3);

  if(isfactor(ob1)) cout << "2 is a factor of 10\n";
  else cout << "2 is not a factor of 10\n";

  if(isfactor(ob2)) cout << "3 is a factor of 13\n";
  else cout << "3 is not a factor of 13\n";

  return 0;
}
```

In this example, **myclass** declares its constructor function and the friend **isfactor( )** inside its class declaration. Because **isfactor( )** is a friend of **myclass**, **isfactor( )** has access to the private parts of it. This is why, within **isfactor( )**, it is possible to refer to **ob.n** and **ob.d**.

It is important to understand that a friend function is not a member of the class for which it is a friend. Thus, it is not possible to call a friend function by using an object name and a class member access operator (a dot or arrow). For example, given the preceding example, this statement is wrong:

```
ob1.isfactor(); // wrong, isfactor is not a member function
```

Instead, friends are called just like regular functions.

Although a friend function has knowledge of the private elements of the class for which it is a friend, it may only access them through an object of the class. That is, unlike a member function of **myclass**, which can refer to **n** or **d** directly, a friend can access these variables only in conjunction with an object declared within or passed to the friend function.

Before continuing, let's review a fundamental concept concerning class member access. When a member function refers to a private element, it does so directly because a member function is executed only in conjunction with an object of that class. Thus, when a member function refers to a private element, the compiler knows which object that private element belongs to by the object that is linked to the function when that member function is called. However, a friend function is not linked to any object. It simply is granted access to the private elements of a class. Thus, inside the friend function, it is meaningless to refer to a private member without reference to a specific object.

Friends will typically be passed one or more objects of the class for which they are defined to operate upon. This is the case with **isfactor( )**. It is passed an object of **myclass**, called **ob**. However, because **isfactor( )** is a friend of **myclass**, it may access **ob**'s private elements. If **isfactor( )** had not been made a friend of **myclass**, it would not be able to access **ob.d** or **ob.n** since **n** and **d** are private members of **myclass**.

A friend function is not inherited. That is, when a base class includes a friend function, that friend function is not a friend of a derived class.

As mentioned at the beginning of this section, one important feature of a friend function is that it may be friends with more than one class. For example, one common use of a friend function occurs when two different types of classes have some quantity in common that needs to be compared. To understand how a friend function can be beneficial in this situation, consider the following program, which creates a class called **car** and a class called **truck**, both of which contain, as a private variable, the speed of each vehicle:

11

```
#include <iostream.h>

class truck; // a forward declaration

class car {
  int passengers;
  int speed;
public:
  car(int p, int s) { passengers = p; speed = s; }
  friend int sp_greater(car c, truck t);
};

class truck {
  int weight;
  int speed;
public:
  truck(int w, int s) { weight = w, speed = s; }
  friend int sp_greater(car c, truck t);
};

/* Return positive if car speed faster than truck.
   Return 0 if speeds are the same.
   Return negative if truck speed faster than car.
*/
int sp_greater(car c, truck t)
{
  return c.speed-t.speed;
}

main()
{
```

```
     int t;
     car c1(6, 55), c2(2, 120);
     truck t1(10000, 55), t2(20000, 72);

     cout << "Comparing c1 and t1:\n";
     t = sp_greater(c1, t1);
     if(t<0) cout << "Truck is faster.\n";
     else if(t==0) cout << "Car and truck speed is the same.\n";
     else cout << "Car is faster.\n";

     cout << "\nComparing c2 and t2:\n";
     t = sp_greater(c2, t2);
     if(t<0) cout << "Truck is faster.\n";
     else if(t==0) cout << "Car and truck speed is the same.\n";
     else cout << "Car is faster.\n";

     return 0;
}
```

This program contains the function **sp_ greater( )**, which is a friend function of both the **car** and **truck** classes. This function returns positive if the **car** object is going faster than the **truck** object, zero if their speeds are the same, and negative if the **truck** is going faster.

This program illustrates another important C++ syntax element: the *forward declaration*. Because **sp_ greater( )** takes parameters of both the **car** and the **truck** classes, it is logically impossible to declare both before including **sp_ greater( )** in either. Therefore, there needs to be some way to tell the compiler about a class name without actually declaring it. This is called a forward declaration. In C++, to tell the compiler that an identifier is the name of a class, use a line like this:

    class *class-name*;

For example, in the preceding program, the forward declaration is

```
class truck;
```

Now, **truck** can be used in the friend declaration of **sp_greater( )** without generating a compile-time error.

The this Pointer

C++ contains a special pointer, called **this**, that relates specifically to classes. **this** is a pointer that is automatically passed to a member function when it is called, and it is a pointer to the object that generates the call. For example, given this statement:

```
ob.f1();   // assume that ob is an object
```

the function **f1( )** is automatically passed a **this** pointer to **ob**—which is the object that generates the call.

It is important to understand that only member functions are passed a **this** pointer. For example, a friend function does not have a **this** pointer.

As you have seen, when a member function accesses another member of a class, it does so without qualifying the member with either a class or an object specification. For example, examine this short program, which creates a simple inventory class:

11

```
#include <iostream.h>
#include <string.h>

class inventory {
  char item[20];
  double cost;
  int on_hand;
public:
  inventory(char *i, double c, int o)
  {
     strcpy(item, i);
     cost = c;
     on_hand = o;
   }
   void show();
};

void inventory::show()
{
  cout << item;
  cout << ": $" << cost;
  cout << "  On hand: " << on_hand << "\n";
}

main()
{
  inventory ob("wrench", 4.95, 4);

  ob.show();

  return 0;
}
```

As you can see, within the constructor **inventory( )** and member function **show( )**, the member variables **item**, **cost**, and **on_hand** are referred to directly. This is because a member function can be called only in conjunction with an object. Therefore, the compiler knows which object's data is being referred to. However, there is an even more subtle explanation.

When a member function is called, it is automatically passed a **this** pointer to the object that generated the call. Thus, the preceding program could be rewritten as shown here:

```
// Demonstrate the this pointer.
#include <iostream.h>
#include <string.h>

class inventory {
  char item[20];
  double cost;
  int on_hand;
public:
  inventory(char *i, double c, int o)
  {
    strcpy(this->item, i); // access members
    this->cost = c;        // through the this
    this->on_hand = o;     // pointer
  }
  void show();
};

void inventory::show()
{
  cout << this->item; // use this to access members
  cout << ": $" << this->cost;
  cout << "  On hand: " << this->on_hand << "\n";
}

main()
{
  inventory ob("wrench", 4.95, 4);

  ob.show();

  return 0;
}
```

Here, the member variables of **ob** are accessed explicitly through the **this** pointer. Thus, within **show( )**, these two statements are equivalent:

```
cost = 123.23;
this->cost = 123.23;
```

In fact, the first form is, loosely speaking, a shorthand for the second.

While no C++ programmer would use the **this** pointer to access a class member as just shown, because the shorthand form is much easier, it is important to understand what the shorthand implies.

The **this** pointer has several uses, including aiding in overloading operators. This use will be described in detail in Chapter 12. For now, the key concept to understand is that by default, all member functions are automatically passed a pointer to the object that invoked the call.

11

Experimenting with the Standard String Class

Aside from I/O (which is discussed at length later in this book) one of the most popular of the standard classes defined by C++ is the **string** class. Although standard C++ strings (which are implemented as null-terminated strings) are highly efficient, they are not always convenient. For the past several years, most C++ programmers at one time or another have defined their own versions of a string class in an attempt to simplify string operations. Of course, each implementation differed from the next. Because string classes were so common, the ANSI C++ standardization committee decided to define once and for all the **string** class. At the time of this writing, not all C++ compilers implement the **string** class. However, since it is now a standard part of the C++ language, all future compilers will support it.

The **string** class fully integrates strings into the C++ environment. It supports several overloaded constructors. The prototypes for two of its most commonly used constructors are shown here.

```
string( ); // creates an empty string
string(const char *str); // creates a string containing str
```

The first form creates an empty **string** object. The second creates an object that contains a string.

A number of operators that make manipulating strings easier are also defined for **string** objects, including:

Operator	Meaning
=	Assignment
+	Concatenation
==	Equality
!=	Inequality
<	Less than
<=	Less than or equal
>	Greater than
>=	Greater than or equal

These operators allow the use of **string** objects in normal expressions and eliminate the need for calls to functions such as **strcpy( )** or **strcat( )**, for example. In general, you can mix **string** objects with normal, null-terminated strings in expressions. For example, a **string** object can be assigned a null-terminated string.

The header file required for the standard string class is **string**. However, at the time of this writing, no commonly available compilers recognize this name. (The sample program shown below uses the header file defined by Borland, which is called CSTRING.H.)

The following program illustrates the use of the **string** class.

```
/* A short demonstration of the standard string class.

   Note: The header file CSTRING.H is specific to
         Borland C++. Check your compiler manual to see
         what the standard string class header file
         is called.
*/
#include <cstring.h>
#include <iostream.h>

main()
{
  string str1("This is a string class object");
  string str2("Testing");
  string str3;

  str3 = str1; // assign a string
  cout << str1 << "\n" << str3 << "\n";

  str3 = str1 + str2; // concatenate two strings
```

```
        cout << str3 << "\n";

      // compare strings
      if(str3 > str1) cout << "str3 > str1\n";
      if(str3 == str1+str2)
        cout << "str3 == str1+str2\n";

      /* A string object can also be
         assigned a normal string. */
      str1 = "This is a normal string.\n";
      cout << str1;

      return 0;
    }
```

11

The output from this program is shown here.

```
This is a string class object
This is a string class object
This is a string class objectTesting
str3 > str1
str3 == str1+str2
This is a normal string.
```

As you can see, objects of type **string** may be manipulated in ways similar to C++'s built-in data types. In fact, this is the main advantage to the **string** class. If **string** is supported by your compiler, you will want to experiment with it. As you will see, it is a powerful class.

As the **string** class and the other standard C++ class libraries are refined, they will find their way into all manner of C++ programs and will become an accepted part of the C++ programming environment.

CHAPTER 12

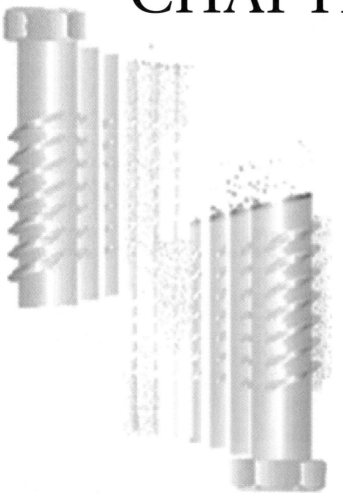

Operator Overloading

This chapter discusses another dimension to overloading: operator overloading. This feature allows you to define the meaning of the C++ operators relative to classes that you create. Operator overloading is one of C++'s most important (and exciting) features because it supports *type extensibility*. Type extensibility is the feature that allows you to seamlessly add new data types to your programming environment. For example, in C++ it is possible to define a new class type and then overload operators related to that class. After this is done, the new class type will be fully integrated and can be used like any of the built-in types.

As you will see, operator overloading is not difficult, but there are several nuances and details that you must understand. Remember that C++ defines a large number of operators and this chapter only demonstrates how to overload a few. However, as you will see, the procedures used to overload operators are quite general and you will not have trouble overloading other operators on your own.

Operator Overloading Fundamentals

Operator overloading resembles function overloading. In fact, operator overloading is really just a special type of function overloading. To overload an operator, you create an *operator function*. Most often an operator function is a member or a friend of the class for which it is defined. However, there is a slight difference between a member operator function and a friend operator function. The first part of this chapter discusses creating member operator functions. Then friend operator functions are discussed.

The general form of a member operator function is shown here:

```
return-type class-name::operator#(arg-list)
{
  // operation to be performed
}
```

For reasons that will become clear, the return type of an operator function is often the class for which it is defined. (However, an operator function is free to return any type of data.) The operator being overloaded is substituted for the #. For example, if the + is being overloaded, then the function name would be **operator+**. The contents of *arg-list* vary depending upon how the operator function is implemented and the type of operator being overloaded.

There are two important restrictions to remember when overloading an operator. First, the precedence of the operator cannot be changed. Second, the number of operands that an operator takes cannot be altered. For example, you cannot overload the + operator so that it takes only one operand. You can, however, choose to ignore an operand.

When an operator is overloaded, that operator loses none of its original meaning. Instead, it gains additional meaning relative to the class for which it is defined.

Most C++ operators can be overloaded. The only operators that you cannot overload are shown here:

.   ::   .*   ?

The .* operator is highly specialized and is beyond the scope of this book.

Except for the assignment operator, operator functions are inherited by a derived class. However, a derived class is free to overload any operator it chooses (including those overloaded by the base class) relative to itself.

While it is permissible for you to have an operator function perform *any* activity—whether related to the traditional use of the operator or not—it is best to have an overloaded operator's actions stay within the spirit of the operator's traditional use. When you create overloaded operators that stray from this principle, you run the risk of substantially destructuring your program. For example, overloading the / operator so that the phrase "I like C++" is written to a disk file 300 times is a fundamentally confusing misuse of operator overloading!

The preceding paragraph notwithstanding, there will be times when you need to use an operator in a way not related to its traditional usage. The two best examples of this are the << and >> operators, which are overloaded for console I/O in the header file IOSTREAM.H. However, even in these cases, the left and right arrows provide a visual "clue" to their meaning. Therefore, if you need to overload an operator in a nonstandard way, make an effort to use an appropriate operator.

12

There is one other restriction that you must follow when implementing operator functions: they may not have default parameters.

It is important to understand that operator functions can be written with many variations. The examples here and elsewhere in this chapter are not exhaustive, but they do illustrate several of the most common techniques.

Overloading Binary Operators

When a member operator function overloads a binary operator, the function will have only one parameter. This parameter will receive the object that is on the right side of the operator. The object on the left side is the object that generated the call to the operator function and is passed implicitly through **this**.

To see how operator functions are written, let's begin with an example. Consider the following program. It overloads the **+** operator relative to the **coord** class. This class maintains X,Y coordinates.

```
// Overload the + relative to coord class.
#include <iostream.h>
```

```
class coord {
  int x, y; // coordinate values
public:
  coord() { x=0; y=0; }
  coord(int i, int j) { x=i; y=j; }
  void get_xy(int &i, int &j) { i=x; j=y; }
  coord operator+(coord ob2);
};

// Overload + relative to coord class.
coord coord::operator+(coord ob2)
{
  coord temp;
  temp.x = x + ob2.x;
  temp.y = y + ob2.y;

  return temp;
}

main()
{
  coord o1(10, 10), o2(5, 3), o3;
  int x, y;

  o3 = o1 + o2; // add two objects - this calls operator+()

  o3.get_xy(x, y);
  cout << "(o1+o2) X: " << x << ", Y: " << y << "\n";

  return 0;
}
```

This program displays the following:

```
(o1+o2) X: 15, Y: 13
```

Let's look closely at this program. The **operator+( )** function returns an object of type **coord** that has the sum of each operand's X coordinates in **x** and the sum of the Y coordinates in **y**. Notice that a temporary object called **temp** is used inside **operator+( )** to hold the result, and it is this object that is returned. Also notice that neither operand is modified. The reason for **temp** is easy to understand. In this situation (as in most), the + is overloaded in a manner consistent with its normal arithmetic use. Therefore, it is important that neither operand be changed. For example, when you add 10+4, the result is 14, but neither the 10 nor the 4 is modified. Thus, a temporary object is needed to hold the result.

The reason that the **operator+( )** function returns an object of type **coord** is that it allows the result of the addition of **coord** objects to be used in larger expressions. For example, the statement

```
o3 = o1 + o2;
```

is valid only because the result of **o1+o2** is a **coord** object that can be assigned to **o3**. If a different type had been returned, this statement would have been invalid. Further, by returning a **coord** object, the addition operator allows a string of additions. For example, this is a valid statement:

```
o3 = o1 + o2 + o1 + o3;
```

Although there will be situations in which you want an operator function to return something other than an object of the class for which it is defined, most of the time it will. The major exception to this rule is when the relational and logical operators are overloaded. As you will see later in this chapter, for these operators, a true/false value is usually required.

12

Because **operator+( )** returns an object of type **coord**, the result of that operation can be used any place a **coord** object can. For example, the following statement is valid:

```
(o1+o2).get_xy(x, y);
```

Here, the temporary object returned by **operator+( )** is used to call **get_xy( )**. Of course, after this statement has executed, the temporary object is destroyed.

Other binary operators can be overloaded in much the same way as the **+**. For example, the following version of the coordinates program overloads the **–** and the **=** operators.

```
// Overload the +, -, and = relative to coord class.
#include <iostream.h>

class coord {
  int x, y; // coordinate values
public:
  coord() { x=0; y=0; }
  coord(int i, int j) { x=i; y=j; }
  void get_xy(int &i, int &j) { i=x; j=y; }
  coord operator+(coord ob2);
  coord operator-(coord ob2);
  coord operator=(coord ob2);
};
```

```cpp
// Overload + relative to coord class.
coord coord::operator+(coord ob2)
{
  coord temp;

  temp.x = x + ob2.x;
  temp.y = y + ob2.y;

  return temp;
}

// Overload - relative to coord class.
coord coord::operator-(coord ob2)
{
  coord temp;

  temp.x = x - ob2.x;
  temp.y = y - ob2.y;

  return temp;
}

// Overload = relative to coord.
coord coord::operator=(coord ob2)
{
  x = ob2.x;
  y = ob2.y;

  return *this; // return the object that is assigned
}

main()
{
  coord o1(10, 10), o2(5, 3), o3;
  int x, y;

  o3 = o1 + o2; // add two objects - this calls operator+()
  o3.get_xy(x, y);
  cout << "(o1+o2) X: " << x << ", Y: " << y << "\n";

  o3 = o1 - o2; // subtract two objects
  o3.get_xy(x, y);
  cout << "(o1-o2) X: " << x << ", Y: " << y << "\n";

  o3 = o1; // assign an object
  o3.get_xy(x, y);
  cout << "(o3=o1) X: " << x << ", Y: " << y << "\n";
```

```
   return 0;
}
```

The **operator–( )** function is implemented similarly to **operator+( )**. However, it illustrates a point that is crucial when overloading an operator for which the order of the operands is important. When the **operator+( )** function was created, it did not matter which order the operands were in. (That is, A+B is the same as B+A.) However, subtraction is order dependent. Therefore, to correctly overload the subtraction operator, it is necessary to subtract the operand on the right from the operand on the left. Because it is the left operand that generates the call to **operator–( )**, the subtraction must be in this order:

```
x - ob2.x;
```

Remember, when a binary operator is overloaded, the left operand is passed implicitly to the function and the right operand is passed as an argument.

Now, look at the assignment operator function. The first thing you should notice is that the left operand (that is, the object being assigned a value) is modified by the operation. This is in keeping with the normal meaning of assignment. The second thing to notice is that the function returns ***this**. That is, the **operator=( )** function returns the object that is the target of the assignment. The reason for this is to allow a series of assignments to be made. As you should know, in C++, the following statement is syntactically correct (and, indeed, very commonly used):

```
a = b = c = d = 0;
```

By returning ***this,** the overloaded assignment operator allows objects of type **coord** to be used in a similar fashion. For example, this is perfectly valid:

```
o3 = o2 = o1;
```

Keep in mind that there is no rule that requires an overloaded assignment function to return the object that receives the assignment. However, if you want the overloaded **=** to behave relative to its class the way it does for the built-in types, then it must return ***this**.

It is possible to overload an operator relative to a class so that the operand on the right side is an object of a built-in type, such as an integer, instead of the class for which the operator function is a member. For example, here the **+** operator is overloaded to add an integer value to a **coord** object. In this case, the integer is added to both the **x** and **y** values.

```
// Overload + for ob + int as well as ob + ob.
#include <iostream.h>

class coord {
  int x, y; // coordinate values
public:
  coord() { x=0; y=0; }
  coord(int i, int j) { x=i; y=j; }
  void get_xy(int &i, int &j) { i=x; j=y; }
  coord operator+(coord ob2); // ob + ob
  coord operator+(int i); // ob + int
};

// Overload + relative to coord class.
coord coord::operator+(coord ob2)
{
  coord temp;

  temp.x = x + ob2.x;
  temp.y = y + ob2.y;

  return temp;
}

// Overload + for ob + int
coord coord::operator+(int i)
{
  coord temp;

  temp.x = x + i;
  temp.y = y + i;
  return temp;
}

main()
{
  coord o1(10, 10), o2(5, 3), o3;
  int x, y;

  o3 = o1 + o2; // add two objects - this calls operator+(coord)
  o3.get_xy(x, y);
  cout << "(o1+o2) X: " << x << ", Y: " << y << "\n";

  o3 = o1 + 100; // add object + int - this calls operator+(int)
  o3.get_xy(x, y);
  cout << "(o1+100) X: " << x << ", Y: " << y << "\n";

  return 0;
}
```

As the preceding example shows, the built-in type must be on the right side of the operator. The reason for this is easy to understand: it is the object on the left that generates the call to the operator function. However, what happens when the compiler sees the following statement?

```
o3 = 19 + o1;  // int + ob
```

There is no built-in operation defined to handle the addition of an integer to an object. The overloaded **operator+(int i)** function works only when the object is on the left. Therefore, this statement generates a compile-time error. (Soon you will see one way around this restriction.)

You can use a reference parameter in an operator function. For example, this is an acceptable way to overload the + operator relative to the **coord** class:

12

```
// Overload + relative to coord class using a reference.
coord coord::operator+(coord &ob2)
{
  coord temp;

  temp.x = x + ob2.x;
  temp.y = y + ob2.y;

  return temp;
}
```

One reason for using a reference parameter is to avoid the trouble caused when a copy of an operand is destroyed. As you know from previous chapters, when an argument is passed by value, a copy of that argument is made. If that object has a destructor function, then when the function terminates, the copy's destructor is called. In some cases it is possible for the destructor to destroy something needed by the calling object. If this is the case, you will want to use a reference parameter instead of a value parameter. Of course, you can also avoid this problem by defining a copy constructor.

Overloading the Relational and Logical Operators

It is possible to overload the relational and logical operators. When you overload the relational and logical operators so that they behave in their traditional manner, you will not want the operator functions to return an object of the class for which they are defined. Instead, they will return an integer that indicates either true or false. This not only allows these operator functions to return a true/false value, it also allows the operators to be integrated into larger relational and logical expressions that involve other types of data.

In the following program, the **==** and **&&** operators are overloaded for the **coord** class:

```cpp
// Overload the == and && relative to coord class.
#include <iostream.h>

class coord {
  int x, y; // coordinate values
public:
  coord() { x=0; y=0; }
  coord(int i, int j) { x=i; y=j; }
  void get_xy(int &i, int &j) { i=x; j=y; }
  int operator==(coord ob2);
  int operator&&(coord ob2);
};

// Overload the == operator for coord.
int coord::operator==(coord ob2)
{
  if(x==ob2.x && y==ob2.y) return 1;
  else return 0;
}

// Overload the && operator for coord.
int coord::operator&&(coord ob2)
{
  return ((x && ob2.x) && (y && ob2.y));
}

main()
{
  coord o1(10, 10), o2(5, 3), o3(10, 10), o4(0, 0);

  if(o1==o2) cout << "o1 same as o2\n";
  else cout << "o1 and o2 differ\n";

  if(o1==o3) cout << "o1 same as o3\n";
  else cout << "o1 and o3 differ\n";

  if(o1&&o2) cout << "o1 && o2 is true\n";
  else cout << "o1 && o2 is false\n";

  if(o1&&o4) cout << "o1 && o4 is true\n";
  else cout << "o1 && o4 is false\n";
```

```
    return 0;
}
```

Overloading a Unary Operator

Overloading a unary operator is similar to overloading a binary operator except that there is only one operand to deal with. When you overload a unary operator using a member function, the function has no parameters. Since there is only one operand, it is this operand that generates the call to the operator function. There is no need for another parameter.

Overloading the Increment and Decrement Operators

The first unary operator that we will overload is **++**. The following program overloads the prefix form of the increment operator (**++**) relative to the **coord** class:

```
// Overload ++ relative to coord class.
#include <iostream.h>

class coord {
  int x, y; // coordinate values
public:
  coord() { x=0; y=0; }
  coord(int i, int j) { x=i; y=j; }
  void get_xy(int &i, int &j) { i=x; j=y; }
  coord operator++();
};

// Overload prefix form of ++ for coord class.
coord coord::operator++()
{
  x++;
  y++;

  return *this;
}

main()
{
  coord o1(10, 10);
  int x, y;

  ++o1; // prefix increment an object
  o1.get_xy(x, y);
```

```
  cout << "(++o1) X: " << x << ", Y: " << y << "\n";

  return 0;
}
```

Since the increment operator is designed to increase its operand by one, the overloaded **++** modifies the object it operates upon. The function also returns the object that it increments. This allows the increment operator to be used as part of a larger statement, such as this:

```
o2 = ++o1;
```

As with the binary operators, there is no rule that says you must overload a unary operator so that it reflects its normal meaning. However, most of the time, this is what you will want to do.

As stated, in the preceding program the **operator++( )** function overloads the prefix form of **++.** In early versions of C++, when overloading an increment or decrement operator, there was no way to determine whether an overloaded **++** or **– –** preceded or followed its operand. That is, assuming the preceding program, these two statements were identical:

```
o1++;
++o1;
```

However, the modern specification for C++ includes a way by which the compiler can distinguish between these two statements. To accomplish this, create two versions of the **operator++( )** function. The first is defined as shown in the preceding example. The second is declared like this:

```
coord coord::operator++(int x) // postfix form
{
  x++;
  y++;

  return *this;
}
```

If the **++** precedes its operand, the **operator++( )** function is called. However, if the **++** follows its operand, the **operator++(int x)** function is used. The **x** is a dummy parameter which will always be zero. On your own, you might want to try putting the postfix version of **operator++( )** into the sample program.

The decrement operator – – is overloaded in precisely the same way as the ++. Of course, you will need to perform a decrement rather than an increment operation.

Overloading the Unary Minus

As you know, the minus sign is both a binary and a unary operator in C++. You might be wondering how you can overload it so that it retains both of these uses relative to a class that you create. The solution is actually quite easy: you simply overload it twice, once as a binary operator and once as a unary operator. This program shows how:

```
// Overload the - relative to coord class.
#include <iostream.h>

class coord {
  int x, y; // coordinate values
public:
  coord() { x=0; y=0; }
  coord(int i, int j) { x=i; y=j; }
  void get_xy(int &i, int &j) { i=x; j=y; }
  coord operator-(coord ob2); // binary minus
  coord operator-(); // unary minus
};

// Overload - relative to coord class.
coord coord::operator-(coord ob2)
{
  coord temp;

  temp.x = x - ob2.x;
  temp.y = y - ob2.y;

  return temp;
}

// Overload unary - for coord class.
coord coord::operator-()
{
  x = -x;
  y = -y;
  return *this;
}

main()
{
  coord o1(10, 10), o2(5, 7);
```

12

```
    int x, y;

    o1 = o1 - o2; // subtraction
    o1.get_xy(x, y);
    cout << "(o1-o2) X: " << x << ", Y: " << y << "\n";

    o1 = -o1; // negation
    o1.get_xy(x, y);
    cout << "(-o1) X: " << x << ", Y: " << y << "\n";

    return 0;
}
```

As you can see, when the minus is overloaded as a binary operator, it takes one parameter. When it is overloaded as a unary operator, it takes no parameter. This difference in the number of parameters is what makes it possible for the minus to be overloaded for both operations. As the program indicates, when the minus sign is used as a binary operator, the **operator–(coord ob2)** function is called. When it is used as a unary minus, the **operator–( )** function is called.

Using Friend Operator Functions

As mentioned at the start of this chapter, it is possible to overload an operator using a friend rather than a member function. The main difference between a member operator function and a friend operator function is the number of parameters each has. As you know, a member operator function is passed the left-hand operand implicitly, through **this**. However, a friend function does not have a **this** pointer. This means that friend operator functions must be passed all parameters explicitly. For binary operators, this means that a friend operator function is passed both operands explicitly. For unary operators, the single operand is passed. All other things being equal, there is no reason to use a friend rather than a member operator function, with one important exception, which is discussed later.

 Note: You cannot use a friend to overload the assignment operator. The assignment operator can be overloaded only by a member operator function.

Let's begin by changing the **operator+( )** function from the preceding examples into a friend function. This change is reflected in the following program.

```
// Overload the + relative to coord class using a friend.
#include <iostream.h>

class coord {
  int x, y; // coordinate values
public:
  coord() { x=0; y=0; }
  coord(int i, int j) { x=i; y=j; }
  void get_xy(int &i, int &j) { i=x; j=y; }
  friend coord operator+(coord ob1, coord ob2);
};

// Overload + using a friend.
coord operator+(coord ob1, coord ob2)
{
  coord temp;

  temp.x = ob1.x + ob2.x;
  temp.y = ob1.y + ob2.y;

  return temp;
}

main()
{
  coord o1(10, 10), o2(5, 3), o3;
  int x, y;

  o3 = o1 + o2; // add two objects - this calls operator+()
  o3.get_xy(x, y);
  cout << "(o1+o2) X: " << x << ", Y: " << y << "\n";

  return 0;
}
```

Notice that the left operand is passed to the first parameter and the right operand is passed to the second parameter.

Overloading an operator by using a friend provides one very important feature that a member function does not have. Using a friend operator function, you can allow objects to be used in operations involving built-in types where the built-in type is on the left side of the operator. As you saw earlier in this chapter, it is possible to overload a binary member operator function so that the left operand is an object and the right operand is a built-in type. But it is not possible to use a member function to allow the built-in type to occur on the left side of the operator. For example, assuming

12

an overloaded member operator function, the first statement shown here is legal; the second is not:

```
ob1 = ob2 + 10; // legal
ob1 = 10 + ob2; // illegal
```

While it is possible, always having to make sure that the object is on the left side of the operand and the built-in type is on the right can be a cumbersome restriction. The solution to this problem is to make the overloaded operator functions friends and define both possible situations.

As you know, a friend operator function is explicitly passed *both* operands. Thus, it is possible to define one overloaded friend function so that the left operand is an object and the right operand is the built-in type. Then, overload the operator again with the left operand being the built-in type and the right operand being the object. The following program illustrates this method:

```
// Use friend operator functions to add flexibility.
#include <iostream.h>

class coord {
  int x, y; // coordinate values
public:
  coord() { x=0; y=0; }
  coord(int i, int j) { x=i; y=j; }
  void get_xy(int &i, int &j) { i=x; j=y; }
  friend coord operator+(coord ob1, int i);
  friend coord operator+(int i, coord ob1);
};

// Overload for ob + int.
coord operator+(coord ob1, int i)
{
  coord temp;

  temp.x = ob1.x + i;
  temp.y = ob1.y + i;

  return temp;
}

// Overload for int + ob.
coord operator+(int i, coord ob1)
{
  coord temp;
```

```
    temp.x = ob1.x + i;
    temp.y = ob1.y + i;

    return temp;
}

main()
{
    coord o1(10, 10);
    int x, y;

    o1 = o1 + 10; // object + integer
    o1.get_xy(x, y);
    cout << "(o1+10) X: " << x << ", Y: " << y << "\n";

    o1 = 99 + o1; // integer + object
    o1.get_xy(x, y);
    cout << "(99+o1) X: " << x << ", Y: " << y << "\n";

    return 0;
}
```

As a result of overloading friend operator functions for both situations, both of these statements are now valid:

```
o1 = o1 + 10; // OK
o1 = 99 + o1; // OK, too
```

If you want to use a friend operator function to overload either the **++** or **– –** unary operator, you must pass the operand to the function as a reference parameter. Remember that the increment and decrement operators imply that the operand will be modified. However, if you overload these operators by using a friend, by default the operand is passed by value as a parameter. Thus, any modifications that occur to the parameter inside the friend operator function will not affect the object that generated the call. And since no pointer to the object is passed implicitly (that is, there is no **this** pointer) when a friend is used, there is no way for the increment or decrement to affect the operand. However, by passing the operand to the friend as a reference parameter, changes that occur inside the friend function affect the object that generates the call.

As with member functions, there is a prefix and postfix form of the increment and decrement friend operator functions. The prefix form has only one parameter: the object being affected. The postfix form takes a second, dummy integer parameter.

Overloading new and delete

Because **new** and **delete** are operators, they too may be overloaded. By overloading **new** and **delete**, you can implement your own, custom allocation scheme. For example, you may want allocation routines that automatically begin using a disk file as virtual memory when the heap has been exhausted. Whatever the reason, it is a simple matter to overload these operators.

The skeletons for the functions that overload **new** and **delete** are shown here.

```
// Allocate an object.
void *operator new(size_t size)
{
  // Allocate memory using your own allocation system.
  return pointer_to_memory;
}

// Delete an object.
void operator delete(void *p)
{
  // Free memory pointed to by p.
}
```

The type **size_t** is a defined type capable of specifying the largest single piece of memory that can be allocated. (**size_t** is essentially an unsigned integer.). When **operator new( )** is invoked, **size** will contain the number of bytes needed to hold the object being allocated. The overloaded **new** function must return a pointer to the memory that it allocates or zero if an allocation error occurs. Beyond these constraints, the overloaded **new** function can do anything else you require.

When you allocate an object using **new** (whether your own version or not), the object's constructor is automatically called. This means that your custom version of **new** need not contain any code of its own to accomplish this.

The **delete** function receives a pointer to the region of memory to free. It must release this memory so that it can be reused. When an object is deleted, its destructor function is automatically called. Your implementation of **delete** need not contain any code of its own to accomplish this.

To allocate and free arrays of objects, you must use these forms of **new** and **delete**.

```
// Allocate an array of objects.
void *operator new[](size_t size)
{
  /* Allocate memory using your own allocation system.
     The constructor for each element is
     automatically called. */
  return pointer_to_memory;
}

// Delete an array of objects.
void operator delete[](void *p)
{
  /* Free memory pointed to by p.
     The destructor for each element is
     automatically called.
  */
}
```

When allocating an array, each element's constructor is automatically called. When freeing an array, each element's destructor is automatically called. You do not have to provide explicit code to accomplish these actions.

Although it is possible to overload **new** and **delete** globally, they are generally overloaded relative to a class. To overload the **new** and **delete** operators relative to a class, simply make the overloaded operator functions class members. You may want to experiment with these operators on your own, trying different dynamic allocation schemes.

More About the Assignment Operator

As you have seen, it is possible to overload the assignment operator relative to a class. By default, when the assignment operator is applied to an object, a bitwise copy of the object on the right is put into the object on the left. If this is what you want, there is no reason to provide your own **operator=( )** function. However, there are cases in which a strict bitwise copy is not desirable—for example when dynamic allocation is involved. (You saw an example of this in Chapter 11.) In these types of situations, you will want to provide a special copy operation.

12

To understand the benefit of overloading assignment, consider the following version of the **strtype** class (which you have seen in various forms in the preceding chapter). **strtype** stores strings in dynamically allocated memory. It maintains a pointer to each string in its **p** member. This version of **strtype** overloads the = operator so that the pointer **p** is not overwritten when one object is assigned to another.

```cpp
#include <iostream.h>
#include <string.h>
#include <stdlib.h>

class strtype {
  char *p;
  int len;
public:
  strtype(char *ptr);
  ~strtype() {
    cout << "Freeing " << (unsigned) p << '\n';
    delete [] p;
  }
  char *get() { return p; }
  strtype &operator=(strtype &ob);
};

strtype::strtype(char *ptr)
{
  int length;

  length = strlen(ptr) + 1;

  p = new char [length];
  if(!p) {
    cout << "Allocation error.\n";
    exit(1);
  }

  len = length;
  strcpy(p, ptr);
}

// Assign an object.
strtype &strtype::operator=(strtype &ob)
{
  // see if more memory is needed
  if(len < ob.len) { // need to allocate more memory
    delete p;
    p = new char [ob.len];
```

```
    if(!p) {
      cout << "Allocation error.\n";
      exit(1);
    }
    len = ob.len;
  }
  strcpy(p, ob.p);
  return *this;
}

main()
{
  strtype a("Hello"), b("There");

  cout << a.get() << '\n';
  cout << b.get() << '\n';

  a = b; // p is not overwritten by this assignment

  cout << a.get() << '\n';
  cout << b.get() << '\n';

  return 0;
}
```

As you can see, the overloaded assignment operator prevents **p** from being overwritten when an assignment takes place. It first checks to see if the object on the left has allocated enough memory to hold the string that is being assigned to it. If it hasn't, that memory is freed and another portion is allocated. Then, the string is copied to that memory. Thus the **p** member of both the source and target objects still points to different regions of memory after the assignment has taken place. If the assignment operator had not been overloaded, then a bitwise copy would have taken place and the **p** member of both objects would point to the same memory. In this case, the destruction of one object would free the memory pointed to by **p**. However, this memory would still be needed by the other object, causing an error. Fortunately, the overloaded assignment operator prevents this error.

Overloading the [ ]

The next operator that we will overload is the **[ ]** array subscripting operator. In C++, the **[ ]** is considered a binary operator for the purposes of overloading. The **[ ]** may only be overloaded by a member function. Therefore, the general form of a member **operator[ ]( )** function is as shown here.

```
type class-name::operator[ ](int index)
{
  // ...
}
```

Technically, the parameter does not have to be of type **int**, but **operator [ ]( )** functions are typically used to provide array subscripting and as such an integer value is generally used.

To understand how the **[ ]** operator works, assume an object called **O** is indexed as shown here.

```
O[3]
```

This index will translate into the following call to the **operator[ ]( )** function:

```
operator[](3)
```

That is, the value of the expression within the subscripting operator is passed to the **operator[ ]( )** function in its explicit parameter. The **this** pointer will point to **O**, the object that generated the call.

In the following program, **atype** declares an array of three integers. Its constructor function initializes each member of the array. The overloaded **operator[ ]( )** function returns the value of the element specified by its parameter.

```
#include <iostream.h>

const int SIZE = 3;

class atype {
  int a[SIZE];
public:
  atype() {
    register int i;
    for(i=0; i<SIZE; i++) a[i] = i;
  }
  int operator[](int i) {return a[i];}
};

main()
{
  atype ob;
```

```
   cout << ob[2];   // displays 2

   return 0;
}
```

The initialization of the array **a** by the constructor in this, and the following programs, is for the sake of illustration only. It is not required.

It is possible to design the **operator[ ]( )** function in such a way that the **[ ]** can be used on both the left and right sides of an assignment statement. To do this, simply specify the return value of **operator[ ]( )** to be a reference. For example, this program makes this change and illustrates its use.

```
#include <iostream.h>

const int SIZE = 3;

class atype {
  int a[SIZE];
public:
  atype() {
    register int i;
    for(i=0; i<SIZE; i++) a[i] = i;
  }
  int &operator[](int i) {return a[i];}
};

main()
{
  atype ob;

  cout << ob[2];   // displays 2
  cout << " ";

  ob[2] = 88;   // [] on left of =

  cout << ob[2];   // now displays 88

  return 0;
}
```

12

Because **operator[ ]( )** returns a reference to the array element indexed by **i**, it can now be used on the left side of an assignment to modify an element of the array. (Of course, it may still be used on the right side as well.)

Creating a Safe Array

One advantage to being able to overload the **[ ]** operator is that it allows a means of implementing safe array indexing. As you know, in C++, it is possible to overrun an array boundary at run time without generating a run-time error message. However, if you create a class that contains the array and allow access to that array only through the overloaded **[ ]** subscripting operator, then you can intercept an out-of-range index. When you do this, you have created a safe array. Earlier in this book, when references were introduced, you saw one way to implement a safe array. As you will see, a better way to accomplish this is by overloading the **[ ]** operator.

To create a safe array, simply add boundary checking to the **operator[ ]( )** function. The **operator[ ]( )** must also return a reference to the element being indexed. For example, this program adds a range check to the array program described in the text and proves that it works by generating a boundary error.

```
// A safe array example.
#include <iostream.h>
#include "stdlib.h"

const int SIZE = 3;

class atype {
  int a[SIZE];
public:
  atype() {
    register int i;

    for(i=0; i<SIZE; i++) a[i] = i;
  }
  int &operator[](int i);
};
```

```
// Provide range checking for atype.
int &atype::operator[](int i)
{
  if(i<0 || i> SIZE-1) {
    cout << "\nIndex value of ";
    cout << i << " is out-of-bounds.\n";
    exit(1);
  }
  return a[i];
}

main()
{
  atype ob;

  cout << ob[2];  // displays 2
  cout << " ";

  ob[2] = 88;  // [] appears on left

  cout << ob[2];  // displays 88

  ob[3] = 1043; // generates run-time error, 3 out-of-range
  return 0;
}
```

12

In this program, when the statement **ob[3] = 1043;** executes, the boundary error is intercepted by **operator[ ]( )** and the program is terminated before any damage can be done.

Because a safe array adds overhead you may not want to use one in all situations. In fact, the added overhead is why C++ does not perform boundary checking on arrays in the first place. However, in applications in which you want to be sure that a boundary error does not take place, a safe array will be worth the effort.

CHAPTER 13

The C++ I/O System

You have been using pieces of the C++ I/O system since the first chapter of this book. It is now time to explore it more fully. The C++ language includes a rich, object-oriented I/O system that is both flexible and powerful. It may also be extended to handle new types of data that you create. As you will see, its type extensibility is one of the C++ I/O system's major advantages.

Although this chapter covers both file and console I/O, the C++ I/O system makes little distinction between the two. File and console I/O are really just different perspectives on the same mechanism. Many examples in this chapter use console I/O, but the information presented is applicable to file I/O, as well.

I/O Fundamentals

Before beginning the discussion of C++ I/O, a few general comments are in order. The C++ I/O system operates through *streams*. You may be familiar with the concept of a stream from your previous programming experience. If not, here is a brief description. A stream is a logical device that either produces or consumes information. A stream is linked to a physical device (such as a disk drive) by the C++ I/O system. All streams behave in the same manner, even if the actual physical devices they are linked to differ. Because all streams act the same, the I/O system can operate on virtually any type of device. For example, the same method that you use to write to the screen can be used to write to a disk file or to the printer.

When a C++ program begins, these four streams are automatically opened:

Stream	Meaning	Default Device
cin	Standard input	Keyboard
cout	Standard output	Screen
cerr	Standard error	Screen
clog	Buffered version of cerr	Screen

If you are familiar with C, the streams **cin**, **cout**, and **cerr** correspond to C's **stdin**, **stdout**, and **stderr**. You have already been using **cin** and **cout**. The stream **clog** is simply a buffered version of **cerr**. By default, the standard streams are used to communicate with the console. However, in environments that support I/O redirection, these streams can be redirected to other devices.

As you learned in Chapter 1, C++ provides support for its I/O system in the header file IOSTREAM.H. In this file, class hierarchies are defined that support I/O operations. There are two related, but different I/O class hierarchies. The first is derived from the low level I/O class called **streambuf**. This class supplies the basic, low-level input and output operations and provides the underlying support for the entire C++ I/O system. Unless you are doing advanced I/O programming, you will not need to use **streambuf** directly. The class hierarchy that you will most commonly be working with is derived from **ios**. This is a high-level I/O class that provides formatting, error-checking, and status information related to stream I/O. **ios** is used as a base for several derived classes, including: **istream**, **ostream**, and **iostream**. These classes are used to create streams capable of input, output, and input/output, respectively.

The **ios** class contains many member functions and variables that control or monitor the fundamental operation of a stream. It will be referred to frequently. Just remember that if you include IOSTREAM.H in your program, you will have access to this important class.

Formatted I /O

Until now, all examples in this book displayed information on the screen using C++'s default formats. However, it is possible to output information in a wide variety of forms. Also, you can alter certain aspects of the way information is input.

Each C++ stream has associated with it a number of format flags that determine how data is displayed. They are encoded into a long integer. (At the time of this writing, the draft ANSI C++ standard suggests the type name **fmtflags** for variables holding format flags, which is some form of long integer. However, this type name is subject to change so this book will simply use **long** to describe the type of the format flags.) The format flags are named and given values within the **ios** class, typically using an enumeration, as shown here:

13

```
// ios format flags
enum {
  skipws = 0x0001,     left = 0x0002,      right = 0x0004,
  internal = 0x0008,   dec = 0x0010,       oct = 0x0020,
  hex = 0x0040,        showbase = 0x0080,  showpoint = 0x0100,
  uppercase = 0x0200,  showpos = 0x0400,   scientific = 0x0800,
  fixed = 0x1000,      unitbuf = 0x2000
};
```

Generally, when a format flag is set, that feature is turned on. When a flag is cleared, the default format is used. The following is a description of these flags.

When the **skipws** flag is set, leading whitespace characters (spaces, tabs, and newlines) are discarded when you are performing input on a stream. When **skipws** is cleared, whitespace characters are not discarded.

When the **left** flag is set, output is left justified. When **right** is set, output is right justified. When the **internal** flag is set, a numeric value is padded to fill a field by the insertion of spaces between any signs or base characters. (You will learn how to specify a field width shortly.) If none of these flags is set, output is right justified by default.

By default, integer values are output in decimal. However, it is possible to change the number base. Setting the **oct** flag causes output to be displayed in octal. Setting the **hex** flag causes output to be displayed in hexadecimal. To return output to decimal, set the **dec** flag.

Setting **showbase** causes the base of numeric values to be shown. For example, if the conversion base is hexadecimal, the value 1F will be displayed as **0x1F**.

Setting **showpoint** causes a decimal point and trailing zeros to be displayed for all floating-point output—whether needed or not.

By default, when scientific notation is displayed, the "e" is in lowercase. Also, when a hexadecimal value is displayed, the "x" is in lowercase. When **uppercase** is set, these characters are displayed in uppercase.

Setting **showpos** causes a leading plus sign to be displayed before positive decimal values.

Setting the **scientific** flag causes floating-point numeric values to be displayed using scientific notation. When **fixed** is set, floating-point values are displayed using normal notation. By default, when **fixed** is set, six decimal places are displayed. When neither flag is set, the compiler chooses an appropriate method.

When **unitbuf** is set, the C++ I/O system flushes its output streams after each output operation.

The format flags just described will be available for all current C++ compilers. But, at the time of this writing, the exact nature of the **ios** format flags is still being determined by the ANSI C++ standardization committee. For example, the **boolalpha** flag has been added, which permits I/O operations on the newly defined **bool** data type. However, this flag is not currently defined by most compilers. (Of course, it will be in the future.) Also, there are three additional format flags that act as shortcuts for combinations of flags. They are **adjustfield**, **basefield**, and **floatfield. adjustfield** is the combination of **left**, **right**, and **internal. basefield** is the combination of **dec**, **oct**, and **hex. floatfield** is the combination of **scientific** and **fixed**. You will want to check your compiler's user manual for information about these and other format flags that may be available for your use.

Setting and Clearing Format Flags

To set a format flag, use the **setf( )** function. This function is a member of **ios**. Its most common form is shown here:

    long setf(long *flags*);

This function returns the previous settings of the format flags and turns on those flags specified by *flags*. (All other flags are unaffected.) For example, to turn on the **showpos** flag, you can use this statement:

> *stream*.setf(ios::showpos);

Here, *stream* is the stream you wish to affect. Notice the use of the scope resolution operator. Remember, **showpos** is an enumerated constant within the **ios** class. Therefore, it is necessary to tell the compiler this fact by preceding **showpos** with the class name and the scope resolution operator. If you don't, the constant **showpos** will simply not be recognized.

It is possible to set more than one flag in one call to **setf( )**, rather than making multiple calls. To do this, OR together the values of the flags you want set.

It is important to understand that **setf( )** is a member function of the **ios** class and affects streams created by that class. Therefore, any call to **setf( )** is done relative to a specific stream. There is no concept of calling **setf( )** by itself. Put differently, there is no concept in C++ of global format status. Each stream maintains its own format status information individually.

Here is an example that illustrates **setf( )**:

13

```
#include <iostream.h>

main()
{
  // display using default settings
  cout << 123.23 << " hello " << 100 << '\n';
  cout << 10 << ' ' << -10 << '\n';
  cout << 100.0 << "\n\n";

  // now, change formats
  cout.setf(ios::hex | ios::scientific);
  cout << 123.23 << " hello " << 100 << '\n';

  cout.setf(ios::showpos);
  cout << 10 << ' ' << -10 << '\n';

  cout.setf(ios::showpoint | ios::fixed);
  cout << 100.0;

  return 0;
}
```

This program displays the following output:

```
123.23 hello 100
10 -10
100
```

```
1.232300e+02 hello 64
a ffffffff6
+100.000000
```

Notice that the **showpos** flag only affects decimal output. It does not affect the value 10 when output in hexadecimal.

The complement of **setf( )** is **unsetf( )**. This member function of **ios** clears one or more format flags. Its most common form is shown here:

   long unsetf(long *flags*);

The flags specified by *flags* are cleared. (All other flags are unaffected.) The previous flag settings are returned.

The following program illustrates **unsetf( )**. It first sets the **uppercase**, **showbase**, and **hex** flags. It then outputs 88 using scientific notation. In this case, the "X" used in the hexadecimal notation is in uppercase. Next, it clears the **uppercase** flag by using **unsetf( )** and again outputs 88 using hexadecimal. This time, the "x" is in lowercase.

```
#include <iostream.h>

main()
{
  cout.setf(ios::uppercase | ios::showbase | ios::hex);

  cout << 88 << '\n';

  cout.unsetf(ios::uppercase);

  cout << 88 << '\n';

  return 0;
}
```

There will be times when you only want to know the current format settings but not alter any. To accomplish this, **ios** also includes the member function **flags( )**, which simply returns the current setting of each format flag encoded into a **long int**. Its prototype is shown here:

   long flags( );

The **flags( )** function has a second form that allows you to set *all* format flags associated with a stream to those specified in the argument to **flags( )**. The prototype for this version of **flags( )** is shown here:

long flags(long *f*);

When you use this version, the bit pattern found in *f* is copied to the variable used to hold the format flags associated with the stream, thus overwriting all previous flag settings. The function returns the previous settings.

Using width( ), precision( ), and fill( )

There are three member functions defined by **ios** that set these format parameters: the field width, the precision, and the fill character. The functions that do these things are **width( )**, **precision( )**, and **fill( )**, respectively.

By default, when a value is output, it occupies only as much space as the number of characters it takes to display it. However, you can specify a minimum field width by using the **width( )** function. Its prototype is shown here:

```
int width(int w);
```

13

Here, *w* becomes the field width, and the previous field width is returned. In some implementations, each time an output operation is performed, the field width returns to its default setting, so it may be necessary to set the minimum field width before each output statement.

After you set a minimum field width, when a value uses less than the specified width, the field is padded by using the current fill character (the space, by default) so that the field width is reached. However, keep in mind that if the length of the value exceeds the minimum field width, the field will be overrun. No values are truncated.

By default, six digits of precision are used. However, you can set this number by using the **precision( )** function. Its prototype is shown here:

```
int precision(int p);
```

Here, the precision is set to *p* and the old value is returned.

By default, when a field needs to be filled, it is filled with spaces. However, you can specify the fill character by using the **fill( )** function. Its prototype is shown here:

```
char fill(char ch);
```

After a call to **fill( )**, *ch* becomes the new fill character, and the old one is returned.

Here is a program that illustrates these functions:

```
#include <iostream.h>

main()
{
  cout.width(10); // set minimum field width
  cout << "hello" << '\n';  // right justify by default
  cout.fill('%'); // set fill character
  cout.width(10); // set width
  cout << "hello" << '\n'; // right justify by default
  cout.setf(ios::left); // left justify
  cout.width(10); // set width
  cout << "hello" << '\n'; // output left justified

  cout.width(10); // set width
  cout.precision(10); // set 10 digits of precision
  cout << 123.234567 << '\n';
  cout.width(10);  // set width
  cout.precision(6);  // set 6 digits of precision
  cout << 123.234567 << '\n';

  return 0;
}
```

This program displays the following output:

```
     hello
%%%%%hello
hello%%%%%
123.234567
123.235%%%
```

Notice that the field width is set before each output statement.

Using I /O Manipulators

There is a second way that you can format information using C++'s I/O system. This method uses special functions called *I/O manipulators*. As you will see, I/O manipulators are, in some situations, easier to use than the **ios** format flags and functions.

I/O manipulators are special I/O format functions that may occur *within* an I/O statement, instead of separate from it the way the **ios** member functions must. The standard manipulators are shown in Table 13-1. As you can see by examining the table, many of the I/O manipulators parallel member functions of the **ios** class. To access manipulators that take parameters, such as **setw( )**, you must include IOMANIP.H in your program. This is not necessary when using a manipulator that does not require an argument.

As stated, the manipulators may occur in a chain of I/O operations. For example:

```
cout << oct << 100 << hex << 100;
cout << setw(10) << 100;
```

The first statement tells **cout** to display integers in octal and then outputs 100 in octal. It then tells the stream to display integers in hexadecimal and then outputs 100 in hexadecimal format. The second statement sets the field width to 10 and then displays 100 in hexadecimal format, again. Notice that when a manipulator does not take an argument, such as **oct** in the example, it is not followed by parentheses.

Keep in mind that an I/O manipulator affects only the stream of which the I/O expression is a part. I/O manipulators do *not* affect all streams currently opened for use.

If you wish to set specific format flags manually by using a manipulator, use **setiosflags( )**. This manipulator performs the same function as the member

13

Manipulator	Purpose	Input/Output
dec	Input/output data in decimal	Input and output
endl	Output a newline character and flush the stream	Output
ends	Output a null	Output
flush	Flush a stream	Output
hex	Input/output data in hexadecimal	Input and output
oct	Input/output data in octal	Input and output
resetiosflags(long *f*)	Turn off the flags specified in *f*	Input and output
setbase(int *base*)	Set the number base to *base*	Output
setfill(int *ch*)	Set the fill character to *ch*	Output
setiosflags(long *f*)	Turn on the flags specified in *f*	Input and output
setprecision(int *p*)	Set the number of digits of precision	Output
setw(int *w*)	Set the field width to *w*	Output
ws	Skip leading white space	Input

The C++ I/O
Manipulators
Table 13-1.

function **setf( )**. To turn off flags, use the **resetiosflags( )** manipulator. This manipulator is equivalent to **unsetf( )**.

This program demonstrates several of the I/O manipulators:

```
#include <iostream.h>
#include <iomanip.h>

main()
{
  cout << hex << 100 << endl;
  cout << oct << 10 << endl;

  cout << setfill('X') << setw(10);
  cout << 100 << " hi " << endl;

  return 0;
}
```

Creating Your Own Inserters

One of the advantages to the C++ I/O system is that you can overload the I/O operators for classes that you create. By doing so, you can seamlessly incorporate your classes into your C++ programs. In this section you learn how to overload C++'s output operator **<<**.

In the language of C++, the output operation is called an *insertion* and the **<<** is called the *insertion operator*. When you overload the **<<** for output, you are creating an *inserter function,* or *inserter* for short. The rationale for these terms comes from the fact that an output operator *inserts* information into a stream.

All inserter functions have this general form:

ostream &operator<<(ostream &*stream, class-name ob*)
{
  // *body of inserter*
  return *stream*;
}

The first parameter is a reference to an object of type **ostream**. This means that *stream* must be an output stream. (Remember, **ostream** is defined within the **ios** class.) The second parameter receives the object that will be output. (This may also be a reference parameter, if that is more suitable to your application.) Notice that the inserter function returns a reference to *stream,* which is of type **ostream**. This is required if the overloaded << is going to be used in compound I/O expressions, such as

```
cout << ob1 << ob2 << ob2;
```

Within an inserter you may perform any type of procedure. What an inserter does is completely up to you. However, for the inserter to be consistent with good programming practices, you should limit the operations inside it to outputting information to a stream.

Although surprising at first, an inserter may *not* be a member of the class on which it is designed to operate. Here is why. When an operator function of any type is a member of a class, the left operand, which is passed implicitly through the **this** pointer, is the object that generates the call to the operator function. This implies that the left operand is an object of that class. Therefore, if an overloaded operator function is a member of a class, then the left operand must be an object of that class. However, when you create an inserter, the left operand is a stream, not a class object, and the right operand is the object that you want output. Therefore, an inserter cannot be a member function.

13

The fact that an inserter cannot be a member function may appear to be a serious flaw in C++ because it seems to imply that all data of a class that will be output using an inserter will need to be public, thus violating the key principle of encapsulation. However, this is not the case. Even though inserters cannot be members of the class upon which they are designed to operate, they can be friends of the class. In fact, in most programming situations you will encounter, an overloaded inserter will be a friend of the class for which it was created.

The following program defines an inserter for the **coord** class, developed in a previous chapter:

```
// Use a friend inserter for objects of type coord.
#include <iostream.h>

class coord {
  int x, y;
public:
  coord() { x = 0; y = 0; }
  coord(int i, int j) { x = i; y = j; }
  friend ostream &operator<<(ostream &stream, coord ob);
};

ostream &operator<<(ostream &stream, coord ob)
{
```

```
    stream << ob.x << ", " << ob.y << '\n';
    return stream;
}

main()
{
  coord a(1, 1), b(10, 23);

  cout << a << b;

  return 0;
}
```

This program displays the following:

```
1, 1
10, 23
```

Exotic Inserters

An inserter need not be limited to displaying only textual information. An inserter can perform any operation or conversion necessary to output information in a form needed by a particular device or situation. For example, it is perfectly valid to create an inserter that sends information to a plotter. In this case, the inserter will need to send appropriate plotter codes in addition to the information. To allow you to taste the flavor of this type of inserter, the following program creates a class called **triangle**, which stores the width and height of a right triangle. The inserter for this class displays the triangle on the screen.

```
// This program draws right triangles
#include <iostream.h>

class triangle {
   int height, base;
public:
   triangle(int h, int b) { height = h; base = b; }
   friend ostream &operator<<(ostream &stream, triangle ob);
};

// Draw a triangle.
ostream &operator<<(ostream &stream, triangle ob)
{
   int i, j, h, k;

   i = j = ob.base-1;
```

```
        for(h=ob.height-1; h; h--) {
          for(k=i; k; k--) stream << ' ';
          stream << '*';

          if(j!=i) {
            for(k=j-i-1; k; k--) stream << ' ';
            stream << '*';
          }

          i--;
          stream << '\n';
        }
        for(k=0; k<ob.base; k++) stream << '*';
        stream << '\n';

        return stream;
    }

    main()
    {
      triangle t1(5, 5), t2(10, 10);

      cout << t1;
      cout << endl << t2;

      return 0;
    }
```

13

Notice that this program illustrates how a properly designed inserter can be fully integrated into a "normal" I/O expression. This program displays the following:

```
    *
   **
  *  *
 *    *
*****



        *
       **
      *  *
     *    *
    *      *
   *        *
  *          *
 *            *
*              *
**********
```

Creating Extractors

Just as you can overload the **<<** output operator, you can overload the **>>** input operator. In C++, the **>>** is referred to as the *extraction operator* and a function that overloads it is called an *extractor*. The reason for this term is that the act of inputting information from a stream removes (that is, extracts) data from it.

The general form of an extractor function is shown here:

```
istream &operator>>(istream &stream, class-name &ob)
{
  // body of extractor
  return stream;
}
```

Extractors return a reference to **istream**, which is an input stream. The first parameter must be a reference to an input stream. The second parameter is a reference to the object that is receiving input.

For the same reason that an inserter cannot be a member function, an extractor may not be a member function. (Of course, it may be a friend.) While you may perform any operation within an extractor, it is best to limit its activity to inputting information.

This program adds an extractor to the **coord** class:

```
// Add a friend extractor for objects of type coord.
#include <iostream.h>

class coord {
  int x, y;
public:
  coord() { x = 0; y = 0; }
  coord(int i, int j) { x = i; y = j; }
  friend ostream &operator<<(ostream &stream, coord ob);
  friend istream &operator>>(istream &stream, coord &ob);
};

ostream &operator<<(ostream &stream, coord ob)
{
  stream << ob.x << ", " << ob.y << '\n';
  return stream;
}

istream &operator>>(istream &stream, coord &ob)
{
  cout << "Enter coordinates: ";
```

```
    stream >> ob.x >> ob.y;
    return stream;
}

main()
{
  coord a(1, 1), b(10, 23);

  cout << a << b;

  cin >> a;
  cout << a;


  return 0;
}
```

Notice how the extractor also prompts the user for input. While not required (or even desired) for most situations, this function shows how a customized extractor can simplify coding when a prompting message is needed.

13

Creating Your Own Manipulators

In addition to overloading the insertion and extraction operators, you can further customize C++'s I/O system by creating your own manipulator functions. Custom manipulators are important for two main reasons. First, a manipulator can consolidate a sequence of several separate I/O operations into one manipulator. For example, it is not uncommon to have situations in which the same sequence of I/O operations occurs frequently within a program. In these cases you can use a custom manipulator to perform these actions, thus simplifying your source code and preventing accidental errors. Second, a custom manipulator can be important when you need to perform I/O operations on a nonstandard device. For example, you might use a manipulator to send control codes to a special type of printer or an optical recognition system.

Custom manipulators are a feature of C++ that supports OOP, but they can also benefit programs that aren't object oriented. As you will see, custom manipulators can help make any I/O-intensive program clearer and more efficient.

As you know, there are two basic types of manipulators: those that operate on input streams and those that operate on output streams. However, in addition to these two broad categories, there is a secondary division: those manipulators that take an argument and those that don't. There are some significant differences between the way a parameterless manipulator and a parameterized manipulator are created. Further, creating parameterized manipulators is substantially more difficult than creating parameterless ones and is beyond the scope of this book. (See my book *C++: The Complete Reference, 2nd Edition* for examples of creating your own parameterized manipulators.) However, writing your own parameterless manipulators is quite easy and is examined here.

All parameterless manipulator output functions have this skeleton:

```
ostream &manip-name(ostream &stream)
{
  // your code here
  return stream;
}
```

Here, *manip-name* is the name of the manipulator. Notice that a reference to a stream of type **ostream** is returned. This is necessary if a manipulator is used as part of a larger I/O expression. It is important to understand that even though the manipulator has as its single argument a reference to the stream upon which it is operating, no argument is used when the manipulator is inserted in an output operation.

All parameterless input manipulator functions have this skeleton:

```
istream &manip-name(istream &stream)
{
  // your code here
  return stream;
}
```

An input manipulator receives a reference to the stream for which it was invoked. This stream must be returned by the manipulator.

It is crucial that your manipulators return *stream*. If this is not done, your manipulators cannot be used in a compound input or output expression.

Here is a simple example that creates an output manipulator called **setup( )** that sets the field width to 10, the precision to 4, and the fill character to *.

```
#include <iostream.h>

ostream &setup(ostream &stream)
{
  stream.width(10);
  stream.precision(4);
  stream.fill('*');
```

```
  return stream;
}

main()
{
  cout << setup << 123.123456;

  return 0;
}
```

As you can see, **setup** is used as part of an I/O expression in the same way that any of the built-in manipulators are used.

The following program creates an input manipulator called **getpass( )** that rings the bell and then prompts for a password:

```
#include <iostream.h>
#include <string.h>

// A simple input manipulator.
istream &getpass(istream &stream)
{
  cout << '\a';  // sound bell
  cout << "Enter password: ";

  return stream;
}

main()
{
  char pw[80];

  do {
    cin >> getpass >> pw;
  } while (strcmp(pw, "password"));
  cout << "Logon complete\n";

  return 0;
}
```

13

File I/O

The remainder of this chapter discusses file I/O. As you will see, file I/O is straightforward because it uses the same I/O system with which you are already familiar. It is just that I/O operations are directed to devices such as disk drives rather than to the console. To perform file I/O, you must include the header file FSTREAM.H in your program. It defines several classes, including **ifstream**, **ostream**, and **fstream**. These classes are derived from **istream** and **ostream**. Remember, **istream** and **ostream** are derived from **ios**, so **ifstream**, **ostream**, and **fstream** also have access to all operations defined by **ios**.

In C++, a file is opened by linking it to a stream. There are three types of streams: input, output, and input/output. Before you can open a file, you must first obtain a stream. To create an input stream, you must declare the stream to be of class **ifstream**. To create an output stream, it must be declared as class **ostream**. Streams that will be performing both input and output operations must be declared as class **fstream**. For example, this fragment creates one input stream, one output stream, and one stream capable of both input and output:

```
ifstream in;   // input
ofstream out;  // output
fstream io;    // input and output
```

Once you have created a stream, one way to associate it with a file is by using the function **open( )**. This function is a member of each of the three stream classes. Its prototype is shown here:

void open(const char *filename*, int *mode*, int *access*=filebuf::openprot);

Here, *filename* is the name of the file, which may include a path specifier. The value of *mode* determines how the file is opened. It must be one (or more) of these values:

```
ios::app
ios::ate
ios::binary
ios::in
ios::nocreate
ios::noreplace
ios::out
ios::trunc
```

You can combine two or more of these values by ORing them together. Let's see what each of these values means.

Including **ios::app** causes all output to that file to be appended to the end. This value can be used only with files capable of output. Including **ios::ate** causes a seek to the end of the file to occur when the file is opened. Although **ios::ate** causes a seek to end-of-file, I/O operations can still occur anywhere within the file.

The **ios::binary** value causes a file to be opened in binary mode. By default, all files are opened in text mode. In text mode, various character translations may take place, such as carriage return, linefeed sequences being converted into newlines. However, when a file is opened in binary mode, no such character translations will occur. Keep in mind that any file, whether it contains formatted text or raw data, can be opened in either binary or text mode. The only difference is whether character translations take place.

The **ios::in** value specifies that the file is capable of input. The **ios::out** value specifies that the file is capable of output. However, creating a stream by using **ifstream** implies input, and creating a stream by using **ofstream** implies output, so in these cases, it is unnecessary to supply these values.

Including **ios::nocreate** causes the **open( )** function to fail if the file does not already exist. The **ios::noreplace** value causes the **open( )** function to fail if the file does already exist.

The **ios::trunc** value causes the contents of a preexisting file by the same name to be destroyed, and the file is truncated to zero length.

The value of *access* determines how the file can be accessed. Its default value is **filebuf::openprot** (**filebuf** is a class derived from **streambuf**), which means a normal file. In DOS/Windows environments, the *access* value generally corresponds to the DOS/Windows file attribute codes. For other operating systems, check your compiler user manual for the valid values of *access*.

13

The following fragment opens a normal output file in a DOS/Windows environment:

```
ofstream out;
out.open("test", ios::out, 0);
```

However, you will seldom (if ever) see **open( )** called as shown because both the *mode* and *access* parameters have default values. For **ifstream**, *mode* is **ios::in**, and for **ofstream**, it is **ios::out**. By default, *access* has a value that creates a normal file. Therefore, the preceding statement will usually look like this:

```
out.open("test");   // defaults to output and normal file
```

To open a stream for input and output, you must specify both the **ios::in** and the **ios::out** *mode* values, as shown in this example. (No default value for *mode* is supplied for this situation.)

```
fstream mystream;
mystream.open("test", ios::in | ios::out);
```

If **open( )** fails, the stream will be zero. Therefore, before using a file, you should test to make sure the open operation succeeded by using a statement like this:

```
if(!mystream) {
  cout << "Cannot open file\n";
  // handle error
}
```

Although it is entirely proper to open a file by using the **open( )** function, most of the time you will not do so because the **ifstream**, **ofstream**, and **fstream** classes have constructor functions that automatically open the file. The constructor functions have the same parameters and defaults as the **open( )** function. Therefore, the most common way you will see a file opened is shown in this example:

```
ifstream  mystream("myfile"); // open file for input
```

As stated, if for some reason the file cannot be opened, the value of the associated stream variable will be zero. Therefore, whether you use a constructor function to open the file or an explicit call to **open( )**, you will want to confirm that the file has actually been opened by testing the value of the stream.

To close a file, use the member function **close( )**. For example, to close the file linked to a stream called **mystream**, use this statement:

```
mystream.close();
```

The **close( )** function takes no parameters and returns no value.

Once a file has been opened, it is very easy to read textual data from it or write formatted, textual data to it. Simply use the **<<** and **>>** operators the same way you do when performing console I/O, except that instead of using **cin** and **cout**, you substitute a stream that is linked to a file. All information is stored in the file in the same format as it would be if displayed on the screen. Therefore, a file produced by using **<<** is a formatted text file and any file read by **>>** must be a formatted text file.

Here is a program that creates an output file, writes information to it, closes the file and opens it again as an input file, and reads in the information:

```
#include <iostream.h>
#include <fstream.h>

main()
```

```
{
  ofstream fout("test");   // create normal output file

  if(!fout) {
    cout << "Cannot open output file.\n";
    return 1;
  }

  fout << "Hello!\n";
  fout << 100 << ' ' << hex << 100 << endl;

  fout.close();

  ifstream fin("test"); // open normal input file

  if(!fin) {
    cout << "Cannot open input file.\n";
    return 1;
  }

  char str[80];
  int i;

  fin >> str >> i;
  cout << str << ' ' << i << endl;

  fin.close();

  return 0;
}
```

13

After you run this program, examine the contents of **test**. It will contain the following:

```
Hello!
100 64
```

As stated, when using the << and >> operators to perform file I/O, information is formatted exactly as it would appear on the screen.

You can detect when the end of an input file has been reached by using the **eof( )** member function. It has this prototype:

    bool eof( );

It returns **true** (nonzero) when the end of the file has been encountered and **false** (zero) otherwise.

The following program copies a text file and, in the process, converts all spaces into ¦ symbols. Notice how **eof( )** is used to check for the end of the input file. Notice also how the input stream **fin** has its **skipws** turned off. This prevents leading spaces from being skipped.

```
// Convert spaces to ¦s.
#include <iostream.h>
#include <fstream.h>

main(int argc, char *argv[])
{
  if(argc!=3) {
    cout << "Usage: CONVERT <input> <output>\n";
    return 1;
  }

  ifstream fin(argv[1]); // open input file
  ofstream fout(argv[2]);  // create output file
  if(!fout) {
    cout << "Cannot open output file.\n";
    return 1;
  }
  if(!fin) {
    cout << "Cannot open input file.\n";
    return 1;
  }

  char ch;

  fin.unsetf(ios::skipws);  // do not skip spaces
  while(!fin.eof()) {
    fin >> ch;
    if(ch==' ') ch = '¦';
    fout << ch;
  }

  return 0;
}
```

Unformatted, Binary I/O

Although formatted text files like those produced by the preceding examples are useful in a variety of situations, they do not have the flexibility of unformatted, binary files. For this reason, C++ supports a wide range of binary (or "raw") file I/O functions.

The lowest level binary I/O functions are **get( )** and **put( )**. You may write a byte by using the member function **put( )** and read a byte by using the member function **get( )**. The **get( )** function has many forms, but the most commonly used version is shown here along with **put( )**:

    istream &get(char &*ch*);
    ostream &put(char *ch*);

The **get( )** function reads a single character from the associated stream and puts that value in *ch*. It returns a reference to the stream which will be null if **EOF** is encountered. The **put( )** function writes *ch* to the stream and returns the stream.

Note: If you will be performing binary operations on a file, be sure to open it using the **ios::binary** mode specifier. Although the binary file functions will work on files opened for text mode, some character translations may occur. Character translations negate the purpose of binary file operations.

13

The following program will display the contents of any file on the screen. It uses the **get( )** function.

```
#include <iostream.h>
#include <fstream.h>

main(int argc, char *argv[])
{
  char ch;

  if(argc!=2) {
    cout << "Usage: PR <filename>\n";
    return 1;
  }
  ifstream in(argv[1], ios::in | ios::binary);
  if(!in) {
    cout << "Cannot open file.\n";
    return 1;
  }

  while(!in.eof()) {
    in.get(ch);
    cout << ch;
  }
```

```
  return 0;
}
```

This program uses **put( )** to write characters to a file until the user enters a period:

```
#include <iostream.h>
#include <fstream.h>

main(int argc, char *argv[])
{
  char ch;

  if(argc!=2) {
    cout << "Usage: WRITE <filename>\n";
    return 1;
  }

  ofstream out(argv[1], ios::out | ios::binary);
  if(!out) {
    cout << "Cannot open file";
    return 1;
  }

  cout << "Enter a period to stop\n";
  do {
    cout << ": ";
    cin.get(ch);
    out.put(ch);
  } while (ch!='.');

  out.close();

  return 0;
}
```

Notice that the program uses **get( )** to read characters from **cin**. This is necessary because using **>>** causes leading whitespace to be skipped. However, **get( )** does not discard spaces.

To read and write blocks of binary data, use C++'s **read( )** and **write( )** functions. Their prototypes are shown here:

>   istream &read(unsigned char *buf, int num);
>   ostream &write(const unsigned char *buf, int num);

The **read( )** function reads *num* bytes from the associated stream and puts them in the buffer pointed to by *buf*. The **write( )** function writes *num* bytes to the associated stream from the buffer pointed to by *buf*.

If the end of the file is reached before *num* characters have been read, **read( )** simply stops, and the buffer contains as many characters as were available. You can find out how many characters have been read by using another member function, called **gcount( )**, that has this prototype:

    int gcount();

It returns the number of characters read by the last binary input operation.

Here is a program that uses **write( )** to write a **double** and a string to a file called **test**:

```
#include <iostream.h>
#include <fstream.h>
#include <string.h>

main()
{
  ofstream out("test", ios::out | ios::binary);
  if(!out) {
    cout << "Cannot open output file.\n";
    return 1;
  }

  double num = 100.45;
  char str[] = "This is a test";

  out.write((char *) &num, sizeof(double));
  out.write(str, strlen(str));

  out.close();

  return 0;
}
```

13

The type cast to **(char *)** inside the call to **write( )** is necessary when outputting a buffer that is not defined as a character array. Because of C++'s strong type checking, a pointer of one type will not automatically be converted into a pointer of another type.

This program uses **read( )** to read the file created by the preceding program.

```
#include <iostream.h>
#include <fstream.h>

main()
{
  ifstream in("test", ios::in | ios::binary);
  if(!in) {
    cout << "Cannot open input file.\n";
    return 1;
  }

  double num;
  char str[80];

  in.read((char *) &num, sizeof(double));
  in.read(str, 15);

  cout << num << ' ' << str;

  in.close();

  return 0;
}
```

As is the case with the program in the preceding example, the type cast inside **read( )** is necessary because C++ will not automatically convert a pointer of one type to another.

More Binary I/O Functions

In addition to the form shown earlier, the **get( )** function is overloaded several different ways. The prototype for the two most commonly used overloaded forms is shown here:

istream &get(char *buf, int *num*, char *delim*='\n');
int get( );

The first overloaded form reads characters into the array pointed to by *buf* until either *num* characters have been read or the character specified by *delim* has been encountered. The array pointed to by *buf* will be null terminated by **get( )**. If no *delim* parameter is specified, by default a newline character acts as a delimiter. If the delimiter character is encountered in the input stream, it is *not* extracted. Instead, it remains in the stream until the next input operation. The second overloaded form of **get( )** returns the next character from the stream. It returns **EOF** if the end of the file is encountered.

Another member function that performs input is **getline( )**. Its prototype is shown here:

   istream &getline(char *buf, int *num*, char *delim*='\n');

As you can see, this function is virtually identical to the **get(buf, num, delim)** version of **get( )**. It reads characters from input and puts them into the array pointed to by *buf* until either *num* characters have been read or until the character specified by *delim* is encountered. If not specified, *delim* defaults to the newline character. The array pointed to by *buf* is null terminated. The difference between **get(buf, num, delim)** and **getline( )** is that **getline( )** reads and removes the delimiter from the input stream.

As you know, when you use **>>** to read a string, it stops reading when the first whitespace character is encountered. This makes it useless for reading a string containing spaces. However, you can overcome this problem by using **getline( )**, as this program illustrates:

```
// Use getline() to read a string that contains spaces.
#include <iostream.h>
#include <fstream.h>

main()
{
  char str[80];

  cout << "Enter your name: ";
  cin.getline(str, 79);

  cout << str << '\n';

  return 0;
}
```

13

In this case, the final parameter to **getline( )** is allowed to default to a newline. This makes **getline( )** act much like the standard **gets( )** function.

You can obtain the next character in the input stream without removing it from that stream by using **peek( )**. It has this prototype:

   int peek( );

It returns the next character in the stream or **EOF** if the end of the file is encountered.

You can return the last character read from a stream to that stream by using **putback( )**. Its prototype is shown here:

istream &putback(char *c*);

where *c* is the last character read.

When output is performed, data is not immediately written to the physical device linked to the stream. Instead, information is stored in an internal buffer until the buffer is full. Only then are the contents of that buffer written to disk. However, you can force the information to be physically written to disk before the buffer is full by calling **flush( )**. Its prototype is shown here:

ostream &flush( );

Calls to **flush( )** might be warranted when a program is going to be used in adverse environments (in situations where power outages occur frequently, for example).

Random Access

In C++'s I/O system, you perform random access by using the **seekg( )** and **seekp( )** functions. Their most common forms are shown here:

istream &seekg(streamoff *offset*, seek_dir *origin*);
ostream &seekp(streamoff *offset*, seek_dir *origin*);

Here, **streamoff** is a type defined in IOSTREAM.H that is capable of containing the largest valid value that *offset* can have. Also, **seek_dir** is an enumeration that has these values:

Value	Meaning
ios::beg	seek from beginning
ios::cur	seek from current location
ios::end	seek from end

The C++ I/O system manages two pointers associated with a file. One is the *get pointer,* which specifies where in the file the next input operation will occur. The other is the *put pointer,* which specifies where in the file the next output operation will occur. Each time an input or output operation takes place, the appropriate pointer is automatically sequentially advanced. However, by using the **seekg( )** and **seekp( )** functions, it is possible to access the file in a nonsequential fashion.

The **seekg( )** function moves the associated file's current get pointer *offset* number of bytes from the specified *origin*. The **seekp( )** function moves the associated file's current put pointer *offset* number of bytes from the specified *origin*.

This program uses **seekg( )** to position the get pointer into the middle of a file and then displays the contents of that file from that point. The name of the file and the location to begin reading from are specified on the command line.

```
// Demonstrate seekg().
#include <iostream.h>
#include <fstream.h>
#include <stdlib.h>

main(int argc, char *argv[])
{
  char ch;

  if(argc!=3) {
    cout << "Usage: LOCATE <filename> <loc>\n";
    return 1;
  }

  ifstream in(argv[1]);
  if(!in) {
    cout << "Cannot open input file.\n";
    return 1;
  }

  in.seekg(atoi(argv[2]), ios::beg);

  while(!in.eof()) {
    in.get(ch);
    cout << ch;
  }

  in.close();

  return 0;
}
```

13

You can determine the current position of each file pointer by using these functions:

> streampos tellg( );
> streampos tellp( );

Here, **streampos** is a type defined in IOSTREAM.H that is capable of holding the largest value that either function can return. The return values

of these functions can be used as arguments to the following versions of
seekg( ) and **seekp( ).**

```
istream &seekg(streampos pos);
ostream &seekp(streampos pos);
```

FAST TRACK TIP

Checking the I /O Status

The C++ I/O system maintains status information about the outcome of
each I/O operation. The current state of the I/O system is held in an
integer, in which the following flags are encoded:

Name	Meaning
eofbit	1 when end of file is encountered, 0 otherwise
failbit	1 when a nonfatal I/O error has occurred, 0 otherwise
badbit	1 when a fatal I/O error has occurred, 0 otherwise

These flags are enumerated inside **ios**. Also defined in **ios** is **goodbit**,
which has the value zero.

There are two ways in which you can obtain I/O status information. First,
you can call the **rdstate( )** member function. It has this prototype:

```
iostate rdstate( );
```

It returns the current status of the error flags encoded into an integer.
(**iostate** is a **typedef** for some variety of integer.) As you can probably
guess from looking at the preceding list of flags, **rdstate( )** returns zero
when no error has occurred. Otherwise, an error bit is turned on.

The other way you can determine if an error has occurred is by using one or
more of these functions:

```
bool bad( );
bool eof( );
bool fail( );
bool good( );
```

The **eof( )** function was discussed earlier. The **bad( )** function returns
true if **badbit** is set. The **fail( )** function returns **true** if **failbit** is set.
The **good( )** function returns **true** if there are no errors. Otherwise they
return **false**.

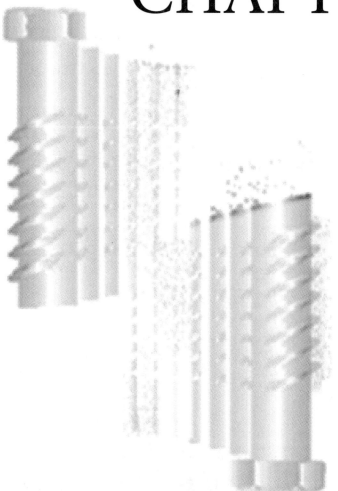

CHAPTER 14

Inheritance and Virtual Functions

You were introduced to the concept of inheritance earlier in this book. Now it is time to explore it more thoroughly. Inheritance is one of the three principles of OOP and, as such, it is an important feature of C++. In C++, inheritance not only supports the concept of hierarchical classification, it also provides support for polymorphism through the creation of virtual functions. Both of these topics are covered in this chapter.

Base Class Access Control

When one class inherits another, it uses this general form:

```
class derived-class-name : access base-class-name {
  // ...
}
```

Here, *access* is one of three keywords: **public, private,** or **protected**. A discussion of the **protected** access specifier is deferred until later in this chapter. The other two are discussed here.

The access specifier determines how elements of the base class are inherited by the derived class. When the access specifier for the inherited base class is **public**, all public members of the base become public members of the derived class. If the access specifier is **private**, all public members of the base class become private members of the derived class. In either case, any private members of the base remain private to it and are inaccessible by the derived class.

It is important to understand that if the access specifier is **private**, then public members of the base become private members of the derived class, but these members are still accessible by member functions of the derived class.

Here is a short base class and a derived class that inherits it (as public):

```
#include <iostream.h>

class base {
  int x;
public:
  void setx(int n) { x = n; }
  void showx() { cout << x << '\n'; }
};

// Inherit as public.
class derived : public base {
  int y;
public:
  void sety(int n) { y = n; }
  void showy() { cout << y << '\n'; }
};

main()
{
  derived ob;
```

```
  ob.setx(10); // access member of base class
  ob.sety(20); // access member of derived class

  ob.showx(); // access member of base class
  ob.showy(); // access member of derived class

  return 0;
}
```

As this program illustrates, because **base** is inherited as public, the public members of **base**—**setx( )** and **showx( )**—become public members of **derived** and are, therefore, accessible by any other part of the program. Specifically, they are legally called within **main( )**.

Here, the same program inherits **base** as private. This change causes the program to be in error, as indicated in the comments.

```
// This program contains an error.
#include <iostream.h>

class base {
  int x;
public:
  void setx(int n) { x = n; }
  void showx() { cout << x << '\n'; }
};

// Inherit base as private.
class derived : private base {
  int y;
public:
  void sety(int n) { y = n; }
  void showy() { cout << y << '\n'; }
};

main()
{
  derived ob;

  ob.setx(10); // ERROR - now private to derived class
  ob.sety(20); // access member of derived class - OK

  ob.showx(); // ERROR - now private to derived class
  ob.showy(); // access member of derived class - OK

  return 0;
}
```

14

As the comments in this (incorrect) program illustrate, both **showx( )** and **setx( )** become private to **derived** and are not accessible outside of it.

It is important to understand that **showx( )** and **setx( )** are still public within **base** no matter how they are inherited by some derived class. This means that an object of type **base** could access these functions anywhere. For example, given this fragment:

```
base base_ob;

base_ob.setx(1); // is legal because base_ob is of type base
```

the call to **setx( )** is legal because **setx( )** is public within **base**. However, relative to objects of type **derived**, **setx( )** is private.

As stated, even though public members of a base class become private members of a derived class when inherited using the **private** specifier, they are still accessible *within* the derived class.

Using protected

As you know from the preceding section, a derived class does not have access to the private members of the base class. This means that if the derived class needs access to some member of the base, then that member must be public. However, there will be times when you want to keep a member of a base class private but still allow a derived class access to it. To accomplish this goal, C++ includes the **protected** access specifier.

The **protected** access specifier is equivalent to the **private** specifier with the sole exception that protected members of a base class are accessible to members of any class derived from that base. Outside the base or derived classes, protected members are not accessible.

The **protected** access specifier may occur anywhere in the class declaration, although typically it occurs after the (default) private members are declared and before the public members. The full general form of a class declaration is shown here:

```
class class-name {
  // private members
protected: // optional
  // protected members
public:
  // public members
};
```

When a protected member of a base class is inherited as **public** by the derived class, it becomes a protected member of the derived class. If the base is inherited as **private**, then a protected member of the base becomes a private member of the derived class.

A base class may also be inherited as **protected** by a derived class. When this is the case, public and protected members of the base class become protected members of the derived class. (Of course, private members of the base class remain private to it and are not accessible by the derived class.)

This program illustrates how public, private, and protected members of a class may be accessed:

```
#include <iostream.h>

class samp {
  // private by default
  int a;
protected: // still private relative to samp
  int b;
public:
  int c;

  samp(int n, int m) { a = n; b = m; }
  int geta() { return a; }
  int getb() { return b; }
};

main()
{
  samp ob(10, 20);

  // ob.b = 99;  Error! b is protected and thus private
  ob.c = 30; // OK, c is public

  cout << ob.geta() << ' ';
  cout << ob.getb() << ' ' << ob.c << '\n';

  return 0;
}
```

14

As you can see, the commented-out line is not permissible in **main( )** because **b** is protected and is thus still private to **samp**.

The following program illustrates what occurs when protected members are inherited as public:

```
#include <iostream.h>

class base {
protected:  // private to base
  int a, b; // but still accessible by derived
public:
  void setab(int n, int m) { a = n; b = m; }
};

class derived : public base {
  int c;
public:
  void setc(int n) { c = n; }

  // this function has access to a and b from base
  void showabc() {
    cout << a << ' ' << b << ' ' << c << '\n';
  }
};

main()
{
  derived ob;

  /* a and b are not accessible here because they are
     private to both base and derived. */
  ob.setab(1, 2);
  ob.setc(3);

  ob.showabc();

  return 0;
}
```

Because **a** and **b** are protected in **base** and inherited as public by **derived**, they are available for use by member functions of **derived**. However, outside of these two classes, **a** and **b** are effectively private and inaccessible.

As mentioned, when a base class is inherited as **protected**, public and protected members of the base class become protected members of the derived class. For example, in the preceding program, if **base** is inherited as **protected** instead of **public,** then **setab( )** becomes a protected member of **derived** and no longer accessible within **main( )**.

Constructors, Destructors, and Inheritance

It is possible for the base class, the derived class, or both to have constructor and/or destructor functions. Several issues that relate to these situations are examined in this section.

When Constructors and Destructors Are Executed

When a base and derived class both have constructor and destructor functions, the constructor functions are executed in order of derivation. The destructor functions are executed in reverse order. That is, the base class constructor is executed before the constructor in the derived class. The reverse is true for destructor functions: the derived class's destructor is executed before the base class's destructor.

If you think about it, it makes sense that constructor functions are executed in order of derivation. Because a base class has no knowledge of any derived class, any initialization it performs is separate from and possibly prerequisite to any initialization performed by the derived class. Therefore, it must be executed first.

On the other hand, a derived class's destructor must be executed before the destructor of the base class because the base class underlies the derived class. If the base class's destructor were executed first, it would imply the destruction of the derived class. Thus, the derived class's destructor must be called before the object goes out of existence.

14

Here is a short program that illustrates when base class and derived class constructor and destructor functions are executed:

```
#include <iostream.h>

class base {
public:
  base() { cout << "Constructing base class\n"; }
  ~base() { cout << "Destructing base class\n"; }
};

class derived : public base {
public:
  derived() { cout << "Constructing derived class\n"; }
  ~derived() { cout << "Destructing derived class\n"; }
};
```

```
main()
{
  derived o;

  return 0;
}
```

This program displays the following output:

```
Constructing base class
Constructing derived class
Destructing derived class
Destructing base class
```

As you can see, the constructors are executed in order of derivation and the destructors are executed in reverse order.

Passing Arguments to Base Class Constructors

So far, none of the preceding examples have passed arguments to either a derived or base class constructor. However, it is possible to do this. When only the derived class takes an initialization, arguments are passed to the derived class's constructor in the normal fashion. However, if you need to pass an argument to the constructor of the base class, a little more effort is needed. To accomplish this, a chain of argument passing is established. First, all arguments necessary to both the base and derived class are passed to the derived class's constructor. Using an expanded form of the derived class's constructor declaration, the appropriate arguments are then passed along to the base class. The syntax for passing along an argument from the derived to the base class is shown here:

```
derived-constructor(arg-list) : base(arg-list) {
  // body of derived class constructor
}
```

It is permissible for both the derived class and the base class to use the same argument. It is also possible for the derived class to ignore all arguments and just pass them along to the base.

In the following example, both the derived class and the base class constructor take an argument. In this specific case, both use the same argument, and the derived class simply passes it along to the base.

```
#include <iostream.h>

class base {
```

```
    int i;
public:
  base(int n) {
    cout << "Constructing base class\n";
    i = n;
  }
  ~base() { cout << "Destructing base class\n"; }
  void showi() { cout << i << '\n'; }
};

class derived : public base {
  int j;
public:
  derived(int n) : base(n) { // pass arg to base class
    cout << "Constructing derived class\n";
    j = n;
  }
  ~derived() { cout << "Destructing derived class\n"; }
  void showj() { cout << j << '\n'; }
};

main()
{
  derived o(10);

  o.showi();
  o.showj();

  return 0;
}
```

Pay special attention to the declaration of **derived**'s constructor. Notice how the parameter **n** (which receives the initialization argument) is both used by **derived( )** and passed to **base( ).**

In most cases, the constructor functions for the base and derived classes will *not* use the same argument. When this is the case and you need to pass one or more arguments to each, you must pass to the derived class's constructor *all* arguments needed by *both* the derived class and the base class. Then, the derived class simply passes along to the base those arguments required by it. Also, it is not necessary for the derived class's constructor to actually use an argument in order to pass one to the base class. If the derived class does not need an argument, it is free to ignore it. For example, in this fragment, parameter **n** is not used by **derived( ).** Instead, it is simply passed to **base( ):**

```
class base {
  int i;
```

```
public:
  base(int n) {
    cout << "Constructing base class\n";
    i = n;
  }
  ~base() { cout << "Destructing base class\n"; }
  void showi() { cout << i << '\n'; }
};

class derived : public base {
  int j;
public:
  derived(int n) : base(n) { // pass arg to base class
    cout << "Constructing derived class\n";
    j = 0; // n not used here
  }
  ~derived() { cout << "Destructing derived class\n"; }
  void showj() { cout << j << '\n'; }
};
```

Multiple Inheritance

There are two ways that a derived class may inherit more than one base class. First, a derived class may be used as a base class for another derived class, creating a multilevel class hierarchy. In this case, the original base class is said to be an *indirect* base class of the second derived class. Second, a derived class may directly inherit more than one base class. In this situation, two or more base classes are combined to help create the derived class. There are several issues that arise when multiple base classes are involved, and these issues are examined in this section.

Class Hierarchies

In a class hierarchy, constructors are called in order of derivation and destructors are called in reverse order. This is a generalization of the principle you learned earlier in this chapter. Thus, if class *B1* is inherited by *D1*, and *D1* is inherited by *D2*, then *B1*'s constructor is called first, followed by *D1*'s, followed by *D2*'s. The destructors are called in reverse order.

When a derived class inherits a hierarchy of classes, each derived class in the chain must pass back to its preceding base any arguments it needs. Here is an example of a derived class that inherits a class derived from another class. Notice how arguments are passed along the chain from **D2** to **B1**.

```
// Multiple Inheritance using a class hierarchy.
#include <iostream.h>

class B1 {
  int a;
public:
  B1(int x) { a = x; }
  int geta() { return a; }
};

// Inherit direct base class.
class D1 : public B1 {
  int b;
public:
  D1(int x, int y) : B1(y) // pass y to B1
  {
    b = x;
  }
  int getb() { return b; }
};

// Inherit a derived class and an indirect base.
class D2 : public D1 {
  int c;
public:
  D2(int x, int y, int z) : D1(y, z) // pass args to D1
  {
    c = x;
  }

  /* Because bases inherited as public, D2 has access
     to public elements of both B1 and D1. */
  void show() {
    cout << geta() << ' ' << getb() << ' ';
    cout << c << '\n';
  }
};

main()
{
  D2 ob(1, 2, 3);

  ob.show();
  // geta() and getb() are still public here
  cout << ob.geta() << ' ' << ob.getb() << '\n';
```

14

```
   return 0;
}
```

The call to **ob.show( )** displays **3 2 1**. In this example, **B1** is an indirect base class of **D2**. Notice that **D2** has access to the public members of both **D1** and **B1**. As you should remember, when public members of a base class are inherited, they become public members of a derived class. Therefore, when **D1** inherited **B1**, **geta( )** became a public member of **D1**, which became a public member of **D2**.

As the program illustrates, each class in a class hierarchy must pass all arguments required by each preceding base class. Failure to do so will generate a compile-time error. The class hierarchy created in this program is illustrated here:

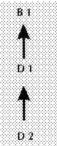

Understanding C++ Inheritance Graphs

C++ class hierarchies are often depicted graphically to aid in their understanding. However, due to a quirk in the way they are usually drawn by C++ programmers, class inheritance graphs are sometimes misleading to newcomers. For example, consider a situation in which class A is inherited by B, which in turn is inherited by C. Using standard C++ graph notation, this situation is drawn like this:

As you can see, the arrows point up, not down. While most people initially find the direction of the arrows to be counterintuitive, it is the style that most C++ programmers have adopted. In C++-style graphs, the arrow points to the base class. Thus, the arrow means "derived from," and not "deriving." While the direction of the arrows may be confusing at first, it is best to become familiar with it since it is commonly used in books, magazines, and users manuals.

Multiple Base Classes

When a derived class directly inherits multiple base classes, it uses this expanded declaration:

```
class derived-class-name : access base1,
                           access base2,
                           ...,
                           access baseN
{
  // ... body of class
}
```

Here, *base1* through *baseN* are the base class names and *access* is the access specifier, which may be different for each base class. When multiple base classes are inherited, constructors are executed in the order, left to right, that the base classes are specified. Destructors are executed in the opposite order.

When a class inherits multiple base classes that have constructors that require arguments, the derived class passes the necessary arguments to them by using this expanded form of the derived class's constructor function:

```
derived-constructor(arg-list) : base1(arg-list),
                                base2(arg-list),
                                ...,
                                baseN(arg-list)
{
  // body of derived class constructor
}
```

Here, *base1* through *baseN* are the names of the base classes.

Here is a reworked version of the preceding program in which a derived class directly inherits two base classes:

14

```
// Inherit multiple base classes.
#include <iostream.h>
// Create first base class.
class B1 {
  int a;
public:
  B1(int x) { a = x; }
  int geta() { return a; }
};

// Create second base class.
class B2 {
  int b;
public:
  B2(int x)
  {
    b = x;
  }
  int getb() { return b; }
};

// Directly inherit two base classes.
class D : public B1, public B2 {
  int c;
public:
  // here, z and y are passed directly to B1 and B2
  D(int x, int y, int z) : B1(z), B2(y)
  {
    c = x;
  }

  /* Because bases inherited as public, D has access
     to public elements of both B1 and B2. */
  void show() {
    cout << geta() << ' ' << getb() << ' ';
    cout << c << '\n';
  }
};

main()
{
  D ob(1, 2, 3);

  ob.show();

  return 0;
}
```

In this version, the arguments to **B1** and **B2** are passed individually to these classes by **D**. This program creates a class that looks like this:

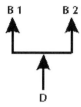

Virtual Base Classes

A potential problem exists when multiple base classes are directly inherited by a derived class. To understand what this problem is, consider the following class hierarchy:

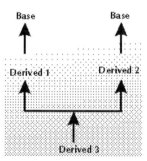

Here, the base class *Base* is inherited by both *Derived1* and *Derived2*. *Derived3* directly inherits both *Derived1* and *Derived2*. However, this implies that *Base* is actually inherited twice by *Derived3*—first, it is inherited through *Derived1*, and second, through *Derived2*. This causes ambiguity when a member of *Base* is referenced by *Derived3*. Since two copies of *Base* are included in *Derived3*, is a reference to a member of *Base* referring to the *Base* inherited indirectly through *Derived1* or to the *Base* inherited indirectly through *Derived2*? To resolve this ambiguity, C++ includes a mechanism by which only one copy of *Base* will be included in *Derived3*. This feature is called a *virtual base class*.

In situations like those just described in which a derived class indirectly inherits the same base class more than once, it is possible to prevent two copies of the base from being present in the derived object by having that base class inherited as **virtual** by any derived classes. Doing this prevents two (or more) copies of the base from being present in any subsequent derived class that inherits the base class indirectly. The **virtual** keyword precedes the base class access specifier when it is inherited by a derived class.

14

Here is an example that uses a virtual base class to prevent two copies of
base from being present in **derived3**.

```cpp
// This program uses a virtual base class.
#include <iostream.h>

class base {
public:
  int i;
};

// Inherit base as virtual.
class derived1 : virtual public base {
public:
  int j;
};

// Inherit base as virtual, here too.
class derived2 : virtual public base {
public:
  int k;
};

/* Here, derived3 inherits both derived1 and derived2.
   However, only one copy of base is present.
*/
class derived3 : public derived1, public derived2 {
public:
  int product() { return i * j * k; }
};

main()
{
  derived3 ob;

  ob.i = 10; // unambiguous because only one copy present
  ob.j = 3;
  ob.k = 5;

  cout << "Product is " << ob.product() << '\n';

  return 0;
}
```

If **derived1** and **derived2** had not inherited **base** as **virtual**, then the
statement

```
ob.i = 10;
```

would have been ambiguous and a compile-time error would have resulted. (You might want to try this on your own.)

It is important to understand that when a base class is inherited as virtual by a derived class, that base class still exists within that derived class. For example, assuming the preceding program, this fragment is perfectly valid:

```
derived1 ob;
ob.i = 100;
```

The only difference between a normal base class and a virtual one occurs when an object inherits the base more than once. If virtual base classes are used, then only one base class is present in the object. Otherwise, multiple copies will be found.

Pointers to Derived Classes

Although Chapter 5 discussed C++ pointers at some length, one special aspect was deferred until now because it relates specifically to inheritance and (as you will soon see) virtual functions. The feature is this: a pointer declared as a pointer to a base class can also be used to point to any class derived from that base. For example, assume two classes called **base** and **derived**, where **derived** inherits **base**. Given this situation, the following statements are correct:

```
base *p; // base class pointer

base base_ob; // object of type base
derived derived_ob; // object of type derived

// p can, of course, point to base objects
p = &base_ob; // p points to base object

// p can also point to derived objects without error
p = &derived_ob; // p points to derived object
```

14

As the comments suggest, a base pointer can point to an object of any class derived from that base without generating a type mismatch error. As you know, normally a pointer can only point to an object of the pointer's base type. Using a base pointer to point to a derived object is an exception to this rule.

Although you can use a base pointer to point to a derived object, you can access only those members of the derived object that were inherited from the base. This is because the base pointer has knowledge only of the base class. It knows nothing about the members added by the derived class.

While it is permissible for a base pointer to point to a derived object, the reverse is not true. A pointer of the derived type cannot be used to access an object of the base class. (A type cast can be used to overcome this restriction, but its use is not recommended practice.)

One final point: remember that pointer arithmetic is relative to the base type of the pointer. Thus, if you point a base pointer to a derived object and then increment that pointer, it will not be pointing to the next derived object. It will be pointing to (what it thinks is) the next base object. Be careful about this.

Virtual Functions

The remainder of this chapter examines another important aspect of C++: the virtual function. What makes virtual functions important is that they are used to support run-time polymorphism. Polymorphism is supported by C++ in two ways. First, it is supported at compile time, through the use of overloaded operators and functions. Second, it is supported at run time, through the use of virtual functions. As you will learn, run-time polymorphism provides the greatest flexibility.

A *virtual function* is a member function that is declared within a base class and redefined by a derived class. To create a virtual function, precede the function's declaration with the keyword **virtual**. When a class containing a virtual function is inherited, the derived class redefines the virtual function relative to the derived class. In essence, virtual functions implement the "one interface, multiple methods" philosophy that underlies polymorphism. The virtual function within the base class defines the *form* of the *interface* to that function. Each redefinition of the virtual function by a derived class implements its operation as it relates specifically to the derived class. That is, the redefinition creates a *specific method*. When a virtual function is redefined by a derived class, the keyword **virtual** is not needed.

A virtual function can be called just like any other member function. However, what makes a virtual function interesting—and capable of supporting run-time polymorphism—is what happens when a virtual function is called by using a pointer. From the preceding section you know that a base class pointer can be used to point to a derived class object. When a base pointer points to a derived object that contains a virtual function and that virtual function is called through that pointer, the compiler determines which version of that function to call based upon the type of object being pointed to by the pointer. Put differently, it is the *type of the object pointed to* that determines which version of the virtual function will be executed.

Therefore, if two or more different classes are derived from a base class that contains a virtual function, then when different objects are pointed to by a base pointer, different versions of the virtual function are executed. This process is the way that run-time polymorphism is achieved. In fact, a class that contains a virtual function is referred to as a *polymorphic class*.

Here is a short example that demonstrates a virtual function:

```cpp
// A simple example using a virtual function.
#include <iostream.h>

class base {
public:
  int i;
  base(int x) { i = x; }
  virtual void func() // a virtual function
  {
    cout << "Using base version of func(): ";
    cout << i << '\n';
  }
};

class derived1 : public base {
public:
  derived1(int x) : base(x) {}
  void func()
  {
    cout << "Using derived1's version of func(): ";
    cout << i*i << '\n';
  }
};

class derived2 : public base {
public:
  derived2(int x) : base(x) {}
  void func()
  {
    cout << "Using derived2's version of func(): ";
    cout << i+i << '\n';
  }
};

main()
{
  base *p;
  base ob(10);
  derived1 d_ob1(10);
  derived2 d_ob2(10);
```

14

```
  p = &ob;
  p->func(); // use base's func()

  p = &d_ob1;
  p->func(); // use derived1's func()

  p = &d_ob2;
  p->func(); // use derived2's func()

  return 0;
}
```

This program displays the following output:

```
Using base version of func(): 10
Using derived1's version of func(): 100
Using derived2's version of func(): 20
```

As you can see, the example program creates three classes. The **base** class defines the virtual function **func( )**. This class is then inherited by both **derived1** and **derived2**. Each of these classes overrides **func( )** with its individual implementation. Inside **main( )**, the base class pointer **p** is declared along with objects of type **base**, **derived1**, and **derived2**. First, **p** is assigned the address of **ob** (an object of type **base**). When **func( )** is called by using **p**, it is the version in **base** that is used. Next, **p** is assigned the address of **d_ob1** and **func( )** is called again. Because it is the type of the object pointed to that determines which virtual function will be called, this time it is the overridden version in **derived1** that is executed. Finally, **p** is assigned the address of **d_ob2** and **func( )** is called again. This time, it is the version of **func( )** defined inside **derived2** that is executed.

The key points to understand from the preceding example are that the type of the object being pointed to determines which version of an overridden virtual function will be executed when accessed via a base class pointer, and that this decision is made at run time.

The redefinition of a virtual function inside a derived class may, at first, seem somewhat similar to function overloading. However, the two processes are distinctly different. First, an overloaded function must differ in type and/or number of parameters. However, a redefined virtual function must have precisely the same type and number of parameters and the same return type. (In fact, if you change either the number or type of parameters when redefining a virtual function, it simply becomes an overloaded function, and its virtual nature is lost.) Further, virtual functions must be class members. This is not the case for overloaded functions. Also, while destructor functions may be virtual, constructors may not. Because of the differences between overloaded functions and redefined virtual functions, the term *overriding* is used to describe virtual function redefinition.

Virtual functions are hierarchical in order of inheritance. Further, when a derived class does *not* override a virtual function, the version of the function defined within its base class is used. For example, if **derived2** had been defined like this in the preceding program:

```
class derived2 : public base {
public:
  derived2(int x) : base(x) {}
  // derived2 does not override func()
};
```

Then the output displayed by the program would have looked like this:

```
Using base version of func(): 10
Using derived1's version of func(): 100
Using base version of func(): 10
```

In this version, **derived2** does not override **func( )**. When **p** is assigned **d_ob2** and **func( )** is called, **base**'s version is used because it is next up in the class hierarchy. In general, when a derived class does not override a virtual function, the base class's version is used.

Here is a more practical example of how a virtual function can be used. This program creates a generic base class called **area** that holds two dimensions of a figure. It also declares a virtual function called **getarea( )** that, when overridden by derived classes, returns the area of the type of figure defined by the derived class. In this case, the declaration of **getarea( )** inside the base class determines the nature of the interface. The actual implementation is left to the classes that inherit it. In this example, the area of a triangle and a rectangle are computed.

```
// Use virtual function to define interface.
#include <iostream.h>

class area {
  double dim1, dim2; // dimensions of figure
public:
  void setarea(double d1, double d2)
  {
    dim1 = d1;
    dim2 = d2;
  }
```

14

```
  void getdim(double &d1, double &d2)
  {
    d1 = dim1;
    d2 = dim2;
  }
  virtual double getarea()
  {
    cout << "You must override this function\n";
    return 0.0;
  }
};

class rectangle : public area {
public:
  double getarea()
  {
    double d1, d2;

    getdim(d1, d2);
    return d1 * d2;
  }
};

class triangle : public area {
public:
  double getarea()
  {
    double d1, d2;

    getdim(d1, d2);
    return 0.5 * d1 * d2;
  }
};

main()
{
  area *p;
  rectangle r;
  triangle t;

  r.setarea(3.3, 4.5);
  t.setarea(4.0, 5.0);

  p = &r;
  cout << "Rectangle has area: " << p->getarea() << '\n';

  p = &t;
```

```
    cout << "Triangle has area: " << p->getarea() << '\n';

    return 0;
}
```

Notice that the definition of **getarea( )** inside **area** is just a placeholder and performs no real function. Because **area** is not linked to any specific type of figure, there is no meaningful definition that can be given to **getarea( )** inside **area**. In fact, **getarea( )** must be overridden by a derived class in order to be useful. In the next section, you will see a way to enforce this.

Pure Virtual Functions and Abstract Classes

Sometimes when a virtual function is declared in the base class, there is no meaningful operation for it to perform. This situation is common because often a base class does not define a complete class by itself. Instead, it simply supplies a core set of member functions and variables to which the derived class supplies the remainder. When there is no meaningful action for a base class virtual function to perform, the implication is that any derived class *must* override this function. To ensure that this will occur, C++ supports *pure virtual functions*.

A pure virtual function has no definition relative to the base class. Only the function's prototype is included. To make a pure virtual function, use this general form:

> virtual *type func-name(parameter-list)* = 0;

The key part of this declaration is the setting of the function equal to zero. This tells the compiler that no body exists for this function relative to the base class. When a virtual function is made pure, it forces any derived class to override it. If a derived class does not, a compile-time error results. Thus, making a virtual function pure is a way to guarantee that a derived class will provide its own redefinition.

When a class contains at least one pure virtual function, it is referred to as an *abstract class*. Since an abstract class contains at least one function for which no body exists, it is, technically, an incomplete type, and no objects of that class can be created. Thus, abstract classes exist only to be inherited. They are neither intended nor able to stand alone. It is important to understand, however, that you can still create a pointer to an abstract class since it is through the use of base class pointers that run-time polymorphism is achieved. (It is also permissible to have a reference to an abstract class.)

14

Here is an improved version of the **area** class from the program in the preceding section. In this version, the function **getarea( )** is declared as pure in the base class **area**.

```
class area { // this is now an abstract class
  double dim1, dim2; // dimensions of figure
public:
  void setarea(double d1, double d2)
  {
    dim1 = d1;
    dim2 = d2;
  }
  void getdim(double &d1, double &d2)
  {
    d1 = dim1;
    d2 = dim2;
  }
  virtual double getarea() = 0; // pure virtual function
};
```

Now that **getarea( )** is pure, it ensures that each derived class will override it.

Virtuality Is Inherited

When a virtual function is inherited, so is its virtual nature. This means that when a derived class inherits a virtual function from a base class and then the derived class is used as a base for yet another derived class, the virtual function may be overridden by the final derived class (as well as the first derived class). For example, if base class B contains a virtual function called *f( )*, and D1 inherits B and D2 inherits D1, then both D1 and D2 may override *f( )* relative to their respective classes.

Consider the following program.

```
// Virtual functions retain their virtual nature when inherited.
#include <iostream.h>

class base {
public:
  virtual void func() { cout << "func() in base\n"; }
};

class derived1 : public base {
public:
  void func() { cout << "func() in derived1\n"; }
```

```
      };

      // Derived2 inherits derived1.
      class derived2 : public derived1 {
      public:
        void func() { cout << "func() in derived2\n"; }
      };

      main()
      {
        base *p, ob;
        derived1 d_ob1;
        derived2 d_ob2;

        p = &ob;
        p->func(); // use base's func()

        p = &d_ob1;
        p->func(); // use derived1's func()

        p = &d_ob2;
        p->func(); // use derived2's func()

        return 0;
      }
```

In this program, the virtual function **func( )** is first inherited by **derived1**, which overrides it relative to itself. Next, **derived2** inherits **derived1**. In **derived2**, **func( )** is again overridden.

Because virtual functions are hierarchical, if **derived2** did not override **func( )**, then when **d_ob2** was accessed, **derived1**'s **func( )** would have been used. If neither **derived1** nor **derived2** had overridden **func( )**, all references to it would have been routed to the one defined in **base**.

14

Applying Polymorphism

Now that you know how to use a virtual function to achieve run-time polymorphism, it is time to consider when it is appropriate to do so. As has been stated many times in this book, polymorphism is the process by which a common interface is applied to two or more similar (but technically different) situations, thus implementing the "one interface, multiple methods" philosophy. Polymorphism is important because it can greatly simplify complex systems. When a single, well-defined interface is used to access a number of different but related actions, artificial complexity is removed. In essence, polymorphism allows the logical relationship of similar actions to become apparent; thus, the program is easier to understand and maintain. When related actions are accessed through a common interface, you have less to remember.

There are two terms that are often linked to OOP in general and to C++ specifically. They are *early binding* and *late binding*. It is important that you know what they mean. Early binding essentially refers to those events that can be known at compile time. Specifically, it refers to those function calls that can be resolved during compilation. Early bound entities include "normal" functions, overloaded functions, and nonvirtual member and friend functions. When these types of functions are compiled, all address information necessary to call them is known at compile time. The main advantage of early binding (and the reason that it is so widely used) is that it is very efficient. Calls to functions bound at compile time are the fastest types of function calls. The main disadvantage is lack of flexibility.

Late binding refers to events that must occur at run time. A late bound function call is one in which the address of the function is not known until the program runs. In C++, a virtual function is a late bound object. When a virtual function is accessed via a base class pointer, the program must determine at run time what type of object is being pointed to and then select which version of the overridden function to execute. The main advantage of late binding is flexibility at run time. Your program is free to respond to random events without having to contain large amounts of "contingency code." Its primary disadvantage is that there is more overhead associated with a function call. This generally makes such calls slower than those that occur with early binding.

Because of the potential efficiency trade-offs, you must decide when it is appropriate to use early binding and when to use late binding.

CHAPTER 15

Templates and Other Advanced Features

This chapter discusses several of C++'s more advanced features. The two most important of these are templates and exception handling. Using templates, it is possible to create generic functions and classes which can be applied to any type of data. Exception handling is the subsystem of C++ that allows you to handle run-time errors in a structured and controlled manner. Using C++ exception handling, your program can automatically invoke an error-handling routine when an error occurs. The principal advantage of exception handling is that it automates much of the error-handling code that previously had to be coded "by hand" in any large program.

Also discussed in this chapter are array-based I/O, conversion functions, the **asm** keyword, the linkage statement, and new keywords recently added to C++.

Generic Functions

A generic function defines a general set of operations that will be applied to various types of data. A generic function has the type of data that it will operate upon passed to it as a parameter. Using this mechanism, the same general procedure can be applied to a wide range of data. As you know, many algorithms are logically the same no matter what type of data is being used. For example, the Quicksort algorithm is the same whether it is applied to an array of integers or an array of **float**s. It is just that the type of the data being sorted is different. By creating a generic function, you can define, independent of any data, the nature of the algorithm. Once this is done, the compiler automatically generates the correct code for the type of data that is actually used when you execute the function. In essence, when you create a generic function you are creating a function that can automatically overload itself.

A generic function is created using the keyword **template**. The normal meaning of the word "template" accurately reflects its use in C++. It is used to create a template (or framework) which describes what a function will do, leaving it to the compiler to fill in the details, as needed. The general form of a **template** function definition is shown here:

```
template <class Ttype> ret-type func-name(parameter list)
{
  // body of function
}
```

Here, *Ttype* is a placeholder name for a data type used by the function. This name may be used within the function definition. However, it is only a placeholder which the compiler will automatically replace with an actual data type when it creates a specific version of the function.

The following program creates a generic function that swaps the values of the two variables it is called with. Because the general process of exchanging two values is independent of the type of the variables, it is a good choice to be made into a generic function.

```
// Function template example.
#include <iostream.h>

// This is a function template.
template <class X> void swap(X &a, X &b)
```

```
{
  X temp;

  temp = a;
  a = b;
  b = temp;
}

main()
{
  int i=10, j=20;
  float x=10.1, y=23.3;

  cout << "Original i, j: " << i << ' ' << j << endl;
  cout << "Original x, y: " << x << ' ' << y << endl;

  swap(i, j); // swap integers
  swap(x, y); // swap floats

  cout << "Swapped i, j: " << i << ' ' << j << endl;
  cout << "Swapped x, y: " << x << ' ' << y << endl;

  return 0;
}
```

As you can see, the keyword **template** is used to define the generic function called **swap( )**. The line

```
template <class X> void swap(X &a, X &b)
```

15

tells the compiler two things: that a template is being created and that a generic definition is beginning. Here, **X** is a generic type that is used as a placeholder. After the **template** portion, the function **swap( )** is declared, using **X** as the data type of the values that will be swapped. In **main( )**, the **swap( )** function is called using two different types of data: integers and **float**s. Because **swap( )** is a generic function, the compiler automatically creates two versions of **swap( )**—one that will exchange integer values and one that will exchange floating-point values.

There are some other terms that are sometimes used when discussing templates and that you may encounter in other C++ literature. A generic function (that is, a function definition preceded by a **template** statement) is also called a *template function*. When the compiler creates a specific version of this function, it is said to have created a *generated function*. The act of generating a function is referred to as *instantiating* it. Put differently, a generated function is a specific instance of a template function.

You may define more than one generic data type in the **template** statement, using a comma-separated list. For example, this program creates a generic function that has two generic types:

```
#include <iostream.h>

template <class type1, class type2>
void myfunc(type1 x, type2 y)
{
  cout << x << ' ' << y << endl;
}

main()
{
  myfunc(10, "hi");

  myfunc(0.23, 10L);

  return 0;
}
```

In this example, the placeholder types **type1** and **type2** are replaced by the compiler with the data types **int** and **char *** and **double** and **long**, respectively, when the compiler generates the specific instances of **myfunc( )**.

Even though a template function overloads itself as needed, you can explicitly overload one, too. If you overload a generic function, then that overloaded function overrides (or "hides") the generic function relative to that specific version. Manual overloading of a template allows you to specially tailor a version of a generic function to accommodate a special situation. However, in general, if you need to have different versions of a function for different data types, you should use overloaded functions rather than templates.

Generic Classes

In addition to generic functions, you may also define a generic class. When you do this, you create a class that defines all algorithms used by that class, but the actual type of the data being manipulated will be specified as a parameter when objects of that class are created.

Generic classes are useful when a class contains generalizable logic. For example, the same algorithm that maintains a queue of integers will also work for a queue of characters. Also, the same mechanism that maintains a linked list of mailing addresses will also maintain a linked list of auto part information. By using a generic class, you can create a class that will maintain a queue, linked list, and so on for any type of data. The compiler will automatically generate the correct type of object based upon the type you specify when the object is created.

The general form of a generic class declaration is shown here.

```
template <class Ttype> class class-name {
    .
    .
    .
}
```

Here, *Ttype* is the placeholder type name which will be specified when a class is instantiated. If necessary, you may define more than one generic data type using a comma-separated list.

Member functions of a generic class are, themselves, automatically generic. They need not be explicitly specified as such using **template**.

Once you have created a generic class, you create a specific instance of that class using the following general form:

class-name <type> ob;

Here, *type* is the type name of the data that the class will be operating upon.

This program creates a very simple generic singly linked list class. It then demonstrates the class by creating a linked list that stores characters.

15

```cpp
// A simple generic linked list.
#include <iostream.h>

template <class data_t> class list {
  data_t data;
  list *next;
public:
  list(data_t d);
  void add(list *node) {node->next = this; next = 0; }
  list *getnext() { return next; }
  data_t getdata() { return data; }
};

template <class data_t> list<data_t>::list(data_t d)
{
  data = d;
  next = 0;
```

```
    }

main()
{
  list<char> start('a');
  list<char> *p, *last;
  int i;

  // build a list
  last = &start;
  for(i=1; i<26; i++) {
    p = new list<char> ('a' + i);
    p->add(last);
    last = p;
  }

  // follow the list
  p = &start;
  while(p) {
    cout << p->getdata();
    p = p->getnext();
  }

  return 0;
}
```

As you can see, the declaration of a generic class is similar to that of a generic function. The actual type of data stored by the list is generic in the class declaration. It is not until an object of the list is declared that the actual data type is determined. In this example, objects and pointers are created inside **main( )** that specify that the data type of the list will be **char**. Pay special attention to this declaration:

```
list<char> start('a');
```

Notice how the desired data type is passed inside the angle brackets.

You should enter and execute this program. It builds a linked list that contains the characters of the alphabet and then displays them. However, by simply changing the type of data specified when **list** objects are created, you can change the type of data stored by the list. For example, you could create another object that stores integers by using this declaration:

```
list<int> int_start(1);
```

You can also use **list** to store data types that you create.

One last point: A template class can have more than one generic data type. Simply declare all the data types required by the class in a comma-separated list within the **template** specification.

A Generic Stack Class

To catch a glimpse of the power of generic classes, consider the following program which reworks the **stack** class first introduced in Chapter 10. In this case, **stack** has been made into a template class. Thus, it can be used to store any type of object. In the example shown here, a character stack and a floating-point stack are created.

```cpp
// This function demonstrates a generic stack.
#include <iostream.h>

const int SIZE=10;

// Create a generic stack class
template <class StackType> class stack {
  StackType stck[SIZE]; // holds the stack
  int tos; // index of top-of-stack
public:
  stack() { tos = 0; }
  void push(StackType ch); // push object on stack
  StackType pop(); // pop object from stack
};

// Push an object.
template <class StackType>
void stack<StackType>::push(StackType ob)
{
  if(tos==SIZE) {
    cout << "Stack is full.\n";
    return;
  }
  stck[tos] = ob;
  tos++;
}

// Pop an object.
template <class StackType> StackType stack<StackType>::pop()
{
  if(tos==0) {
```

15

```
      cout << "Stack is empty.\n";
      return 0; // return null on empty stack
   }
   tos--;
   return stck[tos];
}
main()
{
   int i;

   // Demonstrate character stacks.
   stack<char> s1, s2;  // create two stacks
   s1.push('a'); s1.push('b'); s1.push('c');
   s2.push('x'); s2.push('y'); s2.push('z');

   for(i=0; i<3; i++) cout << "Pop s1: " << s1.pop() << "\n";
   for(i=0; i<3; i++) cout << "Pop s2: " << s2.pop() << "\n";

   // demonstrate double stacks
   stack<double> ds1, ds2;  // create two stacks
   ds1.push(1.1); ds1.push(3.3); ds1.push(5.5);
   ds2.push(2.2); ds2.push(4.4); ds2.push(6.6);

   for(i=0; i<3; i++) cout << "Pop ds1: " << ds1.pop() << "\n";
   for(i=0; i<3; i++) cout << "Pop ds2: " << ds2.pop() << "\n";

   return 0;
}
```

As the **stack** class illustrates, generic functions and classes provide a
powerful tool that you can use to maximize your programming time
because they allow you to define the general form of an algorithm that can
be used with any type of data. You are saved from the tedium of creating
separate implementations for each data type your program uses.

Exception Handling

C++ provides a built-in error handling mechanism that is called *exception
handling*. Using exception handling, you can more easily manage and
respond to run-time errors. C++ exception handling is built upon three
keywords: **try, catch**, and **throw**. In the most general terms, program
statements that you want to monitor for exceptions are contained in a **try**
block. If an exception (that is, an error) occurs within the **try** block, it is

thrown (using **throw**). The exception is caught, using **catch**, and processed. The following elaborates upon this general description.

As stated, any statement that throws an exception must have been executed from within a **try** block. (Functions called from within a **try** block may also throw an exception.) Any exception must be caught by a **catch** statement that immediately follows the **try** statement that throws the exception. The general forms of **try** and **catch** are shown here.

```
try {
  // try block
}
catch (type1 arg) {
  // catch block
}
catch (type2 arg) {
  // catch block
}
  .
  .
  .
catch (typeN arg) {
  // catch block
}
```

The **try** block must contain that portion of your program that you want to monitor for errors. This can be as short as a few statements within one function or as all-encompassing as enclosing the **main( )** function code within a **try** block (which effectively causes the entire program to be monitored).

When an exception is thrown, it is caught by its corresponding **catch** statement which processes the exception. There can be more than one **catch** statement associated with a **try**. Which **catch** statement is used is determined by the type of the exception. That is, if the data type specified by a **catch** matches that of the exception, then that **catch** statement is executed. (And all others are bypassed.) When an exception is caught, *arg* will receive its value. Any type of data may be caught, including classes that you create.

The general form of the **throw** statement is shown here.

throw *exception*;

15

throw must be executed either from within the **try** block, proper, or from any function called (directly or indirectly from within the **try** block); *exception* is the value thrown.

If you throw an exception for which there is no applicable **catch** statement, an abnormal program termination may occur. Throwing an unhandled exception causes the **terminate( )** function to be invoked. By default, **terminate( )** calls **abort( )** to stop your program, but you can specify your own termination handler, if you like. You will need to refer to your compiler's library reference for details.

Here is a simple example that shows the way C++ exception handling operates.

```cpp
// A simple exception handling example.
#include <iostream.h>

main()
{
  cout << "start\n";

  try { // start a try block
    cout << "Inside try block\n";
    throw 10; // throw an error
    cout << "This will not execute";
  }
  catch (int i) { // catch an error
    cout << "Caught One! Number is: ";
    cout << i << "\n";
  }

  cout << "end";

  return 0;
}
```

This program displays the following output:

```
start
Inside try block
Caught One! Number is: 10
end
```

Look carefully at this program. As you can see, there is a **try** block containing three statements and a **catch(int i)** statement that will process an integer exception. Within the **try** block, only two of the three statements will execute: the first **cout** statement and the **throw**. Once an exception has been thrown, control passes to the **catch** expression and the **try** block is terminated. That is, **catch** is *not* called. Rather, program execution is transferred to it. (The stack is automatically reset as needed to accomplish this.) Thus, the **cout** statement following the **throw** will never execute.

After the **catch** statement executes, program control continues with the statements following the **catch**. However, commonly a **catch** block will end with a call to **exit( )**, **abort( )**, and so on, because often exception handling is used to handle catastrophic errors.

As mentioned, the type of the exception must match the type specified in a **catch** statement. For example, in the preceding example, if you change the type in the **catch** statement to **double**, then the exception will not be caught and abnormal termination will occur.

A **try** block can be localized to a function. When this is the case, each time the function is entered, the exception handling relative to that function is reset. For example, examine this program.

```
#include <iostream.h>

// A try/catch can be inside a function other than main().
void Xhandler(int test)
{
  try{
    if(test) throw test;
  }
  catch(int i) {
    cout << "Caught One!  Ex. #: " << i << '\n';
  }
}

main()
{
  cout << "start\n";

  Xhandler(1);
  Xhandler(2);
  Xhandler(0);
  Xhandler(3);

  cout << "end";

  return 0;
}
```

15

This program displays this output:

```
start
Caught One!  Ex. #: 1
Caught One!  Ex. #: 2
Caught One!  Ex. #: 3
end
```

As you can see, three exceptions are thrown. After each exception, the function returns. When the function is called again, the exception handling is reset.

As stated, you can associate more than one **catch** with a **try**. In fact, it is common to do so. However, each **catch** must catch a different type of exception. For example, this version of **Xhandler( )** catches both integers and strings.

```cpp
// Different types of exceptions can be caught.
void Xhandler(int test)
{
  try{
    if(test) throw test;
    else throw "This is a string.";
  }
  catch(int i) {
    cout << "Caught an integer\n";
  }
  catch(char *str) {
    cout << "Caught a string: ";
    cout << str << "\n";
  }
}
```

In general, **catch** expressions are checked in the order in which they occur in a program. Only a matching statement is executed. All other **catch** blocks are ignored.

More About Exception Handling

There are several additional features and nuances to C++ exception handling that make it easier and more convenient to use.

Catching All Expressions

In some circumstances you will want an exception handler to catch all exceptions instead of just a certain type. This is easy to accomplish. Simply use this form of **catch**.

```
catch(...) {
  // process all exceptions
}
```

Here, the ellipsis matches any type of data. One very good use for **catch(...)** is as the last **catch** of a cluster of catches. In this capacity it provides a useful default or "catch all" statement. Also, by catching all exceptions, you prevent an unhandled exception from causing an abnormal program termination.

Restricting throw Expressions

When a function is called from within a **try** block, you can restrict what type of exceptions that function can throw. In fact, you can also prevent that function from throwing any exceptions whatsoever. To establish these restrictions, you must add a **throw** clause to a function definition. The general form of this is shown here.

```
ret-type func-name(arg-list) throw(type-list)
{
  // ...
}
```

Here, only those data types contained in the comma-separated *type-list* may be thrown by the function. Throwing any other type of expression will cause abnormal program termination. If you don't want a function to be able to throw *any* exceptions, then use an empty list.

Attempting to throw an exception that is not supported by a function will cause the **unexpected( )** function to be called. By default, this causes **abort( )** to be called, which causes abnormal program termination. However, you can specify your own termination handler, if you like. You will need to refer to your compiler's library reference for details.

15

The following fragment shows how to restrict the types of exceptions that can be thrown from a function.

```
// This function can only throw ints, chars, and doubles.
void Xhandler(int test) throw(int, char, double)
{
  if(test==0) throw test; // throw int
  if(test==1) throw 'a'; // throw char
  if(test==2) throw 123.23; // throw double
}
```

Here, the function **Xhandler( )** may only throw integer, character, and **double** exceptions. If it attempts to throw any other type of exception, then an abnormal program termination will occur. (That is, **unexpected( )** will be called.)

It is important to understand that a function can only be restricted in what types of exceptions it throws back to the **try** block that called it. That is, a **try** block *within* a function may throw any type of exception so long as it is caught *within* that function. The restriction applies only when throwing an exception outside of the function.

Rethrowing an Exception

If you wish to rethrow an exception from within an exception handler, you may do so by simply calling **throw**, by itself, with no exception. This causes the current exception to be passed on to an outer **try/catch** sequence. The most likely reason for doing so is to allow multiple handlers access to the exception. For example, perhaps one exception handler manages one aspect of an exception and a second handler copes with another. An exception can only be rethrown from within a **catch** block (or from any function called from within that block). When you rethrow an exception, it will not be recaught by the same **catch** statement. It will propagate outward to the next **catch** statement. The following program illustrates rethrowing an exception. It rethrows a **char *** exception.

```
// Example of "rethrowing" an exception.
#include <iostream.h>

void Xhandler()
{
  try {
    throw "hello"; // throw a char *
  }
  catch(char *) { // catch a char *
    cout << "Caught char * inside Xhandler\n";
    throw ; // rethrow char * out of function
  }
}

main()
{
  cout << "start\n";

  try{
    Xhandler();
  }
  catch(char *) {
    cout << "Caught char * inside main\n";
```

```
  }

  cout << "end";

  return 0;
}
```

Static Class Members

It is possible for a class member variable to be declared as **static**. (It is also possible for a member function to be declared as **static**, but this usage is not common and is not examined here.) By using **static** member variables, a number of rather tricky problems can be bypassed.

In short, when you declare a member variable to be **static**, you cause only one copy of that variable to exist—no matter how many objects of that class are created. Each object simply shares that one variable. Remember, for normal member variables, each time an object is created, new copies of those variables are created and are accessible only by that object. (That is, for normal variables, each object possesses its own copies.) However, there is only one copy of a **static** member variable, and all objects of its class share it. Also, the same static variable will be used by any classes derived from the class that contains the **static** member.

Although it may seem odd when you first think about it, a **static** member variable exists *before* any object of its class is created. In essence, a **static** class member is a global variable that simply has its scope restricted to the class in which it is declared. In fact, it is actually possible to access a **static** member variable independent of any object.

All **static** member variables are initialized to zero by default. However, you can give a **static** class variable an initial value of your choosing, if you like.

When you declare a **static** data member within a class, you are not defining it. Instead, you must provide a definition for it elsewhere, outside the class. To do this, you globally redeclare the **static** variable by using the scope resolution operator to identify which class it belongs to.

Here is a simple example that uses a **static** member variable:

```
// A static member variable example.
#include <iostream.h>
class myclass {
  static int i;
public:
  void seti(int n) { i = n; }
  int geti() { return i; }
```

15

```
};

// Definition of myclass::i. i is still private to myclass.
int myclass::i;

main()
{
  myclass o1, o2;

  o1.seti(10);

  cout << "o1.i: " << o1.geti() << '\n'; // displays 10
  cout << "o2.i: " << o2.geti() << '\n'; // also displays 10

  return 0;
}
```

This program displays the following:

```
o1.i: 10
o2.i: 10
```

Looking at the program, you can see that only object **o1** actually sets the value of **static** member **i**. However, since **i** is shared by both **o1** and **o2** (and, indeed, by any object of type **myclass**), both calls to **geti( )** display the same result.

Notice how **i** is declared within **myclass** but defined outside of the class. This second step ensures that storage for **i** is defined. Technically, a class declaration is just that, only a declaration. No memory is actually set aside because of a declaration. Because a **static** data member *implies* that memory is allocated for that member, a separate definition is required that causes storage to be allocated.

Because a **static** member variable exists before any object of that class is created, it can be accessed within a program independent of any object. For example, the following variation of the preceding program sets the value of **i** to 100 without any reference to a specific object. Notice the use of the scope resolution operator to access **i**.

```
// Reference a static independent of any object.
#include <iostream.h>

class myclass {
public:
  static int i;
  void seti(int n) { i = n; }
```

```
    int geti() { return i; }
};

int myclass::i;

main()
{
  myclass o1, o2;

  // set i directly
  myclass::i = 100; // no object is referenced.

  cout << "o1.i: " << o1.geti() << '\n'; // displays 100
  cout << "o2.i: " << o2.geti() << '\n'; // also displays 100

  return 0;
}
```

Keep in mind that the principal reason **static** member variables are supported by C++ is to prevent the need to use global variables. As you can surmise, classes that rely upon global variables almost always violate the encapsulation principle that is so fundamental to OOP and C++.

Array-Based I/O

In addition to console and file I/O, C++ supports a full set of functions that use character arrays as the input or output device. C++'s array-based I/O parallels, in concept, the array-based I/O found in C (specifically, C's **sscanf( )** and **sprintf( )** functions). However, C++'s array-based I/O is more flexible and useful because it allows user-defined types to be integrated into it. In some C++ literature, array-based I/O is referred to as *incore I/O* or *RAM-based I/O*. This book will continue to use the term "array-based" because it is the most descriptive. While it is not possible to cover every aspect of using array-based I/O here, the most important and commonly used features are examined.

15

It is important to understand from the outset that array-based I/O still operates through streams. Everything you learned about C++ I/O in Chapter 13 is applicable to array-based I/O. In fact, you need to learn to use just a few new functions to take full advantage of array-based I/O. These functions link a stream to a region of memory. Once this has been accomplished, all I/O takes place through the I/O functions you have already learned about.

Before you can use array-based I/O, you must be sure to include the header file STRSTREA.H in your file. In this header are defined the classes **istrstream**, **ostrstream**, and **strstream**. These classes create array-based input, output, and input/output streams, respectively. These classes have as a base **ios**, so all the functions and manipulators included in **istream**, **ostream**, and **iostream** are also available in **istrstream**, **ostrstream**, and **strstream**.

To use a character array for output, use this general form of the **ostrstream** constructor:

ostrstream *ostr*(char **buf*, int *size*, int *mode*=ios::out);

Here, *ostr* will be the stream associated with the array *buf*. The size of the array is specified by *size*. Generally, *mode* is simply defaulted to output, but you can use any output mode flag defined by **ios** if you like.

Once an array has been opened for output, characters will be put into the array until it is full. The array will not be overrun. Any attempt to overfill the array will result in an I/O error. To find out how many characters have been written to the array, use the **pcount( )** member function, shown here:

int pcount( );

You must call this function in conjunction with a stream, and it will return the number of characters written to the array.

To open an array for input, use this form of the **istrstream** constructor:

istrstream *istr*(const char **buf*);

Here, *buf* is a pointer to the array that will be used for input. The input stream will be called *istr*. When reading input from an array, **eof( )** will return true when the end of the array has been reached.

To open an array for input/output operations, use this form of the **strstream** constructor:

strstream *iostr*(char **buf*, int *size*, int *mode*);

Here, *iostr* will be an input/output stream that uses the array pointed to by *buf*, which is *size* characters long. For input/output operations, *mode* should be the value **ios::in | ios::out**.

It is important to remember that all I/O functions described earlier operate with array-based I/O, including the binary I/O functions and the random-access functions.

Here is a short example that shows how to open an array for output and write data to it:

```
// A short example using array-based output.
#include <iostream.h>
#include <strstrea.h>

main()
{
  char buf[255]; // output buffer

  ostrstream ostr(buf, sizeof buf); // open output array

  ostr << "Array-based I/O uses streams just like ";
  ostr << "'normal' I/O\n" << 100;
  ostr << ' ' << 123.23 << '\n';

  // you can use manipulators, too
  ostr << hex << 100 << ' ';
  // or format flags
  ostr.setf(ios::scientific);
  ostr << 123.23 << '\n';
  ostr << ends; // ensure that buffer is null-terminated

  // show resultant string
  cout << buf;

  return 0;
}
```

This program displays

```
Array-based I/O uses streams just like 'normal' I/O
100 123.23
64 01.2323e+02
```

15

As you can see, the overloaded I/O operators, built-in I/O manipulators, member functions, and format flags are fully functional when you use array-based I/O. (This is also true of any manipulators or overloaded I/O operators you create relative to your own classes.)

Here is an example of array-based input:

```
// An example using array-based input.
#include <iostream.h>
#include <strstrea.h>

main()
{
  char buf[] = "Hello 100 123.125 a";
```

```
        istrstream istr(buf); // open input array

        int i;
        char str[80];
        float f;
        char c;

        istr >> str >> i >> f >> c;

        cout << str << ' ' << i << ' ' << f;
        cout << ' ' << c << '\n';
        return 0;
}
```

This program reads and then redisplays the values contained in the input array **buf**.

Linkage Specification and the asm Statement

C++ provides two important mechanisms that make it easier to link C++ to other languages. One is the *linkage specifier,* which tells the compiler that one or more functions in your C++ program will be linked with another language that may have different parameter-passing conventions and the like. The second is the **asm** keyword, which allows you to embed assembly language instructions in your C++ source code. Both are examined here.

By default, all functions in a C++ program are compiled and linked as C++ functions. However, you can tell the C++ compiler to link a function so that it is compatible with another type of language. All C++ compilers allow functions to be linked as either C or C++ functions. Some also allow you to link functions with languages such as Pascal, Ada, or FORTRAN. To cause a function to be linked for a different language, use this general form of the linkage specification:

   extern "*language*" *function-prototype*;

Here, *language* is the name of the language you want the specified function to link to. If you want to specify linkage for more than one function, use this form of the linkage specification:

   extern "*language*" {
     function-prototypes
   }

All linkage specifications must be global; they cannot be used inside a function. Also, although not common, you can specify a linkage specification for objects, too.

For example, this line causes **func( )** to be linked as a C, rather than a C++, function:

```
extern "C" int func(int x); // link as C function
```

Although it is generally possible to link assembly language routines with a C++ program, there is often an easier way to use assembly language. C++ supports the special keyword **asm**, which allows you to embed assembly language instructions within a C++ function. These instructions are then compiled as is. The advantage of using **asm** is that your entire program is completely defined as a C++ program and there is no need to link separate assembly language files. The general form of the **asm** keyword is shown here:

asm (*op-code*);

where *op-code* is the assembly language instruction that will be embedded in your program.

Several C++ compilers accept these three slightly different forms of the **asm** statement:

asm *op-code*;
asm *op-code newline*
asm {
  instruction sequence
}

15

Because embedded assembly language instruction tends to be implementation dependent, you will want to read your compiler's user manual on this issue.

Creating a Conversion Function

Sometimes it is useful to convert an object of one type into an object of another. While it is possible to use an overloaded operator function to accomplish such a conversion, there is often an easier (and better) way, called a conversion function. A *conversion function* converts an object into a value compatible with another type, which is often one of the built-in C++ types. In essence, a conversion function automatically converts an object into a value that is compatible with the type of the expression in which the object is used.

The general form of a conversion function is shown here:

operator *type*() { return *value*; }

Here, *type* is the target type you will be converting to and *value* is the value of the object after the conversion has been performed. Conversion functions return a value of type *type*. No parameters may be specified, and a conversion function must be a member of the class for which it performs the conversion. Conversion functions are inherited and they may be virtual.

A conversion function provides an approach to converting an object's value into another type that is generally cleaner than any other method available in C++ because it allows an object to be included directly in an expression involving the target type.

In the following program, the **coord** class contains a conversion function that converts to integer. In this case, the function returns the product of the two coordinates; however, any conversion appropriate to your specific application is allowed.

```
// A simple conversion function example.
#include <iostream.h>

class coord {
  int x, y;
public:
  coord(int i, int j) { x = i; y = j; }
  operator int() { return x*y; } // conversion function
};

main()
{
  coord o1(2, 3), o2(4, 3);
  int i;

  i = o1;  // automatically convert to integer
  cout << i << '\n';

  i = 100 + o2;  // convert o2 to integer
  cout << i << '\n';

  return 0;
}
```

This program displays **6** and **112**.

In this example, notice that the conversion function is called when **o1** is assigned to an integer and when **o2** is used as part of a larger integer expression. As stated, by using a conversion function, you allow classes you create to be integrated into "normal" C++ expressions without having to create a series of complex overloaded operator functions.

Keyword Extensions

In the process of standardization, the ANSI C++ committee has added several new keywords to C++ that were not part of its original specification. At the time of this writing there are no commonly available compilers that implement all of the extended keywords. Also, none of these keywords are technically necessary to fully utilize C++. They exist largely to handle certain special case situations and some are included for convenience. In this section, a brief overview of these features is presented. However, since the exact nature of these keywords is still being defined, you will want to check your compiler's user manual for details concerning their implementation.

const_cast can be used to override **const** and/or **volatile** when performing a type conversion.

dynamic_cast performs a run-time cast for polymorphic class types.

explicit is used to create nonconverting constructors.

mutable allows a member of an object to override **const**ness. That is, a **mutable** member of a **const** object is not **const** and may be modified.

namespace declares a block in which other identifiers may be declared. Thus, an identifier declared within a **namespace** becomes a "sub-identifier" linked to the surrounding **namespace** identifier. (In essence, **namespace** creates a named scope.)

reinterpret_cast casts one type of value into another. For example, it converts a pointer into an integer type.

A **static_cast** is a nonpolymorphic cast. For example, a base class pointer can be cast into a derived class pointer.

typeid obtains the type of an expression.

using specifies a default scope resolution qualifier.

15

What Next?

While this book discusses the fundamentals required to become a C++ programmer, it is really only the beginning. Part of successful C++ programming is knowing the language. The other part is knowing how to apply it. Remember: C++ gives you unprecedented power. It is important that you learn to use the power wisely. And this comes only from experience.

Appendix A

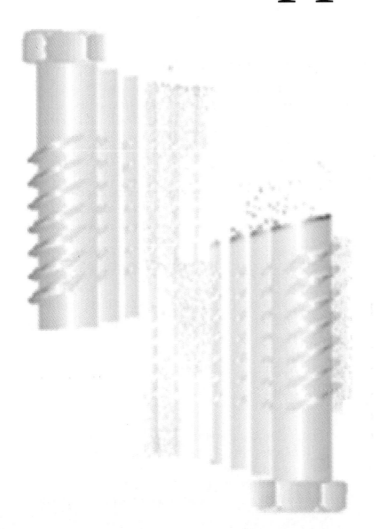

The C++ Preprocessor

This appendix discusses the C++ *preprocessor*. The preprocessor is that part of the compiler that performs various text manipulations on your program prior to the actual translation of your source code into object code. You can give various commands to the preprocessor. These commands are called *preprocessor directives* and, although not technically part of the C++ language, they expand the scope of its programming environment.

The C++ preprocessor contains the following directives.

#if	#ifdef	#ifndef	#else
#elif	#endif	#include	#define
#undef	#line	#error	#pragma

As is apparent, all preprocessor directives begin with a **#** sign. Each will be examined in turn.

Note: The C++ preprocessor is a holdover from C. Some of its features have been rendered redundant by newer and better C++ language elements. In fact, Stroustrup has stated that one of his goals when creating C++ was to render the preprocessor completely redundant and, ultimately, removed from the language entirely. However, since many programmers still use the preprocessor and because it is still part of the C++ language environment, you must be familiar with its capabilities.

#define

#define is used to define an identifier and a character sequence that will be substituted for the identifier each time it is encountered in the source file. The identifier is called a *macro name* and the replacement process is called *macro substitution*. The general form of the directive is

    #define *macro-name character-sequence*

Notice that there is no semicolon in this statement. There may be any number of spaces between the identifier and the character sequence, but once the sequence begins, it is only terminated by a newline.

Here is an example of **#define**. If you wish to use the word UP for the value 1 and the word DOWN for the value 0, then you would declare these two macro **#defines**:

```
#define UP 1
#define DOWN 0
```

This will cause the compiler to substitute a 1 or a 0 each time the name **UP** or **DOWN** is encountered in your source file.

It is important to understand that the macro-substitution is simply the replacing of an identifier with its associated string. Therefore, if you wished to define a standard message you might write something like this:

```
#define GETFILE "Enter File Name"
// ...
cout << GETFILE;
```

The preprocessor will substitute the string "Enter File Name" when the identifier **GETFILE** is encountered. To the compiler, the **cout** statement will actually appear to be

```
cout << "Enter File Name";
```

The **#define** directive has another feature: The macro name can have arguments. Each time the macro name is encountered the arguments associated with it are replaced by the actual arguments found in the program. This creates a *function-like* macro. For example,

```
#define MIN(a,b)   (((a)<(b)) ? a : b)

int x=10, y=20;
cout << "The minimum is " << MIN(x, y);
```

When this fragment is compiled, the expression defined by **MIN(a,b)** will be substituted, except that **x** and **y** will be used as the operands. That is, the **cout** statement will be substituted to look like this.

```
cout << "The minimum is: " << (((x)<(y)) ? x : y);
```

In essence, the function-like macro is a way to define a function that has its code expanded in line rather than called. The use of the (apparently) redundant parentheses in the definition of **MIN** is necessary to ensure its correct evaluation in all cases.

Although still commonly seen in C++ code, the use of function-like macros has been rendered completely redundant by the **inline** specifier, which accomplishes the same goal better and more safely. (Remember, **inline** causes a function to be expanded in line rather than called.) However, function-like macros will almost certainly continue to be a part of C++ programs for some time yet to come because many longtime C/C++ programmers continue to use them out of habit.

A

#error

The **#error** directive forces the compiler to stop compilation when it is encountered. It is used primarily for debugging. The general form of the directive is

```
#error error-message
```

The *error-message* is not between double quotes. When the compiler encounters this directive, it displays information and terminates compilation. What information is actually displayed is implementation dependent.

#include

You have been using the **#include** preprocessor directive since Chapter 1. It instructs the compiler to include another source file with the one that has the **#include** directive in it. The source file to be included must be enclosed between double quotes or angle brackets. For example,

```
#include <iostream.h>
#include "iostream.h"
```

both instruct C++ to read and compile the header for the I/O system. Typically, **#include** is used to include a header file.

Included files may, themselves, contain **#include** directives. That is, include files may be nested.

Whether the file name is enclosed by quotes or angle brackets determines how the search for the specified file is conducted. If the file is enclosed between angle brackets, the file is looked for in one (or more) implementation defined directory. If the file is enclosed between quotes, then the file is looked for in some other implementation defined directory, which is typically the current working directory. If the file is not found in this directory, the search is restarted as if the file name had been enclosed between angle brackets. Since the search path is implementation defined, you will need to check your compiler's user manual for details.

Conditional Compilation Directives

There are several directives that allow you to selectively compile portions of your program's source code. This process is called *conditional compilation* and is used widely by commercial software houses that provide and maintain many customized versions of one program. Each conditional compilation directive is examined here.

#if, #else, #elif, and #endif

The general form of **#if** is

```
#if constant-expression
  statement sequence
#endif
```

If the constant expression following the **#if** is true, then the code that is between it and an **#endif** will be compiled; otherwise it will be skipped over. **#endif** is used to mark the end of an **#if** block. For example,

```
#define MAX 100
#if MAX>10
  cout << "Extra memory required.\n";
#endif
```

This fragment will display the message on the screen because **MAX** is greater than 10. This example illustrates an important point. The expression that follows the **#if** is *evaluated at compile time*. Therefore, it must contain only identifiers that have been previously defined and constants. No variables may be used.

The **#else** works in much the same way as the **else** that forms part of the C++ language: it establishes an alternative if the **#if** fails. The previous example can be expanded as shown here.

```
#define MAX 5
#if MAX>10
  cout << "Extra memory required.\n");
#else
  cout << "Current memory OK.\n";
#endif
```

In this case, **MAX** is defined to be less than 10 so the **#if** portion of the code is not compiled, but the **#else** alternative is. Therefore, the message "Current memory OK" is displayed.

Notice that the **#else** is used to mark both the end of the **#if** block and the beginning of the **#else** block. This is necessary because there can only be one **#endif** associated with any **#if**.

The **#elif** means "else if" and is used to establish an if-else-if ladder for multiple compilation options. The **#elif** is followed by a constant expression. If the expression is true then that block of code is compiled and no other **#elif** expressions are tested. Otherwise, the next in the series is checked. The general form is

```
#if expression
  statement sequence
#elif expression 1
  statement sequence
#elif expression 2
  statement sequence
#elif expression 3
  ...
#elif expression N
  statement sequence
#endif
```

For example, this fragment uses the value of **COMPILED_BY** to define who compiled the program

```
#define JOHN 0
#define BOB 1
#define TOM 2

#define COMPILED_BY JOHN

#if COMPILED_BY == JOHN
  char who[] = "John";
#elif COMPILED_BY == BOB
  char who[] = "Bob";
#else
  char who[] = "Tom";
#endif
```

#ifs and **#elif**s may be nested with the **#endif**, **#else**, or **#elif** associating with the nearest **#if** or **#elif**.

#ifdef and #ifndef

Another method of conditional compilation uses the directives **#ifdef** and **#ifndef** which mean "if defined" and "if not defined" respectively and refer to macro names.

The general form of **#ifdef** is

```
#ifdef macro-name
  statement sequence
#endif
```

If the *macro-name* has been previously defined in a **#define** statement, the statement sequence between the **#ifdef** and **#endif** will be compiled.

The general form of **#ifndef** is

```
#ifndef macro-name
  statement sequence
#endif
```

If *macro-name* is currently undefined by a **#define** statement, then the block of code is compiled. Both the **#ifdef** and **#ifndef** may use an **#else** statement but not the **#elif**.

You may nest **#ifdef**s and **#ifndef**s in the same way as **#if**s.

#undef

The **#undef** directive is used to remove a previously defined definition of the macro name that follows it. The general form is

```
#undef macro-name
```

For example,

```
#undef TIMEOUT
```

The macro name **TIMEOUT** has now been undefined.

Using defined

In addition to **#ifdef**, there is a second way to determine if a macro name is defined. You can use the **#if** directive in conjunction with the **defined** compile-time operator. For example, to determine if the macro **MYFILE** is defined, you can use either of these two preprocessing commands:

```
#if defined MYFILE
#ifdef MYFILE
```

You may also precede **defined** with the **!** to reverse the condition. For example, the following fragment is compiled only if **DEBUG** is not defined.

```
#if !defined DEBUG
  cout << "Final version!\n";
#endif
```

A

#line

The **#line** directive is used to change the contents of _ _**LINE**_ _ and
_ _**FILE**_ _, which are predefined macro names. _ _**LINE**_ _ contains the line
number of the line currently being compiled and _ _**FILE**_ _ contains the
name of the file being compiled. The basic form of the **#line** command is

>   #line *number "filename"*

where *number* is any positive integer and the optional *filename* is any valid
file identifier. The line number is the number of the current source line and
the file name is the name of the source file. **#line** is primarily used for
debugging purposes and special applications.

#pragma

The **#pragma** directive is an implementation-defined directive that allows
various instructions, defined by the compiler's creator, to be given to the
compiler. The general form of the **#pragma** directive is

>   #pragma *name*

where *name* is the name of the **#pragma** you want. If the *name* is
unrecognized by the compiler, then the **#pragma** directive is simply
ignored and no error results.

The # and ## Preprocessor Operators

C++ supports two preprocessor operators: **#** and **##.** These operators are used
in conjunction with **#define**.

The **#** operator causes the argument it precedes to be turned into a quoted
string. For example, given

```
#define mkstr(s)  # s
```

the C++ preprocessor turns a line such as

```
cout << mkstr(I like C++);
```

into

```
cout << "I like C++";
```

The **##** operator is used to concatenate two tokens. For example, given

```
#define concat(a, b)   a ## b
```

the preprocessor transforms a line such as

```
cout << concat(x, y);
```

into

```
cout << xy;
```

If these operators seem strange to you, keep in mind that they are not needed or used in most programs. They exist primarily to allow some special cases to be handled by the preprocessor.

Predefined Macro Names

C++ specifies six built-in predefined macro names. They are

```
__LINE__
__FILE__
__DATE__
__TIME__
__STDC__
__cplusplus
```

The **__LINE__** and **__FILE__** macros were discussed in the **#line** discussion. The other macro names are described here.

The **__DATE__** macro contains a string of the form *month/day/year* that is the date of the translation of the source file into object code.

The **__TIME__** macro contains the time at which the program was compiled. The time is represented in a string having the form *hour:minute:second.*

The meaning of **__STDC__** is implementation-defined. Generally, if **__STDC__** is defined, then the compiler will accept only standard C/C++ code that does not contain any nonstandard extensions.

If your program is compiled as a C++ program then **__cplusplus** is defined. Otherwise, it is not defined.

A

Index

ORDER BOOKS DIRECTLY FROM OSBORNE/McGRAW-HILL

For a complete catalog of Osborne's books, call 510-549-6600 or write to us at 2600 Tenth Street, Berkeley, CA 94710

Call Toll-Free: *1-800-822-8158*
24 hours a day, 7 days a week in U.S. and Canada

Mail this order form to:
McGraw-Hill, Inc.
Customer Service Dept.
P.O. Box 547
Blacklick, OH 43004

Fax this order form to:
1-614-759-3644

EMAIL
7007.1531@COMPUSERVE.COM
COMPUSERVE GO MH

Ship to:

Name _____

Company _____

Address _____

City / State / Zip _____

Daytime Telephone: _____
(We'll contact you if there's a question about your order.)

ISBN #	BOOK TITLE	Quantity	Price	Total
0-07-88				
0-07-88				
0-07-88				
0-07-88				
0-07-88				
0-07088				
0-07-88				
0-07-88				
0-07-88				
0-07-88				
0-07-88				
0-07-88				
0-07-88				
0-07-88				

Shipping & Handling Charge from Chart Below

Subtotal

Please Add Applicable State & Local Sales Tax

TOTAL

Shipping & Handling Charges

Order Amount	U.S.	Outside U.S.
Less than $15	$3.50	$5.50
$15.00 - $24.99	$4.00	$6.00
$25.00 - $49.99	$5.00	$7.00
$50.00 - $74.99	$6.00	$8.00
$75.00 - and up	$7.00	$9.00

Occasionally we allow other selected companies to use our mailing list. If you would prefer that we not include you in these extra mailings, please check here: ☐

METHOD OF PAYMENT

☐ Check or money order enclosed (payable to Osborne/McGraw-Hill)

☐ AMERICAN EXPRESS   ☐ DISCOVER   ☐ MasterCard   ☐ VISA

Account No. ☐☐☐☐☐☐☐☐☐☐☐☐☐☐☐☐

Expiration Date _____

Signature _____

In a hurry? Call 1-800-822-8158 anytime, day or night, or visit your local bookstore.

Thank you for your order   Code BC640SL